SWANSEA
PALS

Dedication
To my soldierly forebears

My Grandfather
*14814 Private **David Thomas Lewis***
The South Lancashire Regiment

Gassed and machine-gunned
on the Western Front during the Great War

My Father
*14623479 Private **Glyndwr Lewis***
2nd Battalion, the Monmouthshire Regiment

Wounded by machine-gun fire in the attack
on the Reichswald Forest, February 1945

And to all the Officers, NCOs and Other Ranks
who served with the
Swansea Battalion (the 14th Welsh)

France and Flanders 1915-1918

*

Brave men, all.

SWANSEA PALS

A History of 14th (Service) Battalion,
Welsh Regiment in the Great War

BERNARD LEWIS

Pen & Sword
MILITARY

First published in Great Britain in 2004, published in this format in 2005 by
PEN & SWORD MILITARY
an imprint of
Pen & Sword Books Limited
47 Church Street
Barnsley
South Yorkshire
S70 2AS

ISBN: 1 84415 252 9

A CIP catalogue record for this book
is available from the British Library

Typeset in 10pt Sabon by Pen & Sword Books Limited

Printed and bound in England by
CPI UK

For a complete list of Pen & Sword titles please contact:
PEN & SWORD BOOKS LIMITED
47 Church Street, Barnsley, South Yorkshire, S70 2AS, England
email: enquiries@pen-and-sword.co.uk • website: www.pen-and-sword.co.uk

Contents

Swansea Battalion officers and men. Simon Peter Lee

Acknowledgements

A work of this nature cannot be completed satisfactorily without the help and assistance of many others. I have been given this help and assistance willingly and in full measure, for which I am very grateful.

Starting with the formal archive repositories, I have to thank Susan Beckley, County Archivist at the West Glamorgan Archive Service (WGAS), in County Hall, Swansea. Susan kindly granted me permission to quote from the records in her care whilst her staff assisted with their usual efficiency in producing the numerous records relating to the formation of the battalion.

Marilyn Jones, Local Studies Librarian at the Swansea Central Library, was very helpful and also enthusiastic regarding the project. Marilyn allowed me to view and photograph certain original records that are not usually made available to the public and I am very grateful for that. The staff at the Swansea Reference Library also assisted me by producing reel after reel of newspaper microfilm.

A generous grant from the Glamorgan County History Trust enabled a week to be spent at the National Archives, formerly the Public Record Office, Kew (PRO) whilst a further week's study was made possible due to the kind loan of a London apartment by Mr Richard Winter of Bryncoch. Staff at the National Archives were always helpful in producing records and giving advice.

John Dart, Curator at the Welch Regiment Museum in Cardiff, also provided assistance and advice. Bernice Cardy at the Swansea Museum kindly allowed me access to certain records and also arranged for the photographing of the Swansea Battalion Cup. Edith Morgan, Registrar of Births, Deaths and Marriages at Swansea also provided some assistance. Staff at the Imperial War Museum (IWM) and the National Army Museum (NAM), London responded to my requests with speed and efficiency. I am grateful to the IWM Photographic Library for permission to reproduce certain photographs from its extensive holdings. The British Library newspaper library at Colindale provided access to the Rhyl Guardian newspaper. Lieutenant Colonel P.A. Crocker (Retd) at the Royal Welch Fusiliers Regimental (RWF) Museum at Caernarvon provided me with copies of certain RWF War Diary entries relating to the Mametz Wood encounter.

It was Dr John Alban, formerly of the Swansea City Council Archives Office but currently County Archivist in Norfolk, who first drew my attention to the existence of the Swansea Battalion. He had himself earlier written an account of its formation and graciously raised no objections when I advised him that I intended to further research the subject. I know that it is a topic that is close to his heart. John assisted by proof reading and commenting on an early draft and I now hope that he finds the finished work a worthy attempt to tell the story of the battalion in its entirety.

My appeal for contact from relatives or friends of those who had served produced a number of responses, all of which have proved extremely helpful. I will list them with respondent name first followed by the name of the serviceman: Connie Evans (Sergeant Haydn David); Denzil Thomas (Private Colin Charles Thomas); Jason Muxworthy (Sergeant David Howell Evans); Kae Warr (Sergeant later Second Lieutenant Dick Lyons); Fred Gammon of Folkestone and John Powell of Mumbles (Private Samuel Thomas Gammon); Hugo and Oliver Brooke (Lieutenant Colonel G.F. Brooke); Ron Strawford and Peter Wright (Sergeant later Lieutenant H.F. Strawford); Bill Beynon (Private Ernie Beynon); H.T. Walters (Private Viv Walters and Sergeant Howard Walters); Danny Rees (Private David John Rees); Shirley Ferguson (Sergeant William Joseph Callaghan); Sue Rouse (Private Edward George Hughes); Ceri Rees-Powell (Private Frederick Bond and Private William Samuel Bond); Diana Stockford (Brigadier General H. C. Rees); John Hartley (Private George Outram Smith);

Hedley Morris (Private Will Williams); Brian Simpson (Private, later Second Lieutenant R. A. Simpson); Ian Milne (Private Willie Williams).

Among others who have helped are:

Jason Muxworthy who, as well as providing information about a family member, also supplied much other information with great enthusiasm. Even his father, John, was roped in on the photographing of soldier's graves and memorials. Simon Lee is actually researching the history of the 6th Welsh Battalion but generously provided much information and some very rare photographs of the Swansea Battalion. David Warren is compiling a service record for all officers who served with the Welsh Regiment in the Great War. This is a truly Herculean task for which I greatly admire him. He willingly provided me with the fruits of his research as regards the Swansea Battalion Officers and filled in many gaps in my knowledge. Oliver Fallon of the Connaught Rangers Association provided further information on the career of Lieutenant Colonel G. F. Brooke as did Charles Messenger. Mike Renshaw (author of *Mametz Wood*) pointed me in the direction of several of his sources. Colin Hughes (author of *Mametz; Lloyd George's 'Welsh Army' at the Battle of the Somme*) did likewise after kindly scrambling about in his loft in search of the details. Richard Ollington allowed me to receive a copy of the poem written by Private R. Thomas on the Mametz Wood action. George Edwards, former editor of the *South Wales Evening Post*, granted me permission to use material from its predecessor, the *South Wales Daily Post*. Harold Evans (of the South Wales branch of the Western Front Association) provided several items relating to the battalion, as did Glyn Samuel of Swansea. Harry Mason of the Royal Welch Fusiliers' Club in Swansea advised me of the current whereabouts of the Swansea Battalion cup. Trevor Tasker provided several photographs from his personal collection. Mrs Teddy Noyes of Flanders Tours directed me to an account of the difficulties of getting uniform cloth in the early days of the war. Chris Baker's website at 1914-1918.net provided much background information and the 'Baker's Pals' who responded to queries posted on the site displayed an awesome knowledge on a wide variety of Great War topics. Alderman Charles Thomas kindly allowed me to use his photographs of the Swansea Territorial Force.

Whilst I was busy researching, writing and corresponding with an ever-lengthening list of 'informers', my wife Elizabeth quietly got on with things at home and cheerfully dealt with all the domestic issues that I had promised to attend to 'in a minute'. My task would have been much harder without her willing and uncomplaining support, for which I am very grateful.

Last, and by no means least, I would like to thank Brigadier Henry Wilson and all at Pen & Sword Books, Barnsley, who read and then accepted an unsolicited manuscript after several local publishers' had praised its qualities but turned it down. I believe that Pen & Sword is doing a great service to the memory of the men who fought in the Great War by regularly taking a commercial risk on works such as this that it knows will have a limited appeal.

My sincere thanks are due to all of the above.

Introduction

I have had a long-standing interest in history, especially of the military kind. When my local history course tutor, Dr John Alban, mentioned an article he had written some years earlier about the formation of a 'Swansea Battalion' in the Great War, I was somewhat intrigued.

However, my Diploma in Local History course dissertation concerned the history of the Swansea Workhouse and the Poor Law, and ongoing research in that area precluded me from immediately devoting any time to the Swansea Battalion story.

Having later tracked down Dr Alban's original article I was surprised to find that, like many other towns and cities, Swansea had actually formed a Pals' Battalion during the First World War. I confess that I had naively assumed that those battalions were largely the creatures of the towns and cities of northern England with little, if any, Welsh involvement.

Eventually with some spare time on my hands I began a brief trawl through the local records and began to realize that, as far as the Swansea Battalion was concerned, there was indeed a story, in my view, well worth telling. Subsequent contact with the relatives of some of those who had served, confirmed my conviction in this area and my researches intensified and spread over a wider range of records.

Swansea was not alone or in any way unique in forming a local battalion during the Great War. Indeed, from the outset of the war local men had flocked to join the colours in various units. This movement was given even greater impetus by Lord Kitchener's famous appeal of August 1914 for 100,000 men, sorely needed to replace the heavy losses of the regular army during the early days of the war and to further expand the size of the army.

The then Mayor of Swansea, Alderman T.T. Corker, became the driving force behind a local movement that sought to provide a battalion of mainly local men, some 1,300 strong, that would clearly show that Swansea was quite prepared to 'do its bit' for King and country. The battalion was duly formed as the 14th Service (Swansea) Battalion, the Welsh Regiment, and, in December 1915, it embarked for France and Flanders where it was to remain for the duration of the war.

As part of the 114th Brigade of the 38th (Welsh) Division the Battalion spent some time in the trenches before taking part in the capture of Mametz Wood on the Somme. This one day it spent fighting in the wood was undoubtedly a defining moment in the history of both the Battalion and, indeed, the town of Swansea.

After rest and reinforcement an element of the Battalion acquitted itself well in a large scale raid on the strongly held High Command Redoubt in November 1916. It was also in action from the start of the Passchendaele offensive in July 1917. It took part in operations around Aveluy Wood in 1918 before playing a part in the offensive actions that led to the final German collapse. Indeed, one of its exploits in crossing a river in August 1918 whilst under fire and in neck-high water was described by Field Marshal Haig as being the highest level of soldierly achievement.

The Battalion returned home to a heroes' welcome at the end of the war. Former members of the Battalion were active thereafter in a number of ways that were designed to keep alive the spirit of comradeship that had been engendered during active service. However, with the passing of time and a diminishing number of members, the memory of the Battalion and its men inevitably faded from the consciousness of Swansea as a whole.

In 1919 and several times thereafter the surviving Battalion members had expressed the wish that the history of the Battalion would soon be committed to print, so that the people of Swansea would better understand the services it had rendered to the country. To the best of my knowledge this task was never completed apart from some coverage of its actions alongside numerous other Battalions in the *History of the Welch Regiment*. I hope that this modest work will at least partly fill the gap left by the passing of the Swansea Battalion and its men into history, with its story left largely untold. They deserve no less than this and in reality a great deal more.

Bernard Lewis, Neath, West Glamorgan.

Foreword

Having spent my childhood days in Swansea, one of my earliest recollections is of the large portraits which hung on the walls of the 'front room' in the house of my paternal grandfather and in that of his own parents in the Hafod. Elaborately framed, one showed my grandfather, Richard, the other his brother, George, in khaki military uniforms, with golden buttons. The portraits looked like paintings; they were, in fact, hand-tinted and -gilded photographs, and they made a huge impression on me.

I learned early that both my grandfather and great-uncle had fought in the Great War. George had died near Ypres and had no known grave, yet even in the 1950s, his passing was still deeply felt within the family. My grandfather had survived, but, perhaps significantly, never spoke about his wartime experiences, other than to say to me once that he felt the Belgians to be more considerate than the French and, on another occasion, that he had always felt sorry for the supply mules. Other family members sometimes made tantalizing passing references to 'the Swansea Pals', 'the Swansea Battalion', 'Mametz', 'Pilckem', and so forth. However, since these comments were made without any further elaboration, I was really none the wiser.

That was until 1974. In that year, I was appointed City Archivist of Swansea, where one of my first tasks was to bring some order to the enormous mass of unsorted records which filled the basement in the Guildhall. In my very first week in post, I discovered a huge trunk, full of documents, entitled 'Swansea Battalion Committee', together with a large quantity of cardboard boxes marked 'Princess Mary's Fund for Soldiers and Seamen, 1915'. These latter were all full of the well-known gilt boxes, originally containing a small greetings card, cigarettes, chocolate, and a pencil in the form of a Lee Enfield .303 bullet, which were presented to serving men at Christmastide. Since they were artefacts, not archives, I subsequently had them transferred to the Glynn Vivian Art Gallery.

Arranging and listing the Swansea Battalion Committee's records (which are now held in the West Glamorgan Archive Service in Swansea) was a very satisfying task. The records were exceptionally full and even contained intriguing items such as military sketch maps, samples of the navy serge cloth from which the battalion's original uniforms were made, and an example of the khaki tins for boiled sweets and other comforts which the committee sent to the battalion when they were in the trenches. I soon understood the meaning of some of the words I had heard spoken by family members all those years before and became very interested in the history of the battalion (which I now knew to be the 14th (Service) Battalion of the Welsh Regiment), quickly realizing what an illustrious and glorious history that had been.

As a consequence, I undertook further research and, in 1974, published an article about the work of the Battalion Committee in Gower, *The Journal of the Gower Society*. My original intention was that this would be the pilot for a more in-depth study on the battalion's history. However, pressure of work, plus the distractions of other research interests, precluded this, and, apart from conducting oral history interviews with some Swansea Battalion veterans, any further published output by me on this subject was, alas, not to be.

My interest in the battalion, however, remained and I always felt that their story needed to be told, a view also shared by others. Indeed, when the battalion's colours were brought back to Swansea in 1919, the hope had been expressed at that time that a full history of the unit would soon be written. In the event, that appears not to have happened, although Part II of *The History of the Welch Regiment* contains a very useful account of the campaigns in which the 14th (Service) Battalion was involved. However, this account is written strictly from the military viewpoint, and does not take note of the other issues involved – social, economic, logistical, human, and so forth.

I was therefore delighted when Bernard Lewis approached me a few years ago and informed me that he was intending to embark upon that long-awaited, detailed study of the battalion. Over the past ten years, Mr Lewis has established himself as one of the leading local historians in the Swansea area, with an excellent track record of scholarly research and publication to his name. He also has a very solid grasp of military issues and that, coupled with his wide experience of the social history of south Wales, rendered him, to my mind, the ideal candidate to write that history.

His work has now been completed and, clearly, it has matched up to those expectations. It is an eminently readable and highly comprehensive account of the 14th (Service) Battalion, the Welsh Regiment, from its inception to its disbandment, and even beyond. Here, we see the battalion in its earliest days under a local authority committee; its handing over to the War Office; its distinguishing itself in many major actions, its return to Swansea and the laying up of its colours; and then, the time in which the memories began to fade, perhaps for some, but never for others.

As such, Mr Lewis's study is a fitting tribute to the fortitude and heroism of those Welshmen and others from the Swansea area 'who gave so much in England's cause', serving in Lord Kitchener's Army. I earnestly commend his work to you.

Dr J. R. Alban,
Hethersett,
Norfolk.
June 2004

The Mayor's newspaper appeal for recruits for Swansea's very own battalion. South Wales Daily Post

Swansea Battalion
(KITCHENER'S ARMY)
Welsh Regiment.

Recruits for the above Battalion are now being enlisted at MOND BUILDINGS, Union Street, Swansea, between 10 a.m. and 8 p.m., and on Saturdays between 10 a.m. and 4 p.m.

Upon being medically passed and attested each man becomes entitled to 1s. per day pay, and, until he is billetted or lodged and maintained in a public building, he will receive besides 2s. per day.

Under the present conditions therefore he will (as the military week consists of seven days) in all be paid each Saturday 21s. per week.

When a recruit is separated from wife and children the latter will be entitled to separation allowances at the following rates:

	s.	d.	
Wife only	12	6	per week
Wife and 1 child	15	0	,,
Wife and 2 children	17	6	,,
Wife and 3 children	20	0	,,

and 2s. per week for each additional child.

The minimum standard for the Battalion is :—

Height, 5ft. 3in.
Chest measurement, 34ins.
Age, 19 to 35, except for ex-soldiers, who will be accepted up to 45, and certain selected ex-N.C.O.'s up to 50.

NOTE.—A few experienced N.C.O.'s are urgently required.

THOMAS T. CORKER,
Guildhall, Swansea.   Mayor.

CHAPTER ONE

Swansea on the Eve of War

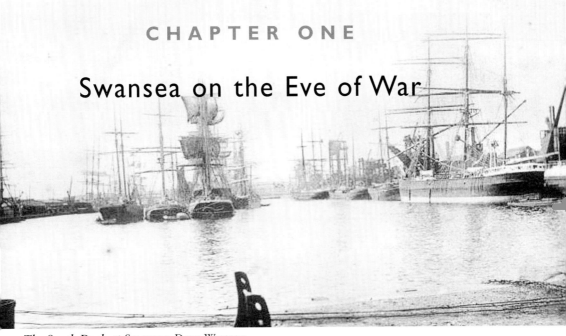

The South Dock at Swansea. Dave Westron

In the early years of the nineteenth century Swansea was a town of many contrasts. Located at the heart of a majestic bay that had been favourably compared with that of Naples, the town had, nevertheless, largely failed in its efforts to become a spa resort. Its wealth was instead firmly rooted in its traditional staple industries. These were principally non-ferrous metal processing and coal production.

Although output had declined somewhat from the heady days of 1845 when Swansea had produced fifty-five per cent of the world's copper, the numerous metal processing works were still major providers of employment in the area. Additionally,

A view of the town of Swansea towards the Docks area, with the east and west piers snaking out to sea. Dave Westron

despite a fall in demand for steam coal, the supply of other coals and anthracite, and the associated demand for transport, kept the local economy reasonably resilient in the face of rising world competition.

However, a short-sighted copper pricing policy and the casual export of technological knowledge had meant that by 1870 Chile had overtaken Swansea as the 'Copperopolis' of the world. America had compounded the difficulties of the local trade by imposing tariffs on imported tinplate in 1890.

Nevertheless, the overall success of its industries meant that for many years Swansea had acted almost as a magnet, drawing to it workers from both near and far. In the early years of the twentieth century the population of the county borough stood at about 115,000, of which only about seventy-one per cent could lay claim to having actually been born even in the broader expanse of Glamorgan, let alone in the town itself.

The four counties of the west of England provided six per cent of the population whilst a further six per cent had been drawn from the predominantly agricultural areas of Carmarthenshire and Pembrokeshire with their fluctuating seasonal demands for labour. The balance of the population came from further afield, including a healthy dose of Irish immigrants.

Inevitably, the heavy industries brought with them problems of smoke pollution as well as the scarring of the landscape, as immense spoil tips proliferated in the vicinity of every works and factory. Indeed, Swansea was gradually becoming one of the most heavily polluted areas in Britain and was developing a legacy of industrial blight that future generations would be unable to sweep away until almost the end of the twentieth century.

The better classes in Swansea society tended to congregate for housing purposes to

The sands at Swansea. The curve of the bay had been favourably compared with that at Naples, even if the weather was not quite as good. Dave Westron

The stark industrial landscape of the Hafod area of Swansea. When the local metal and coal industries declined as a result of worldwide competition, the abandoned works left a scar on the Swansea landscape that was not removed until the twentieth century. Bernard Mitchell

St Helen's Road, Swansea. Like Walter Road this was a relatively affluent part of the town. West Glamorgan Archive Service

the west of the River Tawe, where the prevailing winds kept the worst of the noxious industrial vapours largely at bay and the landscape was still relatively unspoilt. The river ran through the lower Swansea valley. Clustered along its slopes and on both banks of the river itself were many of the worst pollution producing works. The workers themselves lived in nearby housing of a generally poor quality, often perched on the higher reaches of the valley sides, where they were in easy reach of both the works and their poisonous outpourings.

In 1914 the town was well served by railway, canal and other forms of transport. Messrs P. & A. Campbell offered cruises from the Mumbles to Penarth, Cardiff, Newport or Weston. A new police station and library had recently been opened at Alexandra Road, which was also the home of the new offices of the Poor Law Guardians.

The social scene could be lively in nature for those so disposed with the options of the Empire, the Grand Theatre, the Carlton or the Elysium, as well as a number of smaller, district-based halls. A public lecture on 'Wales and the Fine Arts, Past, Present and Future' was advertised in the summer of 1914 as were the Ammanford Horse races and the annual show of the West Gower Horticultural Society (which included a brass band contest). Other attractions included a Temperance Band at Jersey Park, the

Hafod Glee Singers at Manselton Park and the Police Band at Morriston Park.[1]

Messrs Ben Evans Department Store was the principal store for the general needs of the townsfolk though specialist suppliers of many products were also available. For example, Pearce Brothers of Castle Street could provide made-to-measure suits for 'the best dressed men in town' whilst those of a musical bent could purchase or exchange their pianos at the premises of Godfrey & Co. of St Helen's Road.[2]

In June 1914 the Mayor of Swansea was Thomas Taliesyn Corker. At fifty-seven years of age he was a prominent member of the local community and was well known and liked throughout the town. He stood over six feet tall and was correspondingly well proportioned. Born and brought up in Neath, he had had experience in working in the coal trade before he had set up his own company, Thomas T. Corker and Co., with his partner, Mr John Hay, in 1890. A subsequent partnership with Mr George Bevan led him into the commercial trading areas of hay, corn, coal and haulage.

Elected on a Conservative reform ticket to the Swansea Corporation in 1902 he served on several of its committees and chaired the Water and Sewers Committee. A Justice of the Peace, he also acted as the Corporation's representative on the Swansea Harbour Trust.[3]

The local newspaper indicated that at that time Mayor Corker and his Corporation colleagues were understandably interested in a number of issues of a mainly parochial nature. The supply of coal for council buildings, the printing and binding of the Burgess Lists, and the appointment of school caretakers were much to the fore. Events in the wider world could not have been expected to hold many direct implications for the Corporation. However, events in central Europe would soon catapult the Mayor into a role he could never have envisaged at the time of his inauguration.

Alderman T.T. Corker, Mayor of Swansea.
West Glamorgan Archive Service

On 28 June 1914, the Archduke Franz Ferdinand, heir to the Austro-Hungarian Empire, commenced a state visit to the Bosnian capital, Sarajevo. Bosnia had been annexed by Austro-Hungary some years earlier, an action that still rankled with patriotic Bosnian Serbs. As the Archduke began his drive through the city to the Governor's residence, six Bosnian-Serb dissidents, including Gavrilo Princip, watched his progress and waited for an opportunity to strike a blow for Bosnian independence. If it could only be freed from the oppressor's grasp, they saw Bosnia's future as being as an integral element of an enlarged Serbia.

One of Princip's accomplices managed to position himself so that he was able to throw a bomb in the direction of the Archduke's car. The Archduke, sitting nearer to the bomber than his wife, instinctively tried to deflect the object with his hand. In any event the bomb bounced harmlessly off the car before exploding and injuring two officers in an accompanying vehicle. The injured having been taken to hospital, the understandably irate Archduke proceeded to his meeting with the Governor and a chance to berate his host for the hostility to his visit that had been all too readily apparent.

The Archduke Franz Ferdinand and his wife Sophie leaving the town hall at Sarajevo, 28 June 1914. Shortly after this picture was taken they were both dead. Taylor Library

After a frank exchange of views the Archduke decided that he would like further reassurance that his aides were recovering and asked that he be driven to the hospital to speak to the injured. During this journey the driver, having taken a wrong turn, was forced to reverse slowly. At this time Princip, purely by chance, happened to be standing on the pavement barely ten yards from the slow moving car. Seizing this unexpected opportunity he stepped forward and fired two shots at the occupants of the car, neither shot seeming to have any obvious effect. The car now sped off whilst Princip was chased and then arrested. In fact both the Archduke and his wife had indeed been hit by the gunfire and both bled to death before the journey ended.

The assassination set in motion a chain of events that would have cataclysmic consequences. Austria saw the hand of Serbia in the assassination of the royal couple. Germany discreetly promised support for any action deemed necessary by Austro-Hungary in dealing with the troublesome Serbs. In the event of any such action the attitude of Russia, normally a friend to the Serbs, would be of paramount importance. Having carefully weighed up the issues and the associated risks, an Austrian ultimatum was delivered to Belgrade containing terse words and harsh demands which simply invited Serbian rejection.

With Austria planning a partial mobilization of its armed forces the Serbs felt compelled to do likewise and, with the sudden departure of the Austrian Ambassador from Belgrade, the Serbian Government fled to Nis, fearing an imminent attack on their capital. On 29 July 1914 Russia commenced a partial mobilization of some six million men, with full mobilization being ordered a day later. France, allied to Russia since 1894, commenced mobilization amidst a flurry of European diplomatic activity aimed at averting any further escalation of the crisis. Britain, pledged to protect Belgian neutrality by treaty, asked both France and Germany to confirm that Belgian territory would not be entered in the event of any hostilities. Ominously, whilst the French promptly gave the required guarantee, Germany remained silent.

As the situation worsened Germany, keen to support its ally, was nevertheless anxious that in so doing it should not be placed in a position of having to fight a war on two fronts. Its plan was to launch a rapid attack in the west and overrun Paris, before turning its full power against Russia in the east. To this end a German army division was earmarked to seize the Luxembourg railways so that troops could be moved quickly to the western front. While this operation was about to get under way the German Ambassador to Russia handed over a declaration of war. On 2 August 1914, with Russia and Germany now declared enemies, the Germans insisted that the Belgians allow German troops free and unhindered passage to the French border. The Belgians refused. On 3 August Germany declared war on France and German troops violated Belgian neutrality despite having earlier received a British ultimatum that it should not do so.

At 11p.m. on 4 August 1914 Britain, in honour of its treaty obligation to Belgium, declared war on Germany. The train of events that had been set in motion in Sarajevo had begun with an air of pantomime. The Archduke Franz Ferdinand had almost attempted to merely swat away a thrown bomb as one would a troublesome wasp. His subsequent assassination together with that of his wife had led inexorably to the setting of empire against empire. The pantomime element of these events would soon give way to a deadly *danse macabre* that would have most of Europe and beyond twitching convulsively to its murderous melody for more than four long and painful years. The town of Swansea, in common with thousands of other towns and cities across the world, would find this a dance that it was impossible to sit out.

Swansea's tribute to an earlier conflict, the Boer War memorial at Victoria Park, Swansea. The standing figure was modelled on an NCO of the Swansea Territorial Force.
Dave Westron

Notes

1. *South Wales Daily Post* (hereafter SWDP) 1 and 22 July 1914.
2. SWDP, 27 June 1914.
3. SWDP, 8 March 1916.

CHAPTER TWO

The Call to Arms

The heightened international tension during July 1914 gradually filtered through to Swansea as the possibility of war looked ever more likely. Matters reached a climax in early August so that:

...on the Sunday night, August 2nd, [Swansea] was in an uproar. The streets were crowded with agitated throngs, all kind of rumours ran riot – there had been a naval battle in the North Sea, the Germans had attacked Nancy... and so on... the G.W.R. was besieged with reservists hastily summoned up – Navy men and Army men, whose relatives, joking or weeping, crowded the familiar platforms that so many alas trod for the last time...

Meanwhile the local Terriers were flying all over the place, mobilising. Military and police were commandeering horses in the street; the sacred soil of the Vetch Field was transformed into a stable for Howitzer Brigade horses; and a thrill went through the more imaginative of those who saw them, when, on the Tuesday, a trim little khaki block of the 1st Border Regiment marched down to

The Swansea Territorial Force on parade at Hereford prior to the declaration of war on 4 August. Charles Thomas

The drums of the 6th Welsh (Swansea Territorial Force). Charles Thomas

the docks from the G.W.R. to guard the locks and bridges.[1]

With the formal declaration of war, local events moved with an even greater rapidity. A slight rise in the price of foodstuffs was noticed locally as some citizens apparently provoked a run on the available supplies by laying in stocks so as to be better placed to deal with what might be an uncertain future.[2]

Whilst little actual alarm was displayed by the population, nevertheless two German ships that happened to be docked in the port were boarded in a nighttime raid by police and customs officials. As was usual in such cases it was explained to the crew that in the event of their failing to leave port within forty-eight hours the ships would be claimed as British property.[3]

Shortly after this the German Vice-Consul at Victoria Road, Swansea, handed his official documents and seals of office to the safekeeping of the American Consulate prior to his departure from the town. At the same time a local workman removed the address plate from the wall outside the Vice-Consul's office. It was also noted that a list of the names and addresses of all German nationals currently believed to be in Swansea, a number put at about 500, was in the hands of the local police who were keeping a watchful eye on the situation.[4]

The rise in the price of food soon led to some disquiet in the town since it was felt

A civilian detachment designated to guard bridges and waterworks in Swansea against sabotage. South Wales Daily Post

The Docks at Swansea. Dave Westron

To Guard Bridges and Waterworks

that in certain cases local shopkeepers were exploiting the supply and demand situation in order to swell their profits. A large crowd soon gathered and:

...practically every grocer's shop in the centre of the town was visited, and as the demonstrators approached Oxford Street the numbers swelled until traffic was almost impassable and the extraordinary nature of the demonstration may be gauged when it is stated that 'Rule Britannia' was sung alternately with 'The Red Flag'!

...the trouble in Prince of Wales Road, Swansea, at ten o'clock on Friday night, and which lasted till 3.30 on Saturday morning, originated over the price of lump sugar.[5]

Price's Grocers shop was seen as being particularly suspect in its pricing policies with the result that stones were thrown at the windows of the shop, breaking them all.

Despite the warnings issued to the German sailors whose ships were moored at the dock, their subsequent efforts at finalizing their affairs before setting sail seemed too tardy for the authorities with the result that:

There are over 80 German seamen in the Rutland-street Schools, Swansea, under arrest. It is understood they are being held as hostages. The military authorities who have them under guard are awaiting instructions.[6]

Interned Germans at Swansea. South Wales Daily Post

Interned Germans leave Swansea under military guard. South Wales Daily Post

Following the British declaration of war on Germany the country was filled with a great sense of patriotic zeal. Almost inevitably local men of substance felt compelled to use whatever influence they possessed to get things moving in the aid of the homeland. The most obvious way in which help could be rendered by those who were perhaps beyond recruitment age themselves was by using their influence to encourage others to enlist. At the same time Lord Kitchener issued his now famous appeal for 100,000 men to rally to the colours and assist the homeland in the prosecution of the war against Germany and her allies.

At Swansea this led to the idea, to be coordinated by the Mayor of Swansea, of forming a Territorial Reserve Force and a correspondent who contacted the Mayor on this issue was advised that:

As you are no doubt aware active steps are being taken in the Borough to obtain recruits to fill up vacancies in the Territorial units and also to form a Territorial Reserve Force which will be called the Citizen's Guard.[7]

The objectives of such a plan were set out in an undated memorandum drafted by the Mayor and his officials:

Swansea Civil Guard and Special Volunteer Reserve Force
1. To support Lord Kitchener's appeal for one hundred thousand men for the

Regular Forces.
2. To fill up the vacancies in the Territorial Units.
3. To form a force to act as a Volunteer Territorial Reserve.

The duties of those enrolling themselves will be expected to inform [sic] are:-
1. To drill and learn to shoot using every effort in this direction to become efficient and anything that may be required of them in case of invasion.
2. The class of work they may further be asked to undertake will be the protection of property, such as is now being carried out by the Territorial Units now in charge of docks, works, collieries, town and coast line, such as the formation of Guards, Fortress work etc.
3. All men between the ages of 17 and 60 are eligible and urged to become members so long as they are fit and well and capable of marching ten miles.
4. No man within the prescribed ages now appealed for by Lord Kitchener or who can possibly join the Territorials should enrol himself in this force but should particularly at once offer his services to join the colours.
The Mayor of Swansea was one of the first to adopt the formation of a force on these lines having first put himself in communication with the War Office the second day after the formal declaration of war against Germany...[8]

However, Swansea was advised that the creation of home based units was not a priority; the real need was for units that could be trained for deployment on the continent.

Other local organizations were thinking similarly as regards the formation of military style units and at a meeting held on 14 August 1914:

...the idea of forming a Swansea contingent of the Civic Guard from amongst the members of the Swansea Rugby and Cricket Clubs was discussed with

The St Helen's Ground at Swansea, home to the Swansea Cricket and Football Club. A. Thomas

KING and QUEEN,
at S...ea, July 20th, 1904.

A.P.L.B.

Swansea's earlier demonstration of patriotism was seen during the visit of the King and Queen in 1904. Dave Westron

enthusiasm at the Shaftesbury Hall on Friday evening, when a meeting was presided over by Mr A.W. Samuel.

Mr Samuel said no living man could remember when England was faced with such a serious crisis as at present, and it behoved Britishers to stand shoulder to shoulder to the bitter end. Those who could not go to the front could do their best to protect those left behind if such an occasion should arise. Britishers did not want to get shot down like a load of sheep. They wanted to know how to handle a rifle and to learn something about the elements of drill. It was now proposed to erect a rifle range at the St. Helen's field, and to teach drill to those who would like to come forward and feel they were doing something for their country (cheers).[9]

The Swansea Football and Cricket Club's rugby team, the 'All Whites', then struck a patriotic stance by cancelling all matches for the duration of the war. Prime movers in this initiative were Major Perkins, Major Aubrey Smith and Mr Glass. Major Trick was to help establish the rifle range.[10]

The rifle range was, in fact, to be located under the grandstand at the St Helen's Rugby Ground in order that those club members who had joined its civic guard detachment could practice. This detachment soon numbered about 100 men and drilled on Mondays, Wednesdays and Fridays, with shooting practice to be arranged once the range was ready.[11]

While the local authority considered what its next step might be, individual men of the locality were nevertheless still enlisting in a number of existing units of both the Army and the Navy. Indeed, the rate of local recruitment was seen as a matter of some pride

SAFE FROM THE BARBARIANS.

Belgian refugees who had taken shelter in Swansea. Swansea had long standing links with the Belgian metal processing industries. South Wales Daily Post

and anyone casting aspersions on the patriotism of the men of Swansea was likely to be promptly put in their place. On 2 September 1914 the Mayor wrote to the War Office saying:

> *Many statements have been made to the effect that there has been a very poor response in Swansea and district to Lord Kitchener's call to fill up the units of his proposed new army of 100,000 men, and, having felt all along that there was no part of the United Kingdom where young men were more anxious to join the Colours than at Swansea, I have taken the trouble to enquire into this allegation.*
>
> *I find that the Recruiting arrangements here are absolutely inadequate for the needs of the Town, and that there were scores of young men unable to receive any attention at all. One case in particular I have been informed of and that was of a man who tried for five hours to receive attention, but so keen was he to serve his Country that he paid his own expenses to Cardiff (50 miles away) and was enlisted there.[12]*

Teething troubles with the recruitment process were not particularly surprising but despite the practical difficulties being experienced a steady stream of men were nevertheless managing to enlist and were in due course departing the town on being assigned to various units. A repetitive scene was soon being enacted at the town's railway station on an almost daily basis:

> *Fathers, mothers, wives with young children clasped to their bosoms, brothers, sisters, sweethearts and friends, were all there as the 5.30 p.m. train for Cardiff steamed out of High Street Station, Swansea, on Thursday evening to take away 140 men who had enlisted from Swansea and district.*
>
> *The station presented a very animated spectacle, and there must have been some three or four thousand people on the platform. An international football match crowd was nothing to be compared with the dense mass of people who*

hustled and jostled one another in the effort to find their friends and give them a hearty handshake and 'God speed' before they departed...

...advice was given to some of the recruits as to what to do with the Kaiser whilst picture postcards were promised from Berlin at an early date... there were, however, a few who paid little heed to the demonstrations outside the train and seemed to be wondering what the future had in store for them.[13]

In an effort to improve the shortcomings of the prevailing recruitment arrangements the Mayor had already borrowed the Drill Hall for such a purpose and provided it with electric lighting, a refreshment bar, a table and seats so as to provide some limited comfort for the men as they waited to see the recruiting officer.[14]

The Town Clerk took the fight on patriotism to the officer in charge of recruiting at Shrewsbury, pointing out that as regards the Swansea boys:

...it appears that when they 'sign on' they are sent forward to Cardiff to be dispatched to the different regiments to which they are allotted. They are kept there over night, so I am informed, without food or shelter... cannot they be sent direct from Swansea to their regiments? ...I had a wire from one of the stations there... stating that there were 200 Swansea boys in Cardiff, and asking us to be responsible for their food and housing there for the night.[15]

If everything that could be done to ease and speed up the recruiting process for

Sir Alfred Mond (centre) who supported the formation of a Swansea Battalion but later fell under suspicion as to his actual loyalties, being of German descent. West Glamorgan Archive Service

Royal Welsh Fusiliers cap badge. Taylor Library

individuals was being done, there still remained unresolved the question of what precise role the Mayor and Corporation of Swansea could or should play. Sir Alfred Mond was a prominent local industrialist involved in, amongst other things, the nickel trade. He approached the Mayor with a plan to recruit a battalion of local men for service at the front only to be told that Mr Cory Yeo of the Graigola Company had already made a similar proposal that was already under consideration. Mond stated that he was happy to defer to the earlier suggestion of Mr Yeo, which would also receive his full support.[16]

The battalion was the basic infantry building block of the British army. Each regiment of line infantry normally consisted of two battalions, one of which would be serving overseas, while the other remained in Britain and recruited and trained new men to act as replacements or reinforcements. Battalions traditionally had county or regional associations so that the Royal Welsh Fusiliers were linked to North Wales, the South Wales Borderers to Brecon, and the Welsh Regiment to Cardiff.

South Wales Borderers cap badge. Taylor Library

While the Mayor was debating the matter of recruiting a battalion of local men for active service, the town, in fact, already boasted such a unit. This was the 6th (Territorial Force) Battalion of the Welsh Regiment, a unit that was based in Swansea and recruited from the local population. This Battalion was itself busily recruiting new members whilst its trained, albeit part-time, men were prepared for front line action.

A typical 1914 battalion consisted of about 1,000 men, including about thirty officers. It had a battalion headquarters staff and was split into four companies of about 250 men each. Normally an officer with the rank of lieutenant colonel would be in command of the battalion with a major as the nominated second in command. An officer with the rank of captain or lieutenant filled the important role of adjutant, this officer being responsible for administrative matters. This would certainly involve the drafting of detailed orders for the battalion as a whole, or specific companies, intended to put into effect the plans of the higher command. Another officer of similar rank would be responsible for stores and transport (the quartermaster role). A Royal Army Medical Corps doctor would also be attached to the battalion.

A number of non-commissioned soldiers (NCOs) performed specialist roles within the battalion. For example, there would be a need for a cook, a pioneer, a shoemaker, a transport officer, a signaller, an armourer and an orderly room clerk (who assisted the adjutant with routine administration). Each of these NCOs would, in turn, have a small team to deal effectively with their particular speciality, whether it was dealing with the horse-drawn transport, the battalion band, construction and engineering or stretcher bearing. The four companies of the battalion were usually lettered A through D, each with a major or captain in command and a captain as second in command.

Battalion equipment was of a varied nature and included ammunition

Welsh Regiment cap badge. The spelling changed to 'Welch' in the 1920s. Taylor Library

and water carts, wagons for general haulage, and a cart for the medical officer's supplies. General items of battalion equipment, intended to overcome modest obstacles in the field, included shovels, pickaxes, billhooks, felling axes, saws and crowbars. The men themselves would be encumbered with a Lee Enfield rifle and bayonet, and up to 120 rounds of ammunition. A bedding roll and a host of other items for personal use in the field would also be carried in the man's kit.

Battalions were grouped into brigades, a brigade usually consisting of four battalions, under the overall command of a brigadier general. Two or three brigades would be grouped to form a division, under the command of a major general, and several divisions would be grouped to form a corps. Two or three corps, grouped in turn, formed an army.[17]

The Mayor's communication with the War Office received an initially cautious response, requesting that official permission to form such a unit should be obtained before any public announcements were made. The local community would need to provide the initial finance involved in such an enterprise and this was estimated at being between £8,000 and £10,000. It was unclear at that stage whether any sum expended locally in forming a battalion would eventually be refunded by the War Office. In order to gauge the level of support, both moral and financial, that such a suggestion might receive from the township, it was decided to invite the major employers in the area to a meeting with the Mayor. To this end a circular letter was sent out:

> It has been suggested that a Battalion should be raised in Swansea to form part of the Welsh Regiment of Kitchener's Regular Army and being convinced that such a movement would meet with every approval, I approached, as a preliminary measure, the War Office upon it. The suggestion has been considered by the Army Council and they will signify their acknowledgement of what they term a 'patriotic offer' subject to certain conditions... as the movement largely affects the owners of industrial concerns in our district I am inviting them to a Meeting at the Guildhall.[18]

The meeting accepted the idea in principle and it was agreed to arrange a public meeting at the Albert Hall, Swansea, on 16 September 1914, in order to present the proposal to the public at large. Plans for the meeting were promptly set in motion with Mayoral invitations being extended to those in the town who, it was felt, would help fuel the hoped-for patriotic fire. To advance this a noted local singer was advised that:

> The object of the meeting is to arouse enthusiasm for enlistment, and I feel that if you would be good enough to recite a couple of stirring things for us appropriate to the occasion it would do much to foster this.[19]

Given the popularity of community singing at the time it was also planned to regale the audience with songs that were particularly suitable for the predominantly martial atmosphere of the meeting. Thus the songs chosen included God Save the King; Land of My Fathers; Men of Harlech; the French, Russian and Belgian national anthems; God Bless the Prince of Wales; It's a Long Way to Tipperary; Rule Britannia; Cock of the North; The Bay of Biscay and Killarney.[20]

The meeting opened to a packed hall and the Mayor explained:

> The intention of the Meeting today is not so much for the purpose of raising recruits as to discuss the scheme generally, and to go into the question of the cost

If der Swansea Boys af gone by, den I kan kom out.

Postcard showing the supposed German reaction to the formation of a Swansea Battalion. Glyn Samuel

thereof.[21]

On the question of cost, the idea had already garnered significant financial support from the upper echelons of Swansea society. Among the pledges already made were those of a £1,000 contribution and the guarantee of a further £5,000 by Sir Alfred Mond. Mr F. Cory Yeo, of the Graigola Company had guaranteed £1,000 whilst Colonel Wright had donated £500. Mr David Glasbrook and Mr T.J. Williams had each donated 100 guineas and Mr T.W. James had provided a further £25.

After some discussion the Mayor put forward the resolution:

That this meeting heartily approves of the principle of the formation of a Swansea Battalion to be connected to the Welsh Regiment. Carried unanimously.[22]

Having satisfied themselves that the financial structure was largely in place, and the courage and patriotism of the local men undoubted, the result of the meeting was promptly communicated to the War Office which in turn speedily responded by telegram that it had:

Much pleasure in accepting your patriotic offer to raise this battalion.[23]

Interestingly, unlike in England where many towns raised battalions largely on their own initiative, only two areas in Wales apparently went down that route. Swansea was, in fact, the second, the first being the counties of Denbighshire and Flintshire, which received joint sanction to raise a battalion which

A group of workers from the Mond Nickel Works. Alfred Mond was a prominent supporter of the Swansea Battalion despite being of German origin. Bernard Mitchell

subsequently became the 13th Battalion, the Royal Welsh Fusiliers.[24]

Connected events were also unfolding in other quarters. For example, David Lloyd George gave an inspiring speech at the Queen's Hall, London, before two days later hosting a meeting of prominent Welshmen at 11 Downing Street, where he revealed a cherished vision:

> *I should like to see a Welsh Army in the Field. I should like to see the race that faced the Norman for hundreds of years in a struggle for freedom, the race that helped to win Crecy, the race that fought for a generation under Glyndwr against the greatest Captain in Europe – I should like to see that race give a good taste of their quality in this struggle in Europe; and they are going to do it.*[25]

Later that month the Secretary of State for War, Lord Kitchener, gave his approval to the formation of a Welsh Army Corps, and a provisional committee was formed for the purpose of bringing the matter to fruition. The planned corps would, in some quarters, rejoice under the nickname of 'Lloyd George's Welsh Army'. Recruitment in Wales thereafter came largely under the umbrella of the newly formed National Executive Committee in Cardiff and indeed eventual control of the Swansea Battalion would be transferred to that body in mid-October 1914.

On the same day that the sanction of the War Office to raise a battalion was received the Swansea Mayor, Alderman T.T. Corker, promptly set the recruiting wheels in motion locally by way of an advertisement in the *South Wales Daily Post*:

David Lloyd George.
Taylor Library

> Swansea Battalion
> Welsh Regiment
>
> *The sanction of the War Office has now been obtained for the formation of a*
> *Swansea and District Battalion of the Welsh Regiment.*
>
> *Young able-bodied men who desire to rally to the colours in a unit comprised entirely of comrades from the Town & District are asked to call at any time between 10 a.m. and 6 p.m. at the Guildhall (room facing main entrance) where they can be enrolled.*
>
> *T.T. CORKER,*
> *Guildhall, Swansea.*
> *Mayor.*[26]

Guildhall at Swansea. The first recruiting ~ce for the Battalion was based there. A 'new' ~ldhall was opened in 1934 and the one ~ured was eventually converted into a ~ature centre. Dave Westron

The Battalion's latest recruit, Tawe the bulldog. South Wales Daily Post

The newspaper also reported that the minimum height set for recruits, being five feet and six inches, was proving problematic given the fact that many Welshmen were in fact naturally shorter than that. In earlier years the limit for recruits had always been set at five feet and three inches, a figure that was much more in line with the stature almost naturally attained by local men after their preceding generations had spent much of their working lives in cramped, low roofed mining seams. The local newspaper highlighted the problem that this caused:

...recruiting for Lord Kitchener's Army at Swansea on Thursday was not very brisk, only fifteen men signing on at both the Swansea recruiting offices. The sooner the standard is lowered to the original figures, the better it will be for recruiting in Wales.[27]

Being keen to capitalize on the momentum generated by the earlier employers' meeting and the public meeting, the Mayor now arranged a further meeting in order that an executive body could be formed to speedily progress the matter and a number of local dignitaries were contacted regarding the:

Proposed Swansea Battalion for Lord Kitchener's Army.
Referring to the meeting of Employers at the Guildhall on Tuesday last... when the principle of forming the above battalion was agreed upon, and the subsequent Mass Meeting at the Albert Hall... when it was also decided to form this battalion, I shall be glad if you will be good enough to attend a meeting at the Guildhall at 4 p.m. on Tuesday next, the 22nd instant, so that details of the scheme may be discussed, and a small working Committee formed.[28]

The Reverend Canon R.B. Gwydir was unable to attend the meeting since his duty now lay, quite literally, in deeper waters: *'I am commanded by the Admiralty to join the Battle Squadron at once.'*[29]

J.D. Pritchard and Co. felt that their employees had already done all that could reasonably be asked of them:

The Albert Hall, Swansea, once the scene of patriotic recruiting. It later became a bingo hall. Bernard Mitchell

...we need hardly state that the movement has our hearty support. We would point out however that practically all our employees are married and with families and the majority are old having been employed here for many years.

It is with great difficulty that we have been able to keep working since the outbreak of war, due to the shortage of raw material, and it is our desire to keep our men as much employed as possible so as to obviate any of them being

obliged to seek relief from the funds.

> *We are glad to state that the only men who were eligible to join the army have already volunteered.*[30]

With the need to ensure that sufficient funds would be in hand to meet the expenses associated with forming the battalion, and perhaps to provide additional comforts for the men, donations were encouraged and were not slow in coming forth. Among the many contributions made was £50 from the Swansea Improvements and Tramway Co.; £10 from Ben Evans & Co., a surprisingly modest sum from one of Swansea's best known businesses; a £35 cheque from Mr Harry G. Thomas of the Mayals and ten shillings a week from Mr D.A. Rees of Mirador Crescent. It was intimated that the goods staff at the Great Western Railway, Wind Street Goods Office, intended to make a periodic collection for the fund.[31]

Other offers of donations were of a more practical nature. For example, Mr James Steer offered a seven month old goat for use as the battalion mascot. This offer was not taken up, though the offer by Colonel Wright of a bulldog, answering to the name of Tawe (the name of the river on which the town of Swansea stands) was later accepted. Mr Fred Rocke, of Parry and Rocke, offered 1,000 pairs of socks. Mr R.D. Mitchell, LDS (Eng) stated that Swansea dentists would be pleased to attend recruits as to extractions, fillings and dentures at nominal cost. The *South Wales Daily Post* reduced the cost of the recruiting advertisements from £25 to £10[32] while the Swansea

A Swansea tram advertising the Ben Evans store on its front. Bernard Mitchell

Gas and Light Company offered:

> ...to loan without charge Gas Meters, Cookers and Wash Rollers to meet the requirements of the battalion at the Old Training College, provided that the gas supplied is paid for in the usual manner.[33]

Understandably, not all of Swansea's citizens were in favour of the idea of forming a local battalion, one writing to the Mayor to set out his concerns:

> ...as I mentioned to you personally, I do not think our people would be inclined to support this suggestion, to find £8,000 or £10,000 to equip a battalion, specifically for Swansea. I do not want to throw cold water on the suggestion, and therefore I think it is better that I should not attend either of the meetings...if certain wealthy people are anxious to contribute largely to this proposal, of course it would be advisable to encourage them to do so, but my personal feeling is that this is a matter for the Government, and our duty lies in getting the men to enlist, and in looking after their dependants, and also endeavouring to prevent distress and unemployment, and be ready to provide for same should it occur.[34]

Some employers clearly felt that they were being overwhelmed with requests for donations from all sides and an official of the North Central Wagon Company, Rotherham, which had branches at both Swansea and Briton Ferry wrote:

> I am directed to say that in view of the generous contributions we have already made, and are continuing to make, to the National Relief Fund, the Belgian Refugees Fund, etc., etc; the fact that ALL our workmen and the members of our clerical staffs are contributing regularly weekly sums; and the payments we are making week by week to the dependants of married and unmarried men recently in our employ who have joined the colours; they regret they cannot see their way to subscribe to the funds of the above.[35]

However, with the support of most of the local employers and, indeed, the local population, there was good cause for optimism that recruits for the new battalion would not be in short supply.

COL. J. R. WRIGHT.

Colonel J.R. Wright active in Swansea in the recruiting process. South Wales Daily Post

Notes

1. SWDP, 2 August 1915.
2. SWDP, 4 August 1914.
3. SWDP, 5 August 1914.
4. SWDP, 7 August 1914.
5. SWDP, 8 August 1914.
6. SWDP, 10 August 1914.
7. WGAS, TC 26/1.
8. WGAS, TC 26/25.
9. SWDP, 15 August 1914.
10. SWDP, 1 September 1914.
11. SWDP, 27 November 1918.
12. WGAS, TC/26/25
13. SWDP, 4 September 1914.
14. WGAS, TC 26/25.
15. WGAS, TC 26/22.
16. WGAS, TC 26/1.
17. 1914-1918.net (The Long, Long Trail) website information (Mr Chris Baker).
18. WGAS, TC 26/1.
19. WGAS, TC 26/1.
20. ibid.
21. ibid.
22. WGAS, TC 26/3.
23. WGAS, TC 26/5.
24. Alban, J.R., *The Formation of the Swansea Battalion 1914-1915*, Gower Volume 25, 1974, p.28.
25. Welsh Army Corps 1914-1919, Report of the Executive Committee, Cardiff 1921, p. 3. (Hereafter WAC.)
26. SWDP, 18 September 1914.
27. ibid.
28. WGAS, TC 26/1.
29. ibid.
30. ibid.
31. ibid.
32. ibid.
33. ibid.
34. ibid.
35. ibid.

CHAPTER THREE

Kitchener's Men

The embryonic Swansea Battalion was not, of course, the only enlistment option open to the patriotic citizens of the town. Indeed, by 11 September 1914 it was estimated that 8,000 of the young men of Swansea and its surrounds had already rallied to the Colours and were spread amongst a number of units including Swansea's territorial unit, the 6th Battalion of the Welsh Regiment. Patriotic fervour seemed to display the attributes of an infectious disease with workplaces being particularly susceptible to a rapid spread of contagion.

The local newspaper reported on those businesses whose employees had already answered their country's call. The list of men, therefore, also included the names of most of Swansea's well established businesses. The local newspaper, the *South Wales Daily Post*, gave pride of place in the list to those who had enlisted whilst in its own employ.

Also listed were employees of William Hancock and Co., brewers. The trades of these recruits ranged from clerk to fitter to driver and horse keeper. The Hafod-Isha Works, Hutchins and Co. Ltd., Liptons, North's Navigation Collieries and Ben Evans and Co. were all well represented in a list that also included a number of employees of both the Swansea Corporation and the Swansea Board of

High Street, Swansea. The effects of volunteering, and later conscription, meant that more women began to work in traditionally male dominated occupations such as the tramway system. Dave Westron

Guardians. There was a large contingent of dock workers, their numbers probably buoyed up after a mass meeting that had been held some days earlier at which the idea of a local battalion had been warmly welcomed. As Swansea was a town with a long tradition of sporting excellence the list also contained the names of local rugby, soccer and swimming exponents who had embraced the cause with enthusiasm.[1]

It is, therefore, understandable that even with the imminent formation of a Swansea Battalion now a well publicized fact, the local newspaper nevertheless found that, given the amount of competition for recruits, the actual pace of recruiting for the battalion left a little to be desired. There was, however, some limited cause for optimism:

> Although the progress of recruiting for the Swansea Battalion is not quite as brisk as one would desire, the men are coming along steadily, and on Thursday 53 more were enrolled, which brings up the total for this Battalion to 245 in four days.[2]

By the 25 September 1914 the number enlisted had risen to 274 and the recruiting station had moved from the Guildhall at Somerset Place to better suited premises in Mond Buildings, Union Street.[3]

A commanding officer with some local background had also been nominated to lead the battalion. After some doubt as to whether he would, in fact, actually be required by his own regular army unit, the preferred commanding officer of the Swansea Battalion, Major Henry Wightman Benson, finally arrived to take up his command. Benson had previously served with the Surrey Regiment and was a member of the well established Swansea family who resided at Fairy Hill, Gower. One of his ancestors had been Starling Benson, a very prominent personality in Victorian Swansea.[4]

Benson was born in 1855 at the Manor House, Teddington, Middlesex, and was the son of the late General Henry Roxby Benson, CB, who had been Colonel of the 17th Lancers. His mother was Mary Henrietta Benson, the daughter of the late Honourable Sir William Wightman, a Judge of the Queen's Bench.

Educated at Eton and Brasenose College, Oxford, he was an accomplished oarsman, rowing in the Eton Eight in 1873, the Oxford Eight in 1874 and the Leander Eight in 1875. He commenced his military career with the 1st West India Regiment in 1876 before joining the East Surrey Regiment in 1879. During the period 1892-1897 he served with the militia before taking part in the South African campaign with the East Surreys. He saw action in Natal and the Transvaal and was mentioned three times in dispatches as well as being awarded the Distinguished Service Order.[5]

Following his arrival at Swansea, Major Benson took an early opportunity to review those who had so far joined the new formation:

> The members of the Battalion, of whom 228 men have been medically examined and attested, were summoned for their first official parade at the St. Helen's Cricket Field at 10 o'clock on Monday morning.
>
> Major Benson was present and addressed the battalion. The new

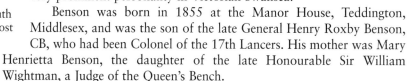

H.W. Benson, commanding officer of the Swansea Battalion. South Wales Daily Post

DIED FOR C

R.E.Benso? who was k in the Batt the Aisne. was the br? of the commandi? officer of t? Swansea Battalion S Wales Dail? Post *commander was enthusiastically received by the men. Col. Wright and Capt. Bransby Williams were also in attendance.*

The men, who are of splendid physique, then received drill instruction by the sergt.-major, and will form the nucleus of a capital fighting force. The pity is that the numbers are not much larger, but big additions are expected during the present week now that the men have commenced their work in earnest.[6]

Major Benson had an early indication of the seriousness of the situation into which he had been pitched, somewhat unexpectedly. Having arrived at Swansea to take up his command, one of his first tasks was to attend the funeral of his brother, Richard Erle Benson. Richard received a full military funeral at Swansea, having died of wounds received in France during the Battle of the Aisne.[7]

Concern continued to grow at what was seen as the apparent apathy of many local men to the plight of their country with the resultant slow pace of recruiting. Another advertisement was placed in the *South Wales Daily Post* on 6 October 1914, in an attempt to reinvigorate the recruitment process:

Swansea Battalion
(KITCHENER'S ARMY)
Welsh Regiment

Recruits for the above Battalion are now being enlisted at MOND BUILDINGS, Union Street, Swansea, between 10 a.m. and 8 p.m., and on Saturdays between 10 a.m. and 4 p.m.

Upon being medically passed and attested each man becomes entitled to 1s. per day pay and, until he is billeted or lodged and maintained in a public building, he will receive besides 2s. per day.

Under the present conditions therefore he will (as the military week consists of seven days) in all be paid each Saturday 21s. per week.

When a recruit is separated from wife and children the latter will be entitled to separation allowances at the following rates:

	s.	d.	
Wife only	12	6	*per week*
Wife and 1 child	15	0	"
Wife and 2 children	17	6	"
Wife and 3 children	20	0	"

And 2s. per week for each additional child.

The minimum standard for the Battalion is:-
Height, 5ft. 3in.
Chest measurement, 34 ins.
Age, 19 to 35, except for ex-soldiers, who will be accepted up to 45, and certain selected ex-N.C.O.'s up to 50.

NOTE - A few experienced N.C.O.'s are urgently required.
THOMAS T. CORKER
Guildhall, Swansea   *Mayor*[8]

A further newspaper appeal in the name of the Mayor was made on 7 October and shortly after that a list of businesses where the recruiting officer could call with hopeful results was passed to Major Anderson. By 15 October the number was up to 436 but was still well short of expectations. Newspaper coverage of progress was becoming subdued:

> Four men joined the Swansea Battalion up to 2 o'clock on Friday, and eight applicants were rejected. Three men joined other units of the Army.
>
> The authorities are disappointed with the progress of recruiting at Swansea, which is getting serious.[9]

A joint parade by soldiers of both the Swansea and the 6th Welsh Battalions was staged in an effort to rekindle what seemed to be the faintly glowing embers of patriotism in Swansea and its surrounds. The *South Wales Daily Post* certainly saw no shortage of prospective candidates even if they were proving difficult to coax into action:

> What effect the joint parade of the Swansea Battalion and the 6th Welsh Regiment on Friday evening will produce upon recruiting remains to be seen. The young men in the district seem to have grown apathetic and need a deal to rouse them to a sense of their responsibilities...
>
> 'Your King and Country need you' are the bold words placarded all over the town and district. None can fail to see them. Yet the response to Lord Kitchener's appeal is, in the majority of cases, made in vain. Meetings are being held all over the district and able speakers come forward and make eloquent appeals to those men who are capable of coming forward to assist in their country's defence at this critical period; recruiting officers visit the big works in the district and appeal

A recruiting parade in Swansea shortly after the declaration of war. Charles Thomas

for recruits, and still much of this effort is wasted for the results are certainly not encouraging and the harvest is poor.

One could not help noticing on Friday evening the thousands and thousands of eligible men who stood about in the principal streets of Swansea waiting to see the march past of the men who had responded to their country's call without asking oneself why the majority were willing and apparently content to allow a handful, comparatively speaking, of men to uphold the honour of Swansea. And when one saw the noble veterans of the old brigade march along in the procession with erect and martial bearing, and, wondered what these old veterans would give if it were possible to place the hands of the clock back thirty or forty years so that they might have the privilege of fighting their battles over again, one could not help contrasting the spirit of these heroes with that of the apathetic eligibles who looked on without a sense of shame and apparently unmoved by the military procession which was organised for the sole purpose of bringing in recruits.[10]

With a growing sense of desperation it seemed necessary to gild even a modest success story beyond that which the facts really justified. A meeting held in Plymouth Street on 16 October 1914 produced ten volunteers for the Swansea Battalion out of an audience of 1,000, a one per cent success rate that was nevertheless greeted with some acclaim in the press.[11]

Despite the disappointing figures from recruitment, work on forming the battalion continued apace though it was undoubtedly hampered by a shortage of uniforms and equipment. The Swansea Battalion was not alone in this since such shortages were being experienced across the entire country as

'Look here, my lad, if you're old enough to walk out with my daughter, you are old enough to fight for her and your Country.'
A cartoon attempts to shame young men into enlisting. South Wales Daily Post

Recruiting Sergeant: 'Now young man! If you object to Conscription the time has come to make good that objecting.'
Another cartoon attempt to reinvigorate the enlisting process. South Wales Daily Post

demand for military items far exceeded the available supply. Regular battalions and even territorial units were slightly better placed since they naturally held some stocks

G. R.

MUNITIONS.

Do not heed all this talk about lack of Munitions, lack of rifles, lack of equipment, lack of readiness for abroad.

JOIN

a Battalion of THE WELSH that has already got

RIFLES & EQUIPMENT

ready and waiting for you to use them.

A LOCAL BATTALION is in the TRENCHES

Come and Help Them!!
Fill the Ranks!!!

Apply to—

Administrative Centre,
6th Battalion The Welsh Regiment,
Central Drill Hall, Swansea.

and you will get UNIFORM, EQUIPMENT and RIFLE IMMEDIATELY YOU JOIN.

A recruiting advertisement highlighting the fact that some units had equipment to hand. South Wales Daily Post

RECRUITS WANTED

1st Welsh (Howitzer) Brigade, R.F.A.

Men are still required to complete the above Brigade.

They must be of good character, and between the ages of 19 and 38.

Height from 5ft. 4ins., Chest measurement 34ins., minimum.

This Brigade depends for Recruits on Swansea, Swansea Valley, Neath, and their adjoining districts.

Local Brigades should receive the full support of all the young and able-bodied men of their own districts, before outside Units are considered.

Saddlers, Shoeing Smiths and Wheelwrights are also urgently required, and when approved become entitled to extra pay.

For full particulars apply to—

OFFICER COMMANDING DEPOT,
1st Welsh (Howitzer) Brigade, R.F.A.,
Drill Hall, Swansea.

Competition in the recruiting process; an advertisement for the Howitzer Brigade.
South Wales Daily Post

of the required items that could be made readily available to recruits. Indeed, this fact was trumpeted loudly in newspaper recruiting advertisements for such units. This probably led to some men choosing to join regular or territorial units in preference to the part-formed Swansea Battalion which must have seemed at the time little more than an ill-equipped bunch of semi-trained civilians.

As the promised delivery date for the much needed items grew near, the press coverage was keen to point out that the previous deficiencies in equipment would soon be remedied. Thus the public were told that the Swansea Battalion men:

> *...will shortly have their guns, their new uniforms, and will be billeted. They will be full blown soldiers. Lieut. Dyson Williams told a 'Daily Post' man... that a portion of the men would be billeted at the Old Swansea Training College, which has now been properly fitted up for the reception of the men, some of whom are expected to go in today... a portion of the men, about 250 at a time, will be billeted at Jersey Marine, where rapid strides are being made with the erection of the 600 yards range. This will be completed in about ten days, and then the men will go out in turn, for musketry instruction.*[12]

Even if they lacked all the necessary equipment, the military training and discipline was beginning to be rewarded:

> *On Wednesday morning over 700 men were at drill at the St. Helens football field, and presented a very smart and soldierly appearance. One could scarcely believe the improvement which has been effected in a few weeks, under the instruction of a capable body of officers.*[13]

On 6 November 1914, with the realization that the departure of the battalion from Swansea for other training areas would not long be delayed, Alderman Corker again resorted to a newspaper appeal with a desperate plea for recruits:

GERMAN MENACE
Swansea Battalion

As Mayor of Swansea, I again make a strong appeal to the Young Men of the Town and District to uphold the Honour and Dignity of their neighbourhood by coming forward to complete the Units of the Swansea Battalion, and assist by so doing to repel the above terrible menace.

There is no doubt 'OUR COUNTRY NEEDS YOU,' and it is far better to gratify that need voluntarily and so destroy all suggestions of Compulsory Service. Over 700 men have already helped to swell the ranks of the Battalion, of which we hope to be so proud. FOLLOW THEIR EXAMPLE, that the Units may be completed

Without Any Further Delay.

I feel sure THAT THIS APPEAL WILL NOT BE IN VAIN. Follow the example of others who have joined. RALLY TO THE COLOURS. HELP TO SAVE YOUR COUNTRY....

GOD SAVE THE KING[14]

WAR WORKERS (?)

GREAT RECRUITING RALLY DEEDS NOT WORDS

Eligible Optimist: 'Say! We're doing jolly well on the West Front this week, what?'
Eligible Pessimist: 'Oh, don't crow! It's a long way to Tipperary yet.'
Recruiting Sergeant (Silent): 'Now I wonder what's the matter with those two?'
Those who have not enlisted are targeted by the local press. South Wales Daily Post

Some of the other needs of the battalion were happily provided for without recourse to public appeals. As the local newspaper reported:

...a Swansea lady who saw the boys of the Swansea Battalion doing a march on the Mumbles-road without a band of any kind was touched to the quick by the absence of this cheering and inspiriting factor. She rightly thought a fife and drum band should at least be provided - fifes take up little room and are most exhilarating these days when the members of brass bands are being turned into ambulance units. 'Please arrange for one for the Swansea Battalion', was the request made to the editor of the "Daily Post" 'and I'll send you £25 to pay for the instruments.'[15]

Men in the town who had attested for service and were now waiting to be summoned to their units were joined by those who had joined other formations earlier and now returned home on leave or as a result of wounds received in action. The sight of many uniformed men within the town resulted in the opening of:

An absolutely free club to our friends of the military - a place where you can smoke and yarn and play games, and not have any straight-laced business about it...

Mr and Mrs G.W. Dorrell and Miss Barrow have organised [this] at the Albert Hall. Refreshments at moderate charges will also be supplied at the club, which will be open daily from 10 a.m. to 10 p.m., daily papers, writing materials, a piano, and, in addition, a committee of ladies is being organised to do darning and sewing for the men who need it...

The Club was then formally opened and wished every success by the new Mayor, Alderman Dan Jones, who had succeeded Alderman Corker. The opening formalities then continued:

> *Major O'Hara, who met with a great reception, seconded, and announced, amid general delight, that Col. Benson, who had been unwell, would be with them again on Wednesday. 'One thing more,' he said. 'We want a few more men. When are you going to come? We want to make up the 1,100. We are going on Tuesday, and are we going to have the full number before we leave? If not, it is of no use talking; you may as well go outside and play your own game; you know what your duty is, but you want other people to do it for you.' (Hear, hear.)...*

> *Surgeon-Capt. Bruce... declared, on the recruiting question, that young men were now divided into two classes – soldiers and those who were afraid of their skins. (Hear, hear.) The latter, he imagined, would be those who, in the event of an invasion, would slink into the corner, and with hands up implore for mercy to an implacable enemy.* [16]

By 24 November 1914 the battalion numbers were up to almost 950. Realistically, a figure in the region of 1,300 was required so there was still a major shortfall. [17] It was expected that the battalion would leave Swansea for North Wales in the next week or so and may well have to depart incomplete in numbers. As the likely day of departure approached a 'Smoking Concert' was held at the Albert Hall on 26 November 1914 and it was noted that:

THE PARIAH.

The Eligible who did not enlist: 'How I wis hadn't held back; I feel a rank outsider. cartoon dig at those who have yet to enl
South Wales Daily Post

> *Swanseaites, it is traditional, never do things by halves, and it was only natural that the dinner in honour of the departure of the Swansea Battalion of the Welsh Regiment, who leave for Rhyl on Tuesday next, should easily eclipse in all respects any function of its kind ever held in Swansea.*

> *Never before has such an inspiring sight been witnessed in the town; never before has there been brought together the flower of Swansea's manhood. A thousand officers and men, drawn from all classes – ready and willing to lay down their lives if necessary for the defence of King and country.*

> *The people of Swansea had decided that these men, many of whom were*

being parted from their wives and children, could not be allowed to depart
without giving these patriotic soldiers a fitting send-off, so they might know that
Swansea was proud of a Swansea Battalion, who had so readily responded to
Lord Kitchener's appeal for men in England's hour of need.

With 1,200 persons present, a special welcome was reserved for the former Mayor, Alderman T.T. Corker, who had played such a prominent role in forming the battalion. Indeed, his eldest son, Frank, was currently serving with it. He stated:

Swansea and its people were proud to have been able to raise a battalion in
the town after having sent away so many thousands of men before. He wanted
to tell them that he was not a Swansea boy himself, but a Neath boy. (Laughter.)
But he had given the battalion his son who was a Swansea boy and he hoped his
son would represent Swansea wherever he went. (Cheers.)

The event continued and:

...the audience were loudly applauding a splendid 'comic' when Colonel
Benson made his appearance. He was quickly 'spotted' and the men as one stood
on their feet cheering the colonel, intermingled with the singing of 'He's a jolly
good fellow'.

The wounded Belgian soldier was given a rousing reception, and his
renderings of the Belgian and French national anthems were most dramatic.[18]

If those who would not join were seen as causing problems, even those who had, in fact, joined sometimes brought with them their own problems. Marshal F. Stonehouse had:

...joined the Swansea Battalion. Mrs Stonehouse the Mother of the recruit is
in very poor circumstances with a large family of young children. The husband
is in Vancouver and has practically left her and the family destitute. The recruit...
when in work contributed to the household exps. To-day Mrs Stonehouse is
receiving 8/- per week which is being earned by one of her boys and she has I
understand help from the Guardians. I know the circumstances of the family well
and can vouch for this being a genuine case for assistance being granted to enable
her to get along without the help of the son who is now serving his country.[19]

Meanwhile, Mr F.W. Border, another recruit, was concerned about the welfare of his wife:

I just drop you a few lines to ask you if my wife will receive anything from
your funds. The reason why I am asking is because others told me to ask you.
That they have receive (sic) something, I have joined the Swansea Battalion last
Wensday (sic) week I have not received anything besides the three shillings a day.
I don't suppose the Separation Allowance will start, untill we gets billeted up...I
expect to be at the front before long. Hope to do my little bit for King and
Country.[20]

The late payment of separation allowances to the families of men who had joined up led to a somewhat exasperated explanation from the officer tasked with making the relevant payments:

I thought when I started this temporary office the work would simmer down,
and I should be in a position to visit the various large towns in south Wales, ere
this. I have, however, found this an impossibility. Every day my post increases,
and I am being regularly bombarded with letters from all over the place, and am

'A' Company outside the George Hotel, Mumbles. John Powell and Fred Gammon

never able to close my office until 8.30.[21]

Some who were anxious to enlist simply failed to meet the medical criteria. Sid Jenkins apparently had a slight rupture and had been rejected as unfit. Bringing his plight to the attention of those he thought might be able to bend the rules in his favour a little, he received a purely practical response:

> *...exceedingly sorry that you have not been able to pass the medical examination, but I am afraid I cannot interfere in the matter in any way... I have heard that for the defect which you have, a slight operation will put things right. What do you think of this?*[22]

Harold Davies of Danygraig Road had initially joined the Docks Corps but had now been transferred to the Swansea Battalion. Not sure of the likely timescales involved in training with the battalion he wondered whether it was worth him starting evening classes at the local Technical College.[23]

The Swansea Battalion was not the only unit that local men might join, of course. As well as the 6th Welsh, the Field Artillery also regularly advertised in the local press for recruits. The Navy was another attractive option for some especially given Swansea's long maritime tradition. Indeed, since the outbreak of war more than 12,000 of Swansea's men had joined the forces in one unit or another, so harsh criticism of the local effort was perhaps not entirely justified. If the rate of recruitment had, to the Battalion Committee and the press at least, proved somewhat pedestrian, nevertheless over 1,000 men had now at last joined the battalion entirely of their own accord.

The Swansea Battalion was clearly a 'Pals' Battalion', the supposed merits of which were openly propagated by the military and civil authorities. The attraction was supposed to be that young men who had grown up together, attended school together and now worked together, would also train and fight together, comfortable in the presence of their long standing pals. At the time no one seems to have quite grasped fully the possibility that in fighting together they might also die together. As the war developed in its first two years this fact became all too apparent as the casualty lists lengthened, leaving entire communities bereft at the loss of scores of local men, many often being killed together in a single engagement.

One of the first to enlist for the embryonic Swansea Battalion was John Stanley Strange of Brynmill, manager of the Old Brewery. In the first newspaper list of volunteers Strange's name appears third. Obviously possessing suitable qualities he was soon commissioned and took up the rank of lieutenant.[24]

Dyson Brock Williams was a well known figure in the Swansea locality being a successful businessman with a solicitor's practice. A keen sportsman, he enjoyed rugby and excelled at cricket as a right-handed batsman. He had captained both the Swansea and Glamorgan cricket teams, appearing for Glamorgan against a touring Australian side. He had some involvement in the raising of the battalion before being himself appointed as a Temporary Major in May 1915.[25]

The Mayor's eldest son, Francis (Frank) Llewellyn Corker, had enlisted at Bridgend in September 1914, at first being assigned as a private in the Glamorgan Yeomanry. However, whether by reason of personal aptitude or some discreet string pulling, he was soon discharged from the ranks and appointed to a commission as a second lieutenant in the battalion formed largely at the instigation of his father. He was nineteen years old.[26]

Colin Charles Thomas was born on 16 January 1894 at Fairfield Terrace in Swansea. Brother to two older sisters, he attended Danygraig School, St Thomas. His father served for a time as a constable in the Swansea Borough Police force before an injury sustained in the course of his duties led to his leaving the force and returning to gardening as a career. He died of tuberculosis at the age of thirty-nine years.

The family then moved to Pontarddulais where Colin attended the National School on Pentre Road until leaving at the age of fourteen years in order to assist the family finances. He worked at the village chemical works before joining the Swansea Battalion as a private in November 1914.[27]

(William) Haydn David was born in 1896 and lived at Scutari Row, Taibach, near Port Talbot. He was employed at the D.R. David Tinplate Works, Port Talbot. In answer to the call for recruits, Haydn joined the Swansea Battalion.[28]

Not all recruits were originally from Swansea or

'For King and Country' – Colin Charles Thomas, posed here by the photographer with a swagger stick and cap badge displayed. Obviously proud to be among those who had volunteered. Denzil Thomas

Haydn David.
Connie Evans

even its surrounds. Charles Henry Mew was a native of Freshwater on the Isle of Wight. Moving to Swansea in 1908 or 1909 he found employment on the tramways and railways of the area. He then moved to the firm of Griff Davies of Paxton Street, a company that was still trading until relatively recent times.

With war having been expected for some time the declaration itself was no great surprise to Mew who also thought it looked as though it would not be the quick affair predicted by the press. The initial recruitment drive in Swansea left Mew largely unmoved, though by late autumn he was beginning to have second thoughts. Matters crystallized during a shopping trip to Swansea in December 1914.

While Mrs Mew shopped, Mr Mew calmly made his way to the Recruiting Office at Mond Buildings, Union Street. Keen to join the Garrison Artillery that he believed had a detachment on his native Isle of Wight, he found himself instead at the mercy of a persuasive recruiting officer. He was promptly enlisted in the Swansea Battalion.

Mrs Mew's subsequent advice that he was not bound to go was politely brushed aside; he would prefer to go now and voluntarily at that, rather than wait and perhaps be compelled to go in the future. He was duly given a free rail pass to Rhyl (the battalion having departed some time earlier) as well as the King's shilling. He left Swansea within a day or two, with little time to order his affairs.[29]

Richard (Dick) Thomas Lyons was born in Ballydavid, near Waterford, Ireland. He was the second of five sons whose father died as a young man following a farming accident. His mother, a 'townie', was unable to run the farm properly and cope with five small boys without the assistance of her late husband. Life became harder and the boys' schooling intermittent. The farm life had eventually to be abandoned and Richard moved to Swansea where he joined the police force. The appeal for recruits for 'Lloyd George's Welsh Army' obviously struck a chord with Richard and both he and his brother joined up; the younger brother falsifying his age; the policeman turning a diplomatic blind eye to the indiscretion. No doubt Richard's ready knowledge of police drill and discipline made him an attractive recruit to what was essentially, at first, a civilian army.[30]

John Henry England lived at Llanishen, near Cardiff. He was educated at Cardiff High School and King's College, Taunton, where he served in the Officer Training Corps, before entering the employment of Messrs Spillers and Bakers as a clerk. He signed up for four years service in the Territorial Force on 24 August 1914, aged seventeen years, meaning he would not be required to serve abroad. He spent almost a year helping guard the north-east coast of England before obtaining a commission in August 1915. The recommendation for his commission was supported by two local worthies, Colonel William Watts and the Earl of Plymouth, Lord Lieutenant of Glamorgan. Seeing the predicament of the country he later voluntarily subjected himself to possible service overseas, with all the risks that that such a decision entailed.[31]

Samuel Thomas Gammon lived with his wife, Gladys, at George Bank, Mumbles, Swansea. He already had two sons, Thomas Samuel and Richard, when he enlisted. Gladys was to give birth to a third son, Fred, in August 1915 while her husband was away, training with the battalion.[32]

Two volunteers who came from even further afield were David Aubrey Sandbrook and Donald Henry Devenish. Sandbrook had links with Swansea (a relative was at one time editor of the *Cambrian* newspaper) though, like Devenish, he was currently living and working in South Africa. With the outbreak of war in Europe both men were determined to return to the homeland and offer their services. Frustrated at not being able to board a suitable sailing vessel as passengers they joined as crew members, together with another comrade, and worked their passages. Both were granted commissions in the Swansea Battalion.[33]

A.A.Perkins, Honorary Recruiting Officer for the Swansea Battalion.
South Wales Daily Post

Even after the departure of the Battalion for north Wales the issue of recruitment did not go away. There was a constant need to provide replacements for units that had suffered losses, as well as new troops to fill out the ranks of the greatly enlarged wartime army. To this end in April 1915 a meeting was arranged in Swansea to discuss the issue of the deployment of female labour. The increasing use of females in a number of previously male dominated areas of work naturally released men for the front. Indeed, it was noted that the Swansea Improvements and Tramway Co. had seen almost thirty per cent of its men enlist, a loss that could not be made up other than by the employment of women. The aim of the meeting:

> ...*was to bring the idea more closely to the employer's notice with a view to*

Southend at the Mumbles, Swansea. A typical Victorian seaside resort on the outskirts of Swansea. Dave Westron

the possibility of releasing a number of men of recruitable age for the forces... Swansea had done undoubtedly well in the way of recruiting, having sent somewhere about 12,000 into His Majesty's Forces but it was clear that the Government wanted every available man... Major Anderson pointed out the absolute necessity for more men and drew attention to the casualty list in the last action of note viz. Neuve Chappelle when over 1,000 officers were lost with the rank and file losses proportionately large.[34]

The urgent nature of the recruitment crisis was reinforced by a letter from Benson in M 1915 stating that:

The strength of the Battalion at present is 39 officers and 1,144 men. Of this number 10 are awaiting discharge and 6 are likely to be struck off as deserters, leaving the number 200 short of the required strength.[35]

In July 1915 Benson was again in contact with Swansea, this time confirming that planned size of the battalion was to be 1,381 NCOs and other ranks. It is doubtful if number was ever achieved in practice.[36]

Major A.A. Perkins, the local recruiting officer, felt that he knew the root cause of problem, advising Alderman Corker in December 1915, after watching the battalion le Winchester for the front:

With reference to our conversation at Winchester re shortage of Men in the Swansea Battalion, the matter is serious and your Committee should really carefully go into the subject. I have, as you know, worked hard to get men for the Battalion for some time passed, but candidly your Committee have not helped me... the Battalion is going to France actually not up to strength and a Draft they sent me down from Rhyl I should imagine were the worst pick of the Training Battalion.[37]

Clearly, the problem of obtaining enough recruits in the absence of a system of compuls conscription was not going to go away.

Notes

1. SWDP, 11 September 1914.
2. SWDP, 24 September 1914.
3. WGAS, TC 26/3.
4. SWDP, 1 October 1914.
5. Information supplied by David Warren of Cardiff, (hereafter Warren).
6. SWDP, 5 October 1914.
7. SWDP, 9 October 1914.
8. SWDP, 6 October 1914.
9. SWDP, 16 October 1914.
10. SWDP, 17 October 1914.
11. SWDP, 17 October 1914.
12. SWDP, 4 November 1914.
13. SWDP, 4 November 1914.
14. SWDP, 6 November 1914.
15. SWDP, 19 November 1914.
16. SWDP, 24 November 1914.
17. SWDP, 24 November 1914.
18. SWDP, 27 November 1914.
19. WGAS, TC 26/1.
20. ibid.
21. WGAS, TC 26/22.
22. WGAS, TC 26/1.
23. ibid.
24. SWDP 17 September 1914.
25. Warren.
26. PRO/WO/339/15332.
27. Information supplied by Mr D. Thomas of Pontarddula Swansea (hereafter Thomas).
28. Information supplied by Mrs C. Evans of Skewen, Nea (hereafter Evans).
29. WGAS, TH 36/A, taped interview (1974) with Charles Henry Mew, (hereafter WGAS/Mew).
30. Information supplied by Mrs K. Warr of Chichester, (hereafter Warr).
31. Warren.
32. Information supplied by Mr John Powell and Mr Fred Gammon hereafter Powell/Gammon.
33. SWDP, 8 August 1917.
34. WGAS, TC 26/26.
35. WGAS, TC 26/3.
36. ibid.
37. WGAS, TC 26/4.

CHAPTER FOUR

Training the Plain Clothes Army

Helping provide equipment for Swansea's new battalion could, to a degree, be seen as a patriotic duty by those businesses that were in the right lines of trade. At the same time the trade could not be done on a no-charge basis and there were clear commercial opportunities to be obtained from meeting the demand for all sorts of items that were suitable for military purposes. Businesses, therefore, were not slow in offering their services in a number of areas. For example, in the case of tents and associated items James's Marquees were able to offer:

...various waterproof tents; Bedding and Blankets with Waterproof Sheets beneath to cover, say, 1,000 men during the training period would cost £500.[1]

Despite such occasional unsolicited approaches from suppliers, the kitting out and equipping of the men proved immediately problematic. Initially, at least, there were simply no uniforms for the new recruits to wear and they paraded in their civilian garb giving rise to the nickname of 'The Plain Clothes Army'. Private Mew, enlisting in the battalion in December 1914 after it had actually left for its training camp at Rhyl, travelled up in his own clothes. On arrival he was, however, given a temporary uniform suit of a blue colour.[2]

In the country generally there was a shortage of the traditional khaki material and this was an important factor in the Welsh National Executive Committee's decision to provide uniforms for the Welsh units in the homespun 'Welsh Grey' or 'Brethyn Llwyd'. Even then supplies of the chosen material proved initially inadequate to meet the enormous demand for uniforms. However, the position as regards the Welsh cloth eased in early 1915 at about the same time that, ironically, khaki also became more readily available. In a relatively short space of time most units had reverted to a uniform in the more traditional khaki colour, the Brethyn Llwyd uniforms being passed down to reserve units.[3]

The supply of footwear was also a problem though the battalion was fortunate in having among its number Sergeant Oakes, who was an accomplished boot maker with easy access to 'some excellent leather'. Having been set to work for the benefit of the battalion his activities and subsequent request for

Sergeant Oakes who helped equip the Battalion with boots. South Wales Daily Post

Private Bebell was one of the lucky early recipients of the scarce uniforms. South Wales Daily Post

reimbursement attracted the attention of a Welsh Army Corps official who, obviously astonished, requested:

...to be informed under what circumstances a Sergeant serving on the Army List came to be a contractor for Army Stores.

After an exchange of correspondence, a cheque for £95-17s-6d eventually arrived from the Welsh Army Corps, much to the relief of Sergeant Oakes who, by that time, was being threatened with legal action by his suppliers.[4]

With demand in the country as a whole for rifles and ammunition understandably at an all time high, supplies were correspondingly scarce. However, Swansea's premiere department store, Messrs Ben Evans & Co. was able to provide the Swansea Battalion Committee with twenty Lee-Enfield .303 match quality rifles at £6 18s 6d each, including delivery to Rhyl. Additionally, 5,000 rounds of suitable ammunition, which was apparently particularly hard to obtain, was offered for sale at £5 18s 6d per 1,000 rounds. Even with such vital items as rifles, prices were still an issue and the Assistant Director of Ordnance at Chester, on considering reimbursement of the local committee, initially baulked at the price paid, feeling that £6 per rifle was quite enough. Messrs Ben Evans & Co. was perplexed at this assertion since it had, itself, paid £6 5s 9d for each rifle.[5]

Alderman Corker and his Battalion Committee were also proving industrious by providing binoculars for the officers, but drew the line at swords, especially as the local committee funds were clearly not inexhaustible. Indeed, Colonel Benson was reminded of the need to obtain clearance for purchases from the committee before incurring expenditure. This advice seemed to be forgotten, or at least went unheeded, as subsequently Benson was dismayed to find that having obtained thirty-eight revolvers for the use of battalion officers the committee would only countenance paying for twenty-nine![6]

With the equipment situation being perceived as increasingly urgent and, with many fingers being firmly in the pie, it was inevitable that the cost conscious sensitivities of the War Office would occasionally be trodden upon. Always anxious to ensure value for money, it was soon making its views known on the profligacy it saw in the purchase of various items by the local committees:

I am commanded by the Army Council to inform you that it has been brought to their notice that the limitations imposed in the Allowance Regulations on the local purchase of articles of Stationary and on local printing are being disregarded, and, amongst other items, Typewriting Machines, expensive duplicating apparatus, India Rubber stamps and other articles are being purchased at a cost which causes unnecessary expense to the public.

GREETINGS!

1915

WELCOME, 1915. MAY IT BE HIS TO SOUND THE "CEASE FIRE."

A New Year cartoon whose optimism proved to be sadly unfounded. South Wales Daily Post

...I am to add that the prohibition of local purchase extends to Official Text Books and Drill Books. Ample stocks of these are available to meet demands from all entitled to them as a free issue, and the Controller of H.M. Stationary Office has notified that he will be unable to continue to authorise the refund of any money spent in the purchase of these books.[7]

Clearly, the local committee and the battalion would have to plan to defeat the might of the Kaiser's Army with less rubber stamps and typewriters than they would have wished for.

If the number of items of equipment ordered and issued was important, so was the fate of even the delivery packing itself. In November 1915 the Ordnance Officer at Pembroke Dock was enquiring about a shipment:

In December last 12 arm chests of sorts were forwarded to C.O.O. Weedon. These had contained arms issued for the Swansea Battalion, The Welch Regt.[8]

With strenuous efforts being made to fully kit the men out for active service it was also necessary to consider provision for the inevitable consequence of engaging the enemy. To this end the question of medical facilities for those invalided home received attention.

Swansea was disappointed to discover that the War Office intended setting up three base hospitals in the Western Division, none of which, however, would be based at Swansea. Manchester, Liverpool and Cardiff were instead the chosen sites. If a base hospital was not to be provided there were, however, other options that might still be of assistance locally.

In March 1915 the Parliamentary Secretary for Education asked that Swansea provide additional hospital accommodation by using school premises. A minimum of 100 beds per building would be required. Private initiative was also apparent with Miss Dulcie Vivian placing her home at Parc Wern at the disposal of the local authority. On inspection it was felt that this would provide room for between 80 and 100 soldiers, together with nurses and attendants. Additionally there was the possibility of erecting wooden structures in the grounds, capable of holding up to 300 more casualties. Given the size of the task of conversion, it was decided to ask the War Office or Red Cross to take over the premises.[9]

Similarly, Mr F. Cory Yeo also placed his home at Danycoed at the disposal of the local authority and this was deemed capable of holding 400 cases if wooden structures were erected in the grounds as with Parc Wern. Mr Cory Yeo's generosity even went so far as to offer to personally bear the cost of conversion and maintenance of the building during its use as a hospital.[10]

In October 1915 the Red Cross took over Parc Wern as an auxiliary hospital whilst also accepting the use of Hedd Fan at Sketty, home to Mr Charles E. Gleaves, who patriotically placed his home at its disposal.[11]

With the mustering of men for service in the 43rd (Welsh) Division being almost complete (though new recruits would continue to come forward for weeks to come), it was necessary to start assembling the division from the various component units in order that proper training on a larger scale could be commenced. The Swansea Battalion therefore departed the town by two special trains on 2 December 1914, and progressed to Rhyl. Large crowds turned out to see the men off:

The first detachment numbered about five-hundred men, and marched into Union-street, Oxford-street, Temple-street, Wind-street, and into the station.

Lieutenant-Colonel Benson and Major O'Hara were at the head of the procession, and the men marched along with splendid swing and soldierly bearing. No one could fail to notice the great strides the battalion have made during the past couple of months, and the officers in charge have reason to be gratified at the smart appearance of the men. Unfortunately a number of the men have not yet been supplied with uniforms and rifles, and this, to a certain extent, militated against the general martial effect.

The men who had rifles carried them with bayonets fixed, and carried the kit under the right arm. As the men marched briskly along, their friends shouted out 'Good Luck!' The whole battalion were in the best of spirit, and sang snatches of many popular songs as they swung past. Along the route cheers were raised but for the most part one was struck by the absence of great enthusiasm on the part of the crowd.

The reason was not far to seek, for here and there a wife or sweetheart would rush out of the crowd, and holding one of the men in fond embrace would shower on him affectionate kisses and tears.

Such scenes as these no doubt do not make for mere cheering. The men of the battalion knew they had hard work in front of them; the crowd knew it also and no one could hazard a guess as to what the future had in store for them.

There was many a sad parting, and at the station some of the women, who struggled bravely to keep back the tears, could do so no longer, and gave way to their grief at being parted from their husbands, how long they knew not.

The men, however, appeared fit for anything. The majority looked grim and determined, but a few of the younger men were so unaffected by their departure that they waltzed in the Victoria Station yard to the strains of the music from the Swansea Telegraph Messengers' Band, who played them to the station with

Swansea Battalion Officers and NCOs. Simon Peter Lee

OFF TO RHYL CAMP.

The Battalion departs Swansea for Rhyl.
South Wales Daily Post

Victoria Station from where the Swansea Battalion departed for Rhyl in December 1914. Bernard Mitchell

'Tipperary,' 'Your King and Country Need You,' 'The Marseillaise,' 'Harlech', etc. The second contingent of the battalion soon followed and was met with similar scenes, the crowd having grown larger as the day progressed:

> *...shouts from the crowd of 'Are you down-hearted?' were answered with an emphatic and vociferous 'No!' The men were in the happiest of moods and sang parodies on the popular songs as they strode along. All along the line friends grabbed hold of their hands and gave them their best wishes.*
>
> *Outside Victoria Station the crowd was impassable, and many friends and relatives could get nowhere near the 'boys' to see them off.*
>
> *Children, wives and sweethearts were held upon the shoulders of men in the crowd and waved farewell with their handkerchiefs, and threw kisses to their men.*[12]

The public were not admitted to the station, it being felt that the likely press of such a large crowd on the narrow station platforms could endanger those attending. This was a matter of much resentment at the time as relatives and friends jostled for a last glimpse of a loved one. A number of local dignitaries were allowed onto the platform to wish the men well and these included Alderman Corker, instrumental in the formation of the battalion, Colonel Edwards Vaughan (of the 6th Welsh Reserves), Colonel Sinclair and Colonel W.D. Rees.

As the special trains brought the battalion into Rhyl, scenes similar to those that

Number 1 Platoon of 'A' company at Rhyl.
South Wales Daily Post

had seen the men off at Swansea occurred:

> *...the Swansea Battalion arrived at Rhyl on Tuesday afternoon under the command of Colonel Benson, D.S.O., two special trains bringing them up from south Wales. They received a very hearty welcome from the towns people, who turned out in large numbers to greet them, and kindly words were spoken at the railway station by Brigadier General Dunn. The bands of the two Rhondda Battalions, which have been training at Rhyl some weeks, headed the procession through the town and along the sea front to the billeting quarters.*[13]

The warmth of the welcome was reflected in the quality of the billeting arrangements since they seemed to receive general acclamation:

> *...the ex-mayor (Alderman T.T. Corker) has received a letter from... Colonel Benson... stating that the men are in splendid billets, and close together and very comfortable. The weather has been a bit against them and made drilling rather difficult, but he feels sure that when Swansea people know how well off the men are in their billets we shall soon have sufficient recruits to fill up the battalion. The ex-mayor points out how very few have been offering themselves during the last few days, but he sincerely hopes that this good account from the commanding officer will induce the young men of Swansea to come forward and complete the battalion without delay for the honour of the town.*[14]

This satisfaction was not merely limited to those higher up the chain of command but extended to the lower ranks as well:

> *The battalion have the best of everything, and one lad writing home says: 'Walter-road is not in it compared with our place; the table was sumptuously*

Ready for anything. Simon Peter Lee

Training at Rhyl. Simon Peter Lee

laid, and the boys swear they will never leave Rhyl. Gee! But we are having a grand time.' [15]

Another commented that:

> The weather at Rhyl has been pretty variable ever since our arrival here, but the Battalion members have quite accustomed themselves to the elements, and up to the present nothing disheartens the 'boys'. One afternoon we drilled through what was practically a sandstorm on the beach. It was alright – I don't think...
>
> ...ours is quite a 'sportsmen's' battalion, but 'togs' are not at hand at present. It is possible our lads when returning from their leave will bring their outfits with them. Probably most of them, however, will be without, so that jerseys, knicks, etc., will be wanted, especially as we shall some day before leaving here issue a challenge to the Rhondda boys to a rugby match...
>
> Corporal Eddie Norman and Private George Thomas have been out singing again, and of course rendered a splendid account of themselves. Quite apart from possessing fine voices, these two young men are an extremely happy couple – real good humorists and very popular everywhere.[16]

The wide distribution of the division's units between Rhyl in the north and Abergavenny in the south, somewhat mitigated against full-scale training manoeuvres at this stage, though the emphasis was still on open warfare training, as far as was practicable. It was felt that there would be ample scope for training in trench warfare techniques once the division arrived in France. Equipment was still a concern, with the limited number of rifles issued to the division being a major problem that would not be fully resolved until two weeks before the battalion sailed for France.

Whilst the battalion was at Rhyl, a number of its members were occasionally back in Swansea, either attending to battalion business or on leave. On one such occasion the locals took the opportunity of collaring Captain Smith, whom they held in high regard and in February 1915:

> ...a smoking concert was held in order to make a presentation to Captain Aubrey Smith, of the Swansea Battalion, who formerly did capital work in

On parade on the beach at Rhyl. Simon Peter Lee

Welsh Brigade recruits in barracks at Rhyl. Flintshire Record Office

Recruits take a break during training in north Wales. Trevor Tasker

helping to organise the Swansea Rugby Training Corps, which is now doing such fine work... the Chairman said they had decided to make a presentation of a handsome luminous watch and compass to Captain Smith as a mark of appreciation of services rendered to the corps, and to his rapid rise in the British Army. Both on the playing field and as a member of the Swansea Rugby Committee they had always found Captain Smith to be a gentleman. (Applause.) He was a sportsman who never left the field with any regrets - unless it was because he hadn't scored a try. (Laughter.)

Captain Smith thanked the members for their kind reception and also for their memento. He said he had noticed the Swansea Training Corps at drill and had been struck by the fine discipline of the men, especially as discipline was very difficult to secure when there was no compulsion. He thanked Major Perkins for his instruction, which proved so valuable to him when he joined the Swansea Battalion, where he at once felt at home because there were so many members from the Swansea Training Corps... he regretted that Swansea people had never seen the Swansea Battalion and probably would never do so now, because the men went away before they had uniforms and rifles.[17]

All pals together – a company sergeant major flanked by two sergeants. Simon Peter Lee

In April 1915 a career soldier, H.C. Rees, arrived at Colwyn Bay to act as a General Staff Officer to the 43rd Welsh Division. Rees was to have an eventful war, having already served with the 2nd Battalion from August 1914. He was to leave the Welsh Division in early 1916 and then saw service with the 31st, 4th and 50th Divisions. He was captured in May 1918 while commanding 150 Brigade and was interviewed by the Kaiser at the end of the month. He was repatriated in December 1918. At Colwyn Bay in early 1915 he found:

General Ivor Phillips was running almost a complete division as regards units, and over strength as regards men, entirely alone. Colonel Morgan was responsible for the medical arrangements, otherwise he had had no staff officers to assist him... it was almost entirely without arms, equipment, guns or transport.[18]

Rees also found that some of the officers were unsuited for their positions of

An officer at Rhyl during training. Trevor Tasker

A happy group during training at Rhyl. Trevor Tasker

Under canvas – sorting out for a kit inspection. Trevor Tasker

Officers observe the progress of training. Trevor Tasker

responsibility and he proceeded to quickly knock the division into shape:

> *As equipment increased and training improved, I launched out into a few divisional exercises. Unfortunately, the standard of knowledge of the Brigadiers and commanding officers was, as a rule, so low that any progress in field training was manifestly impossible... changes of command were absolutely essential. Eventually two Brigadiers and nine of the original commanding officers were replaced before the division sailed for France.*[19]

On 29 April 1915 what had previously been called the 43rd Division was re-designated the 38th (Welsh) Division, consisting of the newly numbered 113, 114 and 115 Infantry Brigades and associated units, the Swansea Battalion forming part of the 114 Brigade. Also in that Brigade were the Carmarthen (15th Welsh) and the two Rhondda battalions (10th and 13th Welsh). At about this time it was becoming clear to the National Executive Committee that the raising of a second Welsh Division, thus enabling the creation of a Welsh Army Corps of two divisions, might not actually make best use of the available manpower. Indeed, the Army Council, a

Officers at Rhyl. Trevor Tasker.

55

An officer lets a car take the strain. Trevor Tasker

very powerful body, was of the firm opinion that future recruiting efforts should be directed at providing drafts for those battalions already at the front, as well as reserve companies for the new army. With these unfavourable developments Lloyd George's dream of a Welsh Army Corps faded slowly away, events having largely overtaken it. The 38th Welsh Division, however, was then a reality and was beginning to hum with activity.[20]

Private Charles Henry Mew found the billeting arrangements at Rhyl quite acceptable even if, at that stage, he still lacked a proper uniform. The first parade he attended consisted of himself, a reservist and a corporal who instructed them both in right and left turns before they were deemed competent enough to join the rest of the battalion. After this gentle introduction to the rigours of army life, the training regime became 'pretty stiff' with physical jerks being completed under the watchful eye of Mr Poole and another civilian instructor, especially sent up from Swansea.

There was some opportunity for unarmed combat training and rifle practice at Rhyl, with dummies taking the brunt of the men's enthusiasm for the bayonet. Route marches could be of fifteen miles length in full kit, all in the burning heat of a splendid summer. Several recruits passed out either on the march or even on parade due to the draining effect of the heat. 'Leave' was a word that was rarely heard and infrequently experienced by the recruits during this time of intense activity.[21]

Corporal Ernest Beynon wrote home to tell his brother about his training experiences at Rhyl. An Orderly Room was located in a large house near to the Water Chute and Marine Lake, these attractions providing clear evidence of the popularity

Fostering the 'offensive spirit'; vigorous bayonet practice at Rhyl. Trevor Tasker

At rest during training. Trevor Tasker

An officer group during training. Trevor Tasker

A mounted officer. Trevor Tasker

Officers at Rhyl. Trevor Tasker

Swansea Battalion recruits at their ease with two civilians. Willie Williams is in the photograph. Ian Milne

Tawe the bulldog once again the centre of attention. Included in the photograph is Willie Williams of the Cuba Hotel, Swansea. Ian Milne

of Rhyl as a pre-war holiday destination. The fields in front of the house provided ample space for drilling the troops while on other occasions the men would parade on the seafront prior to marching for long distances over the nearby sand dunes.[22]

Dick Lyons found his service in the Swansea Police force helpful in securing him a rapid promotion to sergeant. Already familiar from his police days, with the routines of drill and discipline he was sent to Aldershot where he completed courses in physical training and bayonet fighting. On his return to the battalion he then passed on these new found skills to his comrades.[23]

As the training regime progressed, so the need to reassure the high command representatives that all was well grew in importance. Major General Ivor Phillips had been initially appointed to command a brigade in the Welsh Division but, possibly due to his friendship with Lloyd George, he was rapidly promoted to the command of the entire Division. He had represented Southampton as a Liberal MP since 1906. An experienced if unexceptional soldier, he had left the army more than ten years earlier after seeing service in the Burma campaign (1887), the North-West Frontier and China.[24] In February 1915 he reviewed the progress made by elements of his division:

> On Monday, in delightful weather, an inspection of the 2nd Welsh Brigade, now at Rhyl, and consisting of the Swansea Battalion, 1st and 2nd Rhondda Battalions, and the Carmarthen Battalion, took place. An extremely large crowd had gathered in the East Parade. The inspection was made by Major-General Ivor Phillips, D.S.O., commanding the 43rd Division, accompanied by his staff. Afterwards each battalion, headed by their respective bands, 'marched past' the general to the strains of 'See the Conquering Hero Comes.' It was an inspiring sight...and I understand that the general complimented Colonel Benson upon the battalion's smart appearance. The men are a credit to Swansea.[25]

Even if the Swansea Battalion was many months away from active service, casualties, even if not as a result of enemy action, inevitably occurred:

> The funeral of the late Private Cecil John Hopkins, of the Swansea Battalion, and who... died at Rhyl on Sunday from pneumonia, took place on Thursday at Danygraig Cemetery... It was noticed that a relief section of the Swansea Battalion were present, under Lieut. Lewis, and six of the party acted as pall bearers, Sergt. Carey being in charge.[26]

Similarly, Second Lieutenant Ivor Kenneth Colquhoun died while on sick leave from a combination of tonsillitis and heart failure. He was twenty-two years old when he died in September 1915.[27]

At the start of September, the battalion, in concert with the other units of the Division, began the journey to Winchester where training on the divisional level could at last be undertaken. The town of Rhyl turned out readily to say goodbye to what was obviously a very popular band of men:

Second Lieutenant I.K. Colquhoun. Swansea Library Service

> After having been in training at Rhyl for exactly nine months, the Swansea Battalion... left the town on Wednesday night for another camp, whither they had been preceded by the 1st and 2nd Rhondda Battalions. Their departure was the occasion for one of the most enthusiastic demonstrations the town has witnessed for months. They have made Rhyl a home from home, and many of them have entered

All ready for the Western Front – a Welsh recruit at Rhyl wearing the leather straps and ammunition pouches which became synonymous with the Kitchener volunteer battalions. Simon Peter Lee

Colin Charles Thomas (left) and an unidentified pal with a comradely hand placed on his. Denzil Thomas

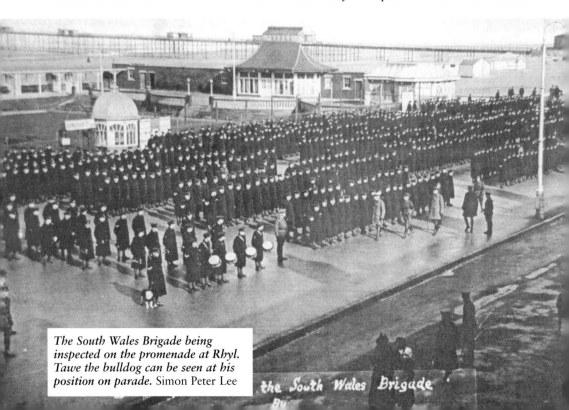

The South Wales Brigade being inspected on the promenade at Rhyl. Tawe the bulldog can be seen at his position on parade. Simon Peter Lee

the South Wales Brigade

A Company on parade at Rhyl. Trevor Tasker

into the life of the town in various ways, while ties of closest association with the town have been formed. It was, therefore, with genuine regret that the townspeople bade them good-bye.

Both residents and visitors turned out in thousands to accord them a hearty send-off, this affording striking testimony to the popularity of the whole battalion.

Major O'Hara was in command owing to the continued indisposition of Colonel Benson, and each company was in turn played to the station by the brigade band, which struck up appropriate music as each special train steamed off, the last leaving at midnight.

Swansea people would have had cause for pride had they seen the battalion depart; every man so bronzed and stalwart in figure and so cheerful in manner and determined to do full justice to the traditions of their regiment.[28]

During August and September 1915 the component parts of the Welsh Division were

Colin Charles Thomas *(centre back row)* and friends from his hut at Rhyl. Note the sun helmets being worn. Some Kitchener divisions had already been sent to the Middle East. In the event the Welsh was not to follow. Denzil Thomas

Colin Charles Thomas and other recruits, including Tawe the Bulldog. Denzil Thomas

finally united at Winchester and, for the first time, it was possible to start training at the operational as well as the tactical level. The surrounding terrain was admirably suited for that purpose and, with the belated arrival of a supply of rifles, the ranges at both Salisbury Plain and Winchester soon became hives of activity.

At Winchester the pace of training quickened noticeably from that which had gone before. Messrs Howells, Home, Bellingham, M.B. Williams and Strange all attended an officers' course at Camberley. Other courses attended by various officers or other ranks included physical training, bayonet fighting, bombing, musketry, range finding, fire direction and control and cookery. Clearly the old adage that an army marches on its stomach had not been forgotten![29]

Field days were held at the level of the battalion, the brigade and the division as both officers and men grappled with the complexities of commanding and controlling thousands of men, each skilled in any one of a number of specialities. Route marches, 'model' attacks and the ever-popular kit inspections also figured prominently in a very busy schedule.

Private Mew recalled travelling to Winchester and being billeted on the hill at South Down Camp. He responded to an appeal for men to train as snipers and went out on Salisbury Plain with a Lee-Enfield rifle equipped with a telescopic sight. During the period of training it rained heavily every day and the trainee snipers' priority became to fire their allotted number of bullets as quickly as possible in order to get in out of the rain. The accuracy of the shots became of purely secondary importance.[30]

| *G. Howells* | *C.F.M. Home* | *R.K. Bellingham* | *M.B. Williams* | *J. S. Stra* |

Chris Jordan

Haydn David at camp (marked with a cross) with the ever popular battalion mascot, Tawe the bulldog. Connie Evans

Haydn David, MM (seated) and his pal, Will Hopkins who is wearing signaller flags, good conduct chevron and a wound stripe. Connie Evans

Haydn David and comrades at Rhyl. Some serious boot polishing can be seen taking place at the rear. Connie Evans

Ration time at Rhyl with Haydn David reclining at front right. Connie Evans

2

General Staff Officer H.C. Rees recalls the pace of his own duties increasing rapidly as the men moved into a camp setting:

> *None of them had ever been in a camp before, result chaos. Chaos would not have mattered so much if office work had not been thrown at me with both hands. I employed three shorthand typists and kept them fully employed all day.*
>
> *No Bde staffs were there, so that I had to correspond with each unit separately.*

While order was being forcibly imposed on the chaos, unwelcome guests also had to be repelled by Rees:

> *Sir Arthur Paget and Sir Pitcairn Campbell both threatened to come over and inspect the troops. I induced them not to come and finally asked Sir P. Campbell to extract the Hdqtrs of the division from Western Command, which he succeeded in doing.*

By the end of October things were at last taking shape when:

> *...guns and arms were at last poured at us from all quarters.*[31]

In the last week of November 1915 the battalion attended a mobilization parade and took part in two rehearsals for a review of the Welsh Division that was to be undertaken by His Majesty the King, prior to the departure of the Division for France. At this time Lieutenant Colonel L.R. King took over the command of the battalion while Major J.H. Hayes became second in command.

King relieved Lieutenant Colonel Benson who was not fit enough for active service overseas and, much to his annoyance, Benson was obliged to follow the medical advice rather than his beloved battalion. He had, however, proved very popular with the men and had helped guide them in good soldierly habits during his tenure, despite being indisposed due to illness on several occasions during their training.

Meanwhile, in Swansea the realization that the town's very own battalion was soon to be setting off for France and Flanders appeared to provoke a late recruiting rush, tinged possibly with feelings of a little guilt by these late converts. This was despite the fact that those enlisting at this time had little realistic chance of immediately joining a battalion that had already been in training for over a year. There were, of course, always the options of their being used in a reserve or reinforcement capacity, as well as the prospect of serving with a battalion other than that of their home town. The local press commented on this rather belated show of patriotic enthusiasm:

> *The record rush was on Saturday, when a large number were attested at the High-street Central Office, and also at Union-street, Morriston, and Trinity... medical examinations had to be dispensed with, so great was the crush, and the men were attested in groups...*
>
> *Doctors and officials can tell many humorous stories and asides of the attesting locally. In the periods of the greatest crushes three or four doctors would be present in one room, and while one would take the height and weight, another would tape the chest and the others would examine with the stethoscope etc. A good rate of passing was 100 per hour, but this was more than the average. The men were stripped and put through - Arm and leg tests for flexibility; bending for pains and ruptures; hopping first on one leg and then on another; chest expansion etc.*

The general survey tapped the heart; searched for varicose veins, tracing for lung trouble and enquiring whether there had been serious illness or discharge from the ears. Eyesight tests were not generally applied, as the men will be examined again later when they are called up.

Mr. W. Crocker told the 'Post' on Sunday evening that when grousers complained of waiting they were told, 'You've been waiting a bit, but we've been waiting for you 16 months.' The effect of this retort, Mr. Crocker says, was magical.

One man asked by the doctor if he ever had fits replied that he had had one or two 'operatic' fits. He meant, of course, epileptic. Another man, asked about gland troubles, admitted he had had an 'emphatic' gland. What he meant was lymphatic.[32]

On 29 November 1915, His Majesty the King was unable to attend due to illness, so the division was reviewed on Crawley Down by Her Majesty, the Queen, accompanied by Her Royal Highness, the Princess Mary. Members of the Battalion Committee were also present, bringing parting gifts of pipes and tobacco for the men. The Queen was able to express her complete satisfaction at the arrangements for the review and the appearance of the men. If the hard work of moulding the men into a competent fighting unit could now be largely regarded as over, the plain fact was that even harder work, of a much more dangerous nature, lay ahead on the continent.

On 2 December the Swansea Battalion left Winchester at 5.15 a.m. for Southampton and an onward sailing to Le Havre in France.[33] It went with the heartfelt prayers and hopes of family, friends and well-wishers for a speedy and safe return home. In fact it would not return home again until after the 1918 Armistice was signed and after it had seen significant action at the front.

Hundreds of the prayers that were offered for the safe return home of a loved one, were destined to remain sadly unanswered.

Notes

1. WGAS, TC 26/1.
2. WGAS/Mew.
3. Hughes, C., *The Welsh Army Corps 1914-1918*, IWM Review Number 1, 1986.
4. WGAS, TC 26/1.
5. ibid.
6. ibid.
7. ibid.
8. ibid.
9. WGAS, TC 26/28.
10. WGAS, TC 26/9.
11. ibid.
12. SWDP, 1 December 1914.
13. *Rhyl Guardian*. 11 December 1914.
14. SWDP, 8 December 1914.
15. ibid.
16. SWDP, 22 December 1914.
17. SWDP, 9 February 1915.
18. IWM/77/179/1 Brigadier General H.C. Rees, *A Personal Record of the War 1915-1916-1917* (hereafter IWM/Rees) p.78-80.
19. ibid.
20. WAC, p.28.
21. WGAS/Mew.
22. Information supplied by Mr W. Beynon of Swansea, hereafter Beynon.
23. Warr.
24. Rhyl Guardian, 22 January 1915.
25. SWDP, 10 February 1915.
26. SWDP, 26 February 1915.
27. PRO/WO/339/25979.
28. SWDP, 2 September 1915.
29. PRO/WO/339/2559.
30. WGAS/Mew.
31. IWM/Rees, op. cit.
32. SWDP, 13 December 1915.
33. PRO/WO/95/2559.

CHAPTER FIVE

France and Flanders

The hectic events of the battalion's departure from the training camp and its subsequent arrival in France was covered by one of the boys, (with village and town names being omitted for censorship reasons):

On Sunday, Nov 28th, we all received our pipes and tobacco from the hands of the deputation from our Council – for which we say in unison – 'Mercy.'

Then our great inspection at Crawley Downs on Monday, the 29th, by Her Majesty Queen Mary. This was an occasion on which I can say every man felt proud to belong to the Army from Wales. The spectacle presented by the Division was simply grand – particularly when, headed by our General the Division marched past Her Majesty in columns of half companies. Those few of Swansea's citizens who witnessed the review had occasion to feel proud of the boys.

On the Thursday following we left our camp at 5 a.m. and marched to Southampton where a great reception awaited us – the good people of the 'village' (?) meeting us with much desired cup of tea and cakes; then on to the steamer.

We embarked later in the day – the passage across is but a memory. We arrived at (?) early on the morning of December 3rd. Disembarking at 8 a.m. we marched through the town to a rest camp. During the march we were met and welcomed by the people of France – (and a nice girl she was!)

Next day we again got on our feet, marching to the station, where we entrained for (?) This journey was not exactly a picnic. Steaming away at 5 p.m. we reached our destination at 2 p.m. the following day. The journey was made in trucks – oh! What a ride! Travelling the streets on the tramlines, we wended our way, vividly bringing to our minds our own dear old express...

Detraining at (?) we again got on the march, to a village, where we were put into billets. Our stay here is indefinite, but while we are here I can assure all at Swansea the boys were never in better spirits. From morn till night one can hear the old marching songs dear to the boys of Abertawe.

We are splendidly equipped, reminiscent of the pirates of old; the only item we are without is a knife between our teeth.

We are experiencing miserable weather, but with the prospect of a very early move to the trenches this passes unnoticed. We expect to be in them within a week. I hope when I next write I will have 'Something' to write about.[1]

In fact, the battalion had disembarked in Le Havre at 7.15 a.m. on 2 December 1915. It had then marched to Number 2 Camp, Bleville. On 4 December it entrained again and departed Havre at 4.15p.m. It reached Aire and then marched to Crecques, arriving at 4.00p.m., where it went into billets. Instruction in musketry and sniping

Sandbagging the trenches at Laventie. Imperial War Museum, Q17402

Trench map of the Richebourg area. National Archives

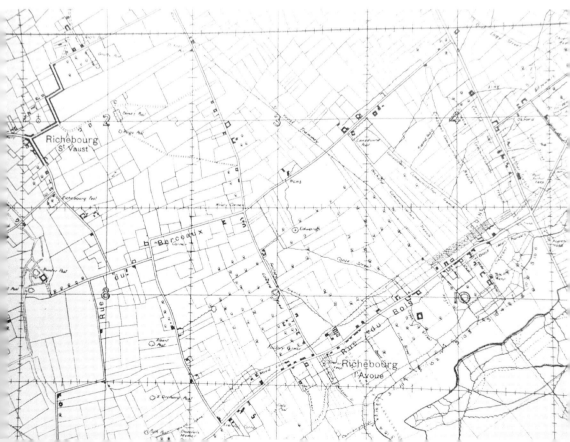

began immediately and a portion of the battalion was deliberately gassed during an exercise. From the 20-27 December the battalion was attached to the 5 Brigade at Richebourg St Vaast, for instruction by the Guards Division in the arcane science of trench warfare.

The battalion was also introduced to the regular rotation of duty, so that a period in the front line would be followed by a spell in support of the front line in the secondary trench system, a little further behind the front. In the event of enemy attacks, support troops could be fed into the front line trench system as reinforcements. There would then follow a period in reserve which was even further away from the front and offered the prospect of some real rest and relaxation. Being in reserve was not risk free, however. German artillery would often target the rear areas hoping to disrupt supply and troop movements and further fray the nerves of those who were meant to be 'resting'.

The battalion was then billeted at Robecq. H.C. Rees recalled the early days at the front in the area of Neuve Chappelle-Richebourg:

Embroidered postcards sent home by Willie Williams who it is thought lived at the Cuba Hotel, Swansea. Willie survived the war. Ian Milne

This part of the line was very quiet and very muddy. The breastworks were in a very bad state of repair and were knee deep in liquid mud.[2]

Private W.E. Hodgens gave his parents an account of the work and the dangers that were ever present in the front line:

Last night about 100 of us formed a working party into the first line of trenches, and were working with the Royal Engineers building up the parapet of the trenches. I shall not say it was not dangerous, because it was. The German trenches were about 40 yards in front of us. Their machine guns were rattling all the time.

The great difficulty lies in getting into the trenches, but once you are in you are fairly safe. Our artillery were playing a tune over us all the time. It was quite an experience, and our boys behaved just like a lot of old veterans.

Our company will spend Christmas Day in the trenches, so I look forward to a novel experience.

Swansea's new Mayor, Alderman Daniel Jones, who succeeded T.T. Corker.
South Wales Daily Post

Although we have a lot of mud to contend with, we cannot help but feel jolly. Nobody seems anxious about the danger they are in.

We came up to 'Mudtown' in London motor buses, and it was like a carnival to see a crowd of fellows on the top of each bus dressed in their 'Teddy Bear' coats, made of goat skins, sheep skins and skins of all colours – anything to keep the cold out.[3]

Private A.E. Norman recorded the experience of a first Christmas on active service in foreign parts:

This is a place and what a Christmas! Still, I did not do so badly. I am back on the transport lines now and we had a bit of dinner – stew. But the poor boys in the trenches are going through it now with a vengeance. Before going into the trenches each man is supplied with a pair of 'waders' so you can surmise what it is like – up to their waists in mud and slush.

We have had about three or four wounded. And one has died in the trenches, and a fine chap he was. We are attached to a regiment that has been out here some time. Our artillery hasn't half given those beggars on the other side a shaking. There's no football with the Prussian Guards this Christmas.

We are still having wet weather, but things are all right generally....[4]

Another of the battalion recalled their first experience of the trenches and the novelty of being exposed to hostile fire:

FOR THE BOYS OF 'SWANSEA'S OWN.'

taken at Messrs. Alf. James's Stores of parcels of cigarettes, from for the lads in the Swansea Battalion.

(Photo: Chapman.)

Gifts from the people of Swansea are dispatched to the front. South Wales Daily Post

The late Pte. Sandywell.

Private Sandywell, one of the first to be killed. He was accidently shot by one of his comrades. South Wales Daily Post

Private's Thomas and Raddenbury who were both wounded by a shell whilst Corporal Harvey was another of those killed. South Wales Daily Post

2,000 killed.

SWANSEA BATTALION MEN WHO WERE HIT.

UNDER DOOR.

Y DRAPER'S AIRS.

BY MONEY-IDER.

e Bankruptcy Court on is, trading as D. Lewis Llewelyn-street Llan- i public examination. bilities were estimated ith his deficiency at

Mr. Wm. Davies, self- ppeared, attributed his s, bad trade, and ill

fficial Receiver, debtor as a collier at Clydach n insurance agent com- menced business as a reet, Llanelly. The cessful, so in 1905 he as a draper, and for it up.

Wm. Davies as to how moneylenders, debtor letter under his door oney, and saying that ld send back £20 in ed to the terms. He name and return the

This class of business ders tempts people. e had business with ter.)

nation was closed.

Pte. L. C. Thomas. Pte. Raddenbury. Both wounded with "Swansea's Own" recently.

Corpl. Rd. Harvey, of Scyborfach-street, who was in the fatal dug-out.

's GRAVE.

APPEAL TO

15½ YEARS OLD SOLDIER!

weather. The presen out by the M and others c was most wel it is but a fe

WITH TH

Germans

A letter se Lewis, machine sea Battalion. "I am in t Davies (editor into the trench were killed th are Lunsdain (already report with the mach fired on us for all they asked f mercifield) got a cap, though it was a lucky m his helmet was Battalion give and more.

A VISITO Sirdailler T. "You must for not writing football, which of us wish to t good old 'Daily reason that I because we ha trenches after "We were v Davies in the were astonished looks in the with the souven "I must no very much for 'Post,' and its

OF "SWANSEA'S OWN."

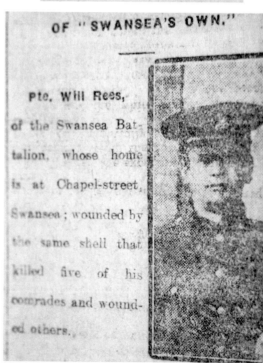

Pte. Will Rees, of the Swansea Bat- talion, whose home is at Chapel-street, Swansea; wounded by the same shell that killed five of his comrades and wound- ed others.

Private Will Rees who was wounded by the shell that killed several comrades. South Wales Daily Post

...(we) were taken in motor buses as near to the firing line as safety permits. Here again we were billeted in a village (which, by the way, was receiving the attention of the German artillery), and we were attached by companies to the several battalions holding the line on our front, to receive instruction in trench warfare, and incidentally our baptism of fire.[5]

Lieutenant W.A.S. Davies was the son of J.A. Davies, manager of the Hafod Copper Works. Lieutenant Davies had a very lucky escape as he went about his duties in the front line trenches as the year drew to a close:

...he was in the trenches when a piece of German shrapnel came hurtling along and took his cap off, with the exception of the lining, which remained on his head. Naturally the shock and impact brought on the concussion Lieutenant Davies is suffering from, and from which his numerous friends trust he will soon recover...(He is) well known in local sporting circles. He has frequently played for the Swansea cricket team and has displayed great promise in the batting department, as well as in fielding. He has also taken a keen interest in Rugby and was a more than useful three-quarter, having played many matches with the Swansea Battalion.[6]

Given the difficulties of sometimes getting supplies to the front line troops it is not surprising that parcels occasionally arrived later than anticipated. That seems to have been the case with the gifts sent by the Swansea Corporation which included 1,000 plum puddings as well as for each man a writing pad, fifty envelopes and a pencil.[7] Though intended for Christmas, the gifts actually arrived on the 2 January 1916. As one of the men recalled:

An event of some importance took place on the 2nd – this was the arrival of some large packages of cakes etc. apparently from the Swansea Corporation. Whether this is so or not, but just to give the impression that we are not averse to receiving gifts of this kind, arrangements were made by companies whereby the men could enjoy a late but none the less welcome Xmas dinner. Our officers entered into the spirit of the event, and supplied the boys with something to drink. The donors of the packages can rest assured that due honour was paid to the good things.[8]

Second-lieutenant W. A. S. Davies, of the Swansea Battalion, who, as reported in Tuesday's "Daily Post," has been wounded by German shrapnel. He is the first of the battalion to figure in the casualties.

Second Lieutenant W.A.S. Davies, an early casualty in the trenches. Happily, he was only wounded. South Wales Daily Post

At about this time the appointment of Lieutenant Colonel King to command the battalion was proving somewhat problematic, through no fault of the officer himself.

In late 1915 Leonard Reginald King was resident at Crowland, Manor Road, Barnet. He had seen some service with the 1/7th Battalion (TF), the Middlesex Regiment. Appointed to command the Swansea Battalion in November 1915 he had actually assumed command on 1 December 1915.

However, King was suffering from eczema and this condition was aggravated by life in the trenches. He was forced to leave the battalion on 9 January 1916 and embark for Southampton from Rouen. He did this on 26 January 1916 aboard the St Andrew. This was his only 'leave' since joining the battalion in December.

He attended a Medical Board on 31 January 1916 at the Queen Alexandra Military Hospital, Millbank, London, where he was found unfit for one month. Leave was accordingly granted for the period 31 January to 29 February 1916, he being deemed unfit for General Service, service at home, or light duty at home. At this time he was thirty-seven years old with fifteen years' Army service.

On 18 February 1916 King wrote to the War Office requesting re-examination by Medical Board and on 4 March 1916 a further Medical Board assembled at Bedford and found he was now recovered and therefore fit for General Service. On 11 March 1916 King was ordered to 'rejoin unit Expeditionary Force and report personally Embarkation Officer, Folkestone'.

He embarked at Folkestone on 15 March 1916 for passage to Boulogne. However,

Commemorative plaque and dedication including the Battalion's first active service casualty, Private T. Fisher. Autho

THE ELECTRICAL EQUIPMENT IN THIS HOSPITAL WAS INSTALLED BY THE DIRECTORS AND EMPLOYEES OF THE PORT TALBOT STEEL Cᵒ LTᴰ IN NOVᴿ 1920, AS A *Memorial* TO THE UNDER-MENTIONED MEN WHO MADE THE SUPREME SACRIFICE IN THE GREAT WAR.

ROLL OF HONOUR

IN MEMORY OF THE MEMBERS OF THE STAFF OF THE PORT TALBOT STEEL COMPANY, LIMITED

BISH. E.J. Pte 11ᵀᴴ Welsh Regᵀ
BOWDEN, G. Cpl King's Shrop L Infᵀ
BEDDOES, F.W. Cpl Royal Irish Rifles
BRADDICK. J. Pte Welsh Regᵀ
CHARLTON. H. Pte Northumberland Fus
CRAIG. W. J. Pte King's Shrop L Infᵀ
DONOVAN T. Pte Royal Irish Rifles
DAYCOCK J. Pte Welsh Reg
DAVIES. D. H. 2ᴺᴰ Lt Wiltshire Regᵀ
EVANS T. L. Pte Welsh Regᵀ
FISHER. T. Pte 14ᵀᴴ Welsh Regᵀ
FIELDING. J. Capt 7ᵀᴴ Welsh Regᵀ

GURR. J. Pte Royal Sussex
HICKS-BEACH. Rt Hon... Lennington Major Gloster Yeo
HEYCOCK. J. Pte 12ᵀᴴ Welsh Regᵀ
HEBBRON. B. Pte King's Shrop Lt Infᵀ
JOHNS. A. OS Royal Navy
JONES. V. Pte Royal Welsh Fusiliers
JONES. W. Pte Royal Berks
JENKINS. D. Pte South Wales Borderers
LUDLOW. J. Gnr Royal Field Artillery
LEWIS. S. T. Regᵀ Sgt Grenadier Guards
MORAN. P. Pte Royal Dublin Fusiliers
PHILLIPS. D. B. Pte Sot Welsh Reg
PHILLIPS. T. Pte Welsh Reg

PRICE. G. Royal Navy
REES. S. Pte Grenadier Guards
RICHARDS. E. Pte Royal Welsh
RICHARDS. W. Gnr Royal Horse A
ROWLANDS. F.
RYAN. J. Pte Royal Munster Fus
RYAN. S. Sig Royal Horse Artill
SMITH. C. Pte Grenadier Guards
VENNESS. J. Pte Royal Sussex
WATSON. H. Pte 2ᴺᴰ Welsh Regᵀ
WHITWORTH. C. Pte King's Shrop
WHITWORTH. W.

JARRETT. H. Gunner R.H.A.

JENKINS. W. Gunner R.H.A.

though the records are unclear, it appears likely that the condition returned and in due course he was again compelled to return home to recuperate. In April 1916 he was replaced by his former second in command, J.H. Hayes.[9]

Towards the end of January 1916 further news on casualties was filtering back to Swansea and the local newspaper reported that:

> It is with regret that we have to report the death of the first Swansea Battalion man at the front, in the person of Pte. W.J. Sandywell, who was accidentally shot in the front line trenches exactly a week ago.[10]

Regarding the death of Private Sandywell, Lieutenant Frank Corker, eldest son of Alderman Corker and himself serving with the battalion, wrote to the family:

> Perhaps it will help you to bear up in your great trouble to know that he died without pain. He was unconscious throughout.
>
> No idle words of mine can recompense you in such a time as this, but after a little while you will read my letter again, perhaps, and know that your husband was one of the best soldiers in our regiment. He did his duty always and never wavered in the cause for which he gave his life. He was in my own platoon, and he was an example to many, and liked by all.[11]

Private Sandywell was a married man with five children aged between eleven and four years of age. He had three brothers-in-law serving in the forces, one of whom was actually still with the Swansea Battalion. The local press recorded the sad proceedings of a memorial service held at Christ Church, Swansea, for the late Private Sandywell:

> The Vicar, in the course of a short discourse, said there were problems and dark passages in life, that we could not comprehend, but there was a purpose, and God had a great reason. He told the five little children, who were present with the rest of the family, to be good, and God with all his mercies, would look after them, and do all that was necessary.[12]

Private Sandywell may well have been the first Swansea man to die whilst on active service with the battalion but the records indicate that a battalion fatality had, in fact, occurred on Christmas Day. The newspaper might have been differentiating between battalion casualties who had lived in Swansea at the outbreak of war and those who had not. The difference seems academic but it is difficult to see any other logic. In any event the records show that Thomas Fisher was born in Aberavon, Port Talbot and had also enlisted there. He was reported as having died on Christmas Day rather than the more usual being 'killed in action' and thus became the first battalion fatality on active service. Private George Gent of 'A' Company referred to the incident, stating that two men were wounded at the same time:

> Harry Hardy in the shoulder, and James Owen in the head, whilst another man died of shock.[13]

Presumably the other man was Private Fisher who may have been killed though left unmarked by the concussion blast as the shell exploded. He was later commemorated on a plaque that has recently been removed from its original location and reinstalled at the new Baglan Hospital, near Port Talbot.

Despite not being involved in any heavy fighting, the battalion casualty lists nevertheless began to increase steadily as intermittent sniping and artillery fire began to exact a toll. Another loss was soon being reported:

...we were unfortunate in losing one of our most popular N.C.O.'s – Lance-corporal P.K. Finch, who received a bullet in the neck whilst taking aim, which proved fatal.[14]

With the battalion being new to active service, training was still ongoing in a number of specialities. On 17 January 1916 some men were being trained in bomb throwing near the La Bassée Canal. Private Herbert Lake later recalled:

I was throwing grenades under the instruction of Lieutenant Bellingham. I took a grenade out of the box, the pin was stiff and I failed to take it out. Lieutenant Devenish who was standing behind me told me to give him the grenade and said he would take the pin out himself. Lieutenant Bellingham told me to take another grenade and to remove the pin when he blew one whistle and carry my arm well back and throw the grenade when he blew twice. After Lieutenant Bellingham had blown twice when I was throwing, my arm caught in Mr Devenish's arm who was standing behind me, and the grenade was jerked out of my hand and fell to the ground behind me. I told Mr Bellingham to get out of the way, shouted to Lieutenant Devenish that the grenade had dropped. I gave Lieutenant Bellingham a push round the traverse and jumped round myself and we both crouched down and I heard the grenade explode and we both went round to see if Lieutenant Devenish was hurt. Devenish was hurt, and we found him lying on his back, with his feet towards the spot where the grenade had burst.

In fact Lieutenant Devenish, who had worked his passage from South Africa to Britain in company with Aubrey Sandbrook, in order to enlist, was dead. A Court of Inquiry

The war of the guns. A German gun team prepares. Taylor Library

The British reply in kind. Taylor Library

held in the field attached no blame to the other participants in this unhappy incident, returning a finding of 'accident'.[15]

With interest in the battalion understandably at a high level back in Swansea, a special correspondent for the local newspaper was able to visit the men at the front in order to report back on their progress. For someone who was in all probability more used to reporting on the potential dangers to pedestrians of the Swansea tramway system, this must have been an exciting, if not terror inducing assignment. As the reporter duly reported:

> Artillery duels seemed to be nearly continuously maintained; only once did we see guns turned upon the trenches. The shells went shrieking and wailing overhead, but for the trench-men, except when an assault in force is contemplated, the greatest peril was presented in the rifle bullets which came whistling over the parapets, the 'sausage' shells discharged by the small mortars, and the grenades thrown by hand.
>
> There is no water in the trenches occupied by 'Swansea's Own,' or, to be more precise, when the rain falls heavily it drains away without causing discomfort, because the wooden pathway is fixed some feet above the bottom of the trench...The dug-outs are simply great. The many odds against chance occurrence of a shell dropping at the mouth of one, killing five and wounding four of the occupants, does not modify the opinion that, as a rule, they afford adequate protection.[16]

The reference to the shell dropping at the mouth of a dugout referred to a recent incident that had resulted in the deaths of five men. These were Privates Lumsdaine, Smitham, Gilchrist, Jones and Paterson. Rattenbury and Rees, and two other men were wounded in the same incident.

Sergeant F.A. Lewis was a machine gun instructor to the battalion and his reaction to the five deaths was purely practical and provoked a German response that he had apparently not anticipated:

> That day I opened fire with the machine guns, and their artillery fired on us for all their worth. I gave them all they asked for. One of my fellows (Summerfield) got a shot through his helmet and cap though it did not touch his head. He was a lucky man. I was by his side when his helmet was knocked off.[17]

At the end of January there was very bad news for the mother of Lance Corporal P.W. Chapple, Aubrey Sandbrook advising her by letter that:

> He was carrying out a very dangerous duty on the morning of January 30, when he was fired on by a German patrol. He was brought in by Lieut. Roderick and the company sergeant-major, very badly wounded, and died today. Everything possible was done for him but with no success...although badly wounded he never failed to summon up a smile to reassure his anxious comrades as he was carried away to the dressing station.[18]

One of the men noted how different things now were from the busy but enjoyable days in happy billets at Rhyl:

> Billeting out here bears a remarkable contrast to the style we had become accustomed to whilst in our infancy at Rhyl. Here, if we are lucky, we get a roof to the barns or stables allotted to us. But this is a minor detail compared with the realities of war. When we come out to rest-billets, and look around for the boys who were our own familiar friends – 'tis then we begin to realise.
>
> To pay our respects to the lads of the battalion who have given their lives for the cause, a memorial service was conducted by our chaplain, the Rev. Alban Davies, on the steps of what must have once been a beautiful church. The four walls only were standing; the tower had been shattered, and the roof blown away. Even the pillars in one transept had been hurled down. Alongside these ruins lies a peaceful graveyard with hardly a stone touched – almost a living testimony to the accuracy of modern gun fire...
>
> Last Sunday some of us took part in another service, which so far has been quite unique in the history of the battalion. We hardly knew what day of the week it was, until we saw to our surprise our chaplain standing amongst us in

The Revd. Alban Davies who surprised members of the Swansea Battalion by visiting them in the front lines.
A. Thomas

the front line and greeting us in his usual fashion: 'Hello! Boys, how are you?' On our replying that we were very fit he informed us: 'If the boys cannot come to church, the church will come to the boys.'...In front of us, not very far away, stood our rifles ready for any emergency; behind us were the ruins of a village, battered out of recognition. It was a service, however, which we all appreciated, for services are sometimes few and far between owing to frequent movements.[19]

Sapper Winch of Eversley Road, Sketty, was reported as being the first member of the battalion to be allowed home on leave (six days) without his having been wounded. He told the local newspaper that:

Private Tom Hughes who was hit in the head and killed. South Wales Daily Post

...when he left the front all the boys and their officers were as happy as could be and enjoying good health. All the four companies have had their turns in the trenches, even the new drafts. They have been in three or four times, and have succeeded in holding all the trenches despite their warm work. The majority of the men would sooner be up in the first line trenches than in the reserves and the supporting trenches, as the latter trenches are more frequently subjected to severe bombardment by the Germans...

The Minstrel Troupe, organised by Major Dyson Williams, over twenty strong, contains a lot of talent. Included in the company are Lance-Corpl. G.B. Thomas (baritone), Sergt. W. Stevens, Quartermaster-Sergt. E. Norman, Sergt. Bidder, and they arrange excellent concerts which create much-needed diversion after having a spell in the trenches.[20]

Private Hill of 'B' Company had a lucky escape as he recounted to his family back home:

I was in the trench making a nice tin of tea when a 'whizz bang' exploded near and a piece of it hit my canteen of tea over, and I consequently lost the lot. I didn't half call Fritz, the dirty dog. I am going to keep that piece of shell and, with a bit of luck, will show it to you when I come home.[21]

Private Phillips served with 'C' company and described for his family his recent experiences in the front line trenches with due regard to the sensitivities of the censor:

We have had a busy time out here since we arrived in France. We have been in the first line of trenches for – hours, and – hours in the supports, and – days about a mile from the firing line staying in cellars. I was very much surprised to see how close the German lines are to ours; in some places they are only 20 yards apart. We were on a working party on Christmas Eve, and the Germans started to shell the roads by where we were standing. They sent over six big shells, but only one burst – a lucky job for us or I don't suppose I should have been able to write these few lines, as the first one dropped about seven yards away. You should have seen us make a dive for cover; some of the chaps fell into a shell-hole, and they did look a sight.

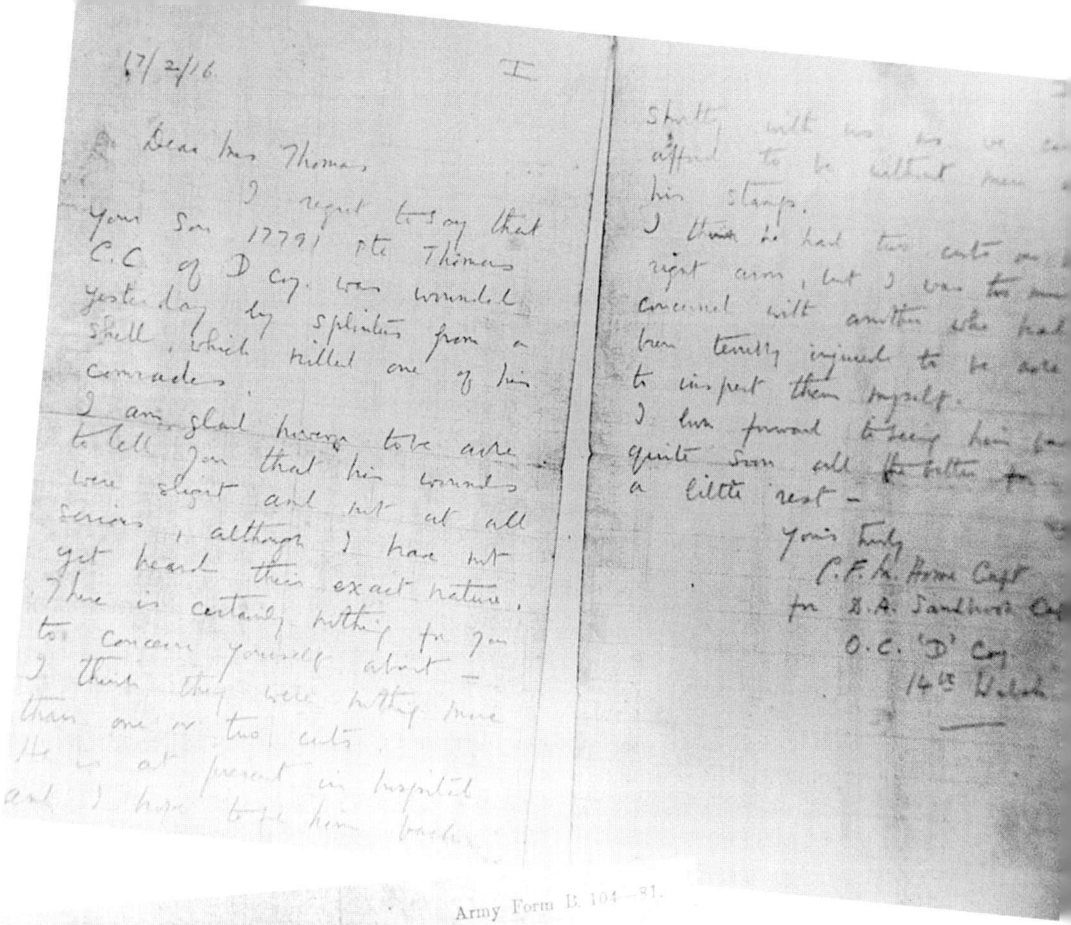

17/2/16. I

Dear Mrs Thomas,

I regret to say that Your Son 17791 Pte Thomas C.C. of D Coy. was wounded yesterday by splinters from a shell, which killed one of his comrades.

I am glad however to be able to tell you that his wounds were slight and not at all serious, & although I have not yet heard their exact nature, there is certainly nothing for you to concern yourself about — I think they were nothing more than one or two cuts.

He is at present in hospital and I hope to see him back shortly with us as we cannot afford to be without men of his stamp.

I think he had two cuts on the right arm, but I was too much concerned with another who had been terribly injured to be able to inspect them myself.

I look forward to seeing him quite soon all the better for a little rest —

Yours truly

C.F.M. Home Capt

for S.A. Sandhurst Capt

O.C. 'D' Coy

14th Welsh

Letter to the family of Colin Charles Thomas from Captain Home, February 1916. Denzil Thomas

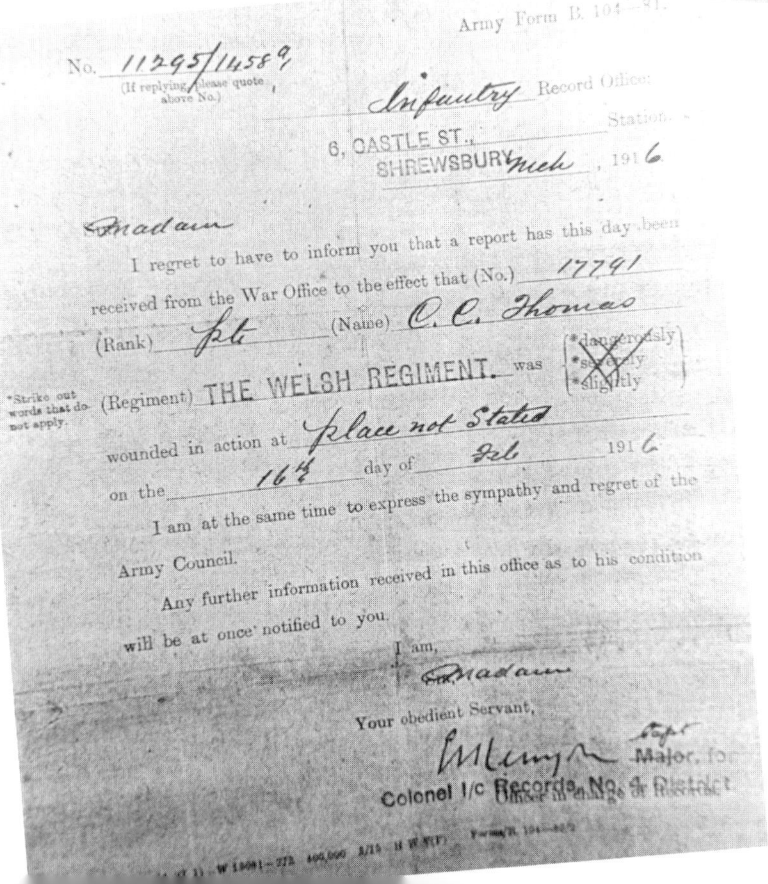

Army Form B. 104—81.

No. 11295/14589 (If replying, please quote above No.)

Infantry Record Office:

6, CASTLE ST., SHREWSBURY Station.

Mch, 1916.

Madam

I regret to have to inform you that a report has this day been received from the War Office to the effect that (No.) 17791 (Rank) Pte (Name) C. C. Thomas (Regiment) THE WELSH REGIMENT. was ~~*dangerously~~ ~~*severely~~ *slightly wounded in action at place not Stated on the 16th day of Feb 1916.

*Strike out words that do not apply.

I am at the same time to express the sympathy and regret of the Army Council.

Any further information received in this office as to his condition will be at once notified to you.

I am,
Madam
Your obedient Servant,

Capt Major, for
Colonel i/c Records, No. 4 District.
Officer in charge of Records.

Letter notifying the family of Colin Charles Thomas that he had been wounded, February 1916. Denzil Thomas

Last Monday the Germans shelled the village we were staying at. They sent over about 150 'coal-boxes,' and they made a terrible mess of the church and graveyard; it was bad enough before. I went over the following day to see the damage they had done; it was something terrible. One of the shells did not burst; it was about 3ft. long and weighed 2 cwt; so you can guess the mess they were making. But for every one shell they send us our artillery sends them twenty; so those bounders must be very nearly driven mad.[22]

F.C. Vivian, who came from the village of Mumbles as did Samuel Gammon. Both were fated not to return. John Powell and Fred Gammon

Colin Charles Thomas of Pontarddulais was wounded by shell splinters on 16 February 1916. Private Thomas was, in one way, a lucky man, for the same shell killed one of his comrades. This was Private George Cottle who had been born in Landra, Cornwall but had enlisted at Aberavon. Captain Home was able to reassure the Thomas family back home that the wound was relatively minor and Private Thomas was expected to be back with the battalion in the near future where he could yet again face the dangers of active service with the infantry.[23]

On 22 February 1916 Private Tom Hughes died from a wound to the head. Lieutenant Bellingham wrote to his widow to say that:

...one could not wish for a better soldier, as he always did his duty, however hard it might be. If only more would leave their homes and do their duty as your husband did the war would soon be over.[24]

Signaller R.E. Davies was from the St Thomas area of Swansea though he had since moved to Ridge House at the Mayals. He had been wounded and Captain Sandbrook was, at first, unable to provide all the information that the family might require at this worrying time:

The wounds were caused by shrapnel shell, and I fear they are more serious than those of others who have suffered. I have not been able to ascertain the exact nature of the wounds as I myself have been in the thick of things till now...it is hard to see one's comrades being killed and wounded one by one but we must always bear in mind the cause for which they suffer.[25]

Sadly, Sandbrook's fears proved well founded and Signaller Davies died of his wounds on 12 February 1916. Soon, there was another casualty to report, this time Sergeant A. Kennedy, whose wife was given the sad news that:

Your husband was on duty with his platoon in the trenches on the morning of 14 February when he was shot through the head by a enemy sniper. Death was instantaneous...we have lost a good comrade.[26]

Another who was wounded but happily still alive, W.C. Sandry, wrote home to reassure his family and friends that he was:

...progressing as favourably as possible, being well looked after and carefully nursed. (I have) gone through a very bad time, and (am) thankful to get no more than shrapnel wounds through the fleshy part of (my) legs and arms.[27]

Signaller Rees Atherton was another who had a lucky escape, carrying on his person:

...a folded copy of the 'Penny Pictorial' and a packet of cigarettes, which

SHOT BY HUN SNIPER.

Sketty has been deprived of a bright and promising life in Private W. H. Rees, son of Mr. and Mrs. Harry Rees, Llewellyn-street, Sketty, who, at daybreak recently, whilst on sentry-go, was fatally shot by a sniper "somewhere in France." Capt. Aubrey Smith conveyed the sad tidings to the heart-broken parents in a beautifully sympathetic letter on Tuesday morning, and spoke in high appreciation of the lad's sterling qualities. His body was reverently laid to rest in the churchyard near where he fell, and the burial service was attended by the many Sketty boys in the company. Private Rees had a wide circle of friends, was an active member of Sketty English Congregational Church, and an energetic worker in the Band of Hope connected with that place of worship. His brother George is in the 7th Welsh.

Private W.H. Rees, killed by a sniper while on sentry duty. South Wales Daily Post

FATHERLESS GREENHILL CHILDREN.

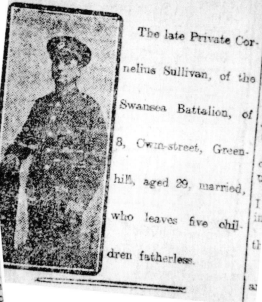

The late Private Cornelius Sullivan, of the Swansea Battalion, of 8, Cwm-street, Greenhill, aged 29, married, who leaves five children fatherless.

Private Cornelius Sullivan who was killed in action and was a father of five. South Wales Daily Post

A MIRACULOUS ESCAPE.

News has been received that Private Gilbert Morgan, of the Swansea Battalion, son of Mr. and Mrs. Morgan, Waunroad, Morriston, has been wounded in action in France. A bullet pierced his capbadge and grazed his head, causing a scalp wound.

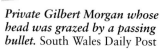

Private Gilbert Morgan whose head was grazed by a passing bullet. South Wales Daily Post

LATE MUMBLES SERGEANT.

Sergt. J. A. Griffiths, of the Swansea Battalion, killed in action. Prior to joining the Army at the outbreak of war he was a member of the Glamorgan Police Force, stationed at Mumbles. In a letter to his father, Lieut. H. Jones Williams says: "I assure you that you have the heartfelt sympathy of every officer and man in our company. I, personally, shall miss your son very much, and I feel as if I had lost one of my best friends. He was a splendid soldier, and in your great sorrow you have the consolation of knowing that he fell bravely fighting for King and Country and his loved ones at home."

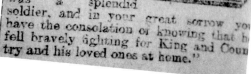

Sergeant J.A. Griffiths killed in action. South Wales Daily Post

The front line trenches at Givenchy. Imperial War Museum, Q6481

> *stopped a shell splinter from piercing his thigh. A rifle he was carrying was*
> *blown to pieces by the same shell, which wounded a number of his comrades.*[28]

Sadly, one who was not so fortunate was Private William Lewis who was described as being:

> *A strapping youth, standing 5ft 10in., 18 years of age, and weighing 12 stone;*
> *a good soldier, inoffensive, always willing, and never a grumble.*

Private Lewis was killed in action on 18 February 1916, his death being described as 'painless'.[29]

Private Charles Henry Mew knew all about the dangers of sniping, both for the hunter and the hunted. Sniping was an activity that brought with it particular dangers since snipers often operated in relatively exposed locations. It was, of course, essential that to be a successful sniper you had to be able to see the enemy. By the same token, if you could see him, there was a good chance that he could see you too, with all the danger that entailed. Additionally, a well-trained and successful sniper would inevitably be a prime target for the enemy, whether by counter-sniping or even, in the case of a particularly troublesome sniper, shellfire. Private Mew had volunteered and been specially trained for this arduous duty.

Captain Jones-Williams was the battalion sniping officer and the men worked under him in pairs. While one wielded the rifle (equipped with telescopic sights) the other observed the enemy positions with a telescope or binoculars, trying to locate suitable targets. Duty extended from the stand-to in the trenches at dawn until the fall of darkness. Conditions were often cramped and the possibility of free movement very limited, lest one should draw enemy fire on oneself.

A German sniper marks his target. Taylor Library

While on sniping duty the opportunity was taken to use the telescope or binoculars to examine the barbed wire for damage or gaps. Occasionally the Germans would be seen observing the British snipers observing them. To give the snipers some protection they were often given steel plates that could be placed on the trench parapet or the rim of a shell crater with a sighting slot in the middle some four inches long by one and a quarter inches wide. Mew recalls an incident where the Germans managed to put a bullet through the slot and injure the man behind it. On another occasion one of Mew's comrades managed to hit the glass of a German trench periscope at a range of 250 yards.[30]

Corporal Watkins was a signaller and part of his duty was to lay or repair communication wires between trenches and, indeed, on occasion into the nether region of no man's land, where danger was a constant companion. If Watkins' letter was at least frank and truthful, its contents can have done little to assuage the worries of his family back home as regards his personal safety:

We have just come out for a little rest after being in the trenches, and I can assure you we appreciate the change very much. The snow has fallen at last, and covered the country with its whiteness and showing its beauty, defying the great machinery of war and destruction.

My duties here are varied, and while I was in the trenches looking after the lines I found the boys in excellent spirits through all. Yet the boys were very cold after being exposed to the weather at night. But, despite all, they still have the grit in them which our forefathers had in the olden fighting days.

My only wish is that the war will soon end. Yes, with victory on our side. May God grant us that the day will soon come and that the boys will be back once more marching through the streets of dear old Swansea triumphantly.

We linesmen have very difficult tasks to perform. In many cases we have to run a line in the open, exposed to the fire of the enemy, and when it comes to cut wire entanglements it is very dangerous. Our sappers don't cut the wire quickly enough, and the result is that we have to fray the insulation, wishing at the same time that some kind friend would make us a present of a substantial pair of nippers. Some time ago we had to run a line in the open and the Germans were only 25 yards away. The enemy spotted us just as we were going to joint another reel of cable. They threw up night lights and we were exposed to their machine and rifle fire. We laid as low as possible till the danger was over, then we proceeded with our task until it was completed.

On another occasion the Germans sent a 'whiz bang' over, which fell about six yards from us. Luckily not one of us was hit.[31]

In the first week of March 1916 the battalion moved into the reserve billets at Gorre. Private D. Jones of 'D' company took the opportunity to update his family on developments:

I am back safe out of the trenches again. We came out last night (March 1st). I was in for ten days and did not take my boots off all the time. I suppose I was in one of the worst places in the whole line, and was doing sentry duty at night.

I had to lie down flat in the mud as I was only about 10 or 15 yards away from the German sentry, one watching the other just like two cats. Not one of us dare move. If he had attempted to move any way, I had plenty of bombs by me, and I should have thrown one of them and 'put his lights out'. Of course, he'd have done the same to me. I think these trenches are about the closest on the whole of the front.

Private R. A. Simpson. Serving initially with the Swansea Battalion he was later granted a commission and saw action with the 15 Welsh.
Brian Simpson

It is very dangerous here. One of the chaps of another regiment, who came to relieve us, was hit in the right leg. It came through the dug-out. I was thankful to come out of that hole, I can tell you. The worst of a sentry's job is that the feet get numbed. When I was lying there in the pitch dark night in the rain, there was a dummy attack made. You should have heard the noise of those thousands of guns, and hundreds of flashlights. It was like day. The bullets were whizzing in all directions. It was quite exciting, and livened things up a bit.[32]

Another wrote and was able to tell his family that there were obvious dangers while the men were in the trenches:

For the past few days that battalion has been making the most of a short respite ere returning to the trenches. During their 'all too short' rests they make every endeavour to get a little enjoyment after their perilous stay in the lines...

Our recent visit to the trenches has, up to the present, been the longest and, incidentally, the hottest we've had since our arrival in France. On the evening of 29th February we were subjected to a very warm bombardment with some most injurious missiles, known as 'whiz bangs,' rifles, grenades and trench mortar bombs, which did a lot of damage to our dug-outs. Happily no lives were lost.[33]

Out of the line and in reserve at La Vert Lannot, the battalion was able to enjoy some much needed relaxation and the apparently much maligned battalion minstrel troupe gave a concert, deciding that it must:

> '...take arms against a sea of criticism'. Our divisional recreation room was made a splendid arena for the 'trials'. At the appointed hour the hall was packed to its utmost, there being several hundreds present, officers and men. Major Hayes, commanding officer, attended, accompanied by his brother officers of the battalion. Major Dyson Williams had arranged a splendid programme which opened with a chorus by the troops, in conjunction with a solo by Lance-corporal George Thomas (Kilvey)...General Sir Ivor Phillips stepped on to the platform and addressed the gathering (said) how pleased he was with the work of the 38th Welsh Division, both in and out of the trenches.[34]

Back in the front line trenches at Givenchy between 12-15 March 1916 the battalion suffered losses every day. On the 12th it was one killed and one wounded; on the 13th it was one killed and eleven wounded; on the 14th it was two killed and three wounded whilst on the 15th it was one killed and two wounded. Private W.A. Seely left a widow and one child after he:

> ...was shot while on duty on the afternoon of 12 March. Death was instantaneous. His loss to the battalion will be very great as he was reputed to be one of the best of our grenadiers.[35]

The damage being inflicted was certainly not all one way and the battalion was involved in bombing raids on the enemy trenches. During one of these, Alf Rice who, in peacetime, had worked at the Gorseinon Colliery, was reported killed.[36]

The *South Wales Daily Post* was happy to include stories that it felt showed those back home who, despite the regular appeals for recruits, still hesitated about enlisting, exactly what sort of public spiritedness was required in the present troubled times:

> Much-to-do is being made over the married men with businesses being called up nowadays. Q.M.S. Jarvis Jones, of the Swansea Battalion, was one of the first to join, without waiting for the Derby scheme, leaving his business in the hands of his plucky wife – a model to others similarly situated, and a fine example of patriotic self-sacrifice under conditions of unusual hardship...
>
> The last time he was in the trenches he had a good illustration of what the British artillery can do, for their guns and mortars have been throwing shells into the German saps with deadly accuracy, and the saps were blown to atoms, and if there were any men in them they must have suffered terribly. The Germans hardly replied at all to the British bombardment.
>
> The Battalion have had a few days' rest. A heavy fall of snow makes things a bit unpleasant, but a concert party has been trying to liven things up a bit.[37]

During March 1916 sad news reached the battalion from Swansea. The former Mayor of Swansea, Alderman Thomas Taliesyn Corker, had passed away suddenly. Although Alderman Corker had not seemed his usual breezy self at the Corporation committee meeting he had chaired earlier in the day, no one had been prepared for the events that were to unfold that evening at the Ffynone Club, Swansea. Having shared a joke with his Corporation colleague, Councillor W.W. Holmes, the Alderman had suddenly and without warning collapsed and slumped sideways, his head resting on Holmes' shoulder. Doctor Marks, who happened to be in the club, attended the scene immediately and attempted to resuscitate him but to no avail. In the space of a minute or so Alderman Corker had passed away without uttering a word.[38]

A few days later the funeral procession left the family home in Sketty, Swansea, and began its sombre journey to the cemetery. It was noted that along the route many blinds were drawn as a mark of respect and the whole area wore a general aspect of mourning. At Oystermouth Cemetery, in front of a large gathering, the remains of Alderman Corker were laid to rest after a Masonic funeral service. He left a wife, two sons and four daughters.[39]

The local press and former colleagues were all agreed that, of all his public works, the one of which he had been most proud and that which had given him the most pleasure, was his role in the formation of the Swansea Battalion. He had also been very proud of the fact that his eldest son, Frances (Frank) Llewellyn Corker, was currently serving as a lieutenant with the battalion in France. As a further mark of respect, Colonel Wright donated a trophy to the battalion in memory of the late Mayor in the form of a large silver cup. This could be competed for on battalion sports days and would help perpetuate the memory of a man who had done so much work in raising the battalion.

At around this time in Swansea, local recruiting tribunals were at work hearing appeals from some of those who found themselves subject to the newly introduced conscription regime but claimed to have pressing business elsewhere. For example the New Cross Hands Colliery claimed to have already had 163 of its employees join the armed forces. It requested an exemption from service for a twenty-year old assistant fitter, stating that the colliery could not do without him. The tribunal was only prepared to countenance a one month postponement.[40]

Another applicant claimed that he had recently got married in order that his wife could then look after his aged mother in the event that he was called to the colours. Having been so called he now had doubts as to just how the ladies would manage without him and requested exemption. With exemption being refused he advised the tribunal that he would have to be dragged to the front.[41]

A slaughter man who was aged twenty-five and single requested exemption on the grounds that his butchering work was of greater value to the war effort than would be his active service. It was established that the applicant's mother also ran a butchery business though the son did the slaughtering for both. It being felt that the mother could look after both concerns and arrange an alternative slaughter man the request for exemption was refused.[42]

The cup presented to the Swansea Battalion by Colonel J.R. Wright in memory of the late Mayor of Swansea T. T. Corker. On loan from the R.R.W. Comrades Association, Swansea Museum.

With the conscription regime now in force, seemingly fit and able young men who were observed on the streets of Swansea came under some suspicion. The local authorities commenced periodic operations designed to assess whether those men, in fact, had good cause to be still at home:

Commencing operations in the early part of Saturday afternoon, the police, in conjunction with the military authorities, conducted a 'round-up' of any person who may have succeeded in evading the military authorities up to date. In the main streets of Swansea parties were stationed who stopped every man of military age and required him to produce some evidence of exemption from military service. If these could not produce their papers they were taken to the Central Police Station (and subjected) to a searching examination. If still they could not satisfy the military authorities that they were excused from or unfit for service, they were informed that they would receive a notice calling them up for service next week.[43]

In April 1916 command of the Swansea Battalion had formally passed from Lieutenant Colonel L.R. King to Lieutenant Colonel John Higson Hayes. Born on New Year's Eve 1876, Hayes had been educated at Harrow and was a professional soldier who had joined the 3rd Dragoon Guards as a Second Lieutenant in January 1899. He had seen service in the Transvaal, Zululand and the Cape Colony in 1901, and in the Orange River Colony in 1902. He had been mentioned in dispatches for his Boer War service and had gained the Queen's Medal with five clasps. He had resigned from the Dragoon Guards with the rank of Captain in 1909 before joining the Shropshire Yeomanry in 1911. Appointed District Remount Officer (Western Command) in 1914, he had joined the Swansea Battalion in June 1915 and was to prove to be one of its finest officers.[44]

April 1916 saw the battalion relieving the 15th Welsh in the vicinity of Festubert. Le Touret, Robermetz and Laventie were also familiar areas at this time as the battalion carried out the usual duties of reserve, support and front line. A number of drafts were received amounting to about 100 other ranks and three officers. Casualties were very light during this period and a German soldier was captured. Back in Swansea the funeral of Private Smitham took place:

The military funeral of Pte. Ben Smitham, Tontine Street, Swansea, a member of the Swansea Battalion, who died at Bangor Military Hospital while in training took place...at Danygraig Cemetery. The funeral procession was headed by a firing party, the Tramways Band (Inspector Maimone), a number of troops, and many comrades from the Swansea Battalion.[45]

At the beginning of May 1916 the battalion occupied the front line trenches at Laventie. On 1 May three men were killed and eleven wounded. The wounded included Temporary Captain Graham Howells. As he was leaving the trench he was hit in the forehead by a machine-gun bullet. He had been born in 1895 and lived at Brynymor Crescent, Swansea. An old boy of the Swansea Grammar School, he had been employed as a clerk prior to enlisting in the Swansea Battalion as a private in October 1914. He was later granted a commission and remained with his hometown battalion. After being wounded he was transferred to the 7th Casualty Clearing Station where he died on 2 May 1916. Howells' father, having received the customary War Office telegram at Weston-Super-Mare where he was Postmaster, responded that he learned:

...with very much regret of the death of my son, Capt. Graham Howells, of the 14th Welsh Regiment. My wife and I deeply appreciate the expression of

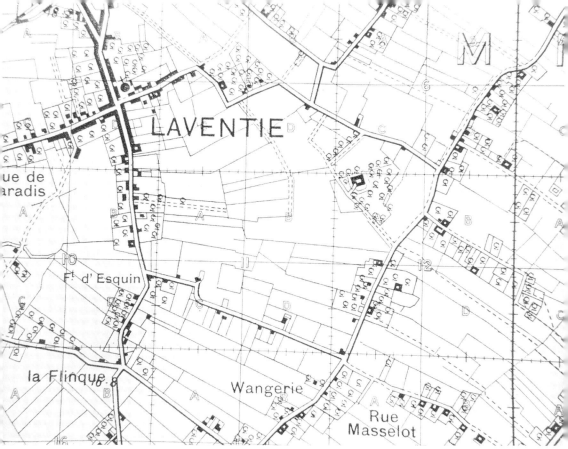

The Laventie area where Captain Graham Howells was fatally wounded. National Archives

fact that our son died in doing his duty for King and country.[46]

The Howells' family was destined to have a very hard war. On the same day in 1918 that the 'In Memoriam' column of the *South Wales Daily Post* contained an entry remembering Graham, further down the page was a report on the death in action of his brother, Denzil:

'Fought Like a Hero'
Tributes to dead Swansea Officer

Mr. J. Howells, late Chief Clerk at Swansea G.P.O., and now postmaster of Weston-super-Mare, has received a letter from Lieut.-Col Brinson (himself wounded), alluding to his son, the late Lieut. Denzil Howells, in which he says:- 'Your son was a most hard-working and useful officer, whose loss the whole battalion deplores. Though he came to us disappointed at not going to his own regiment, he quickly settled down in a way which filled one with admiration, and he did extremely good work for us.'

The assistant adjutant, Lieutenant Hallam, wrote

THIRD SWANSEA OFFICER OF SAME FAMILY.

Lieutenant Denzil Howell, the third son of Mr. J. Howell, formerly chief clerk at the Swansea Post Office, and now postmaster at Weston-super-Mare, killed in action.

Denzil Howells.
South Wales Daily Post

Captain G. Howells.
Swansea Library Service

He...fought like a hero to the last. He was beloved by all the men and his brother officers, and his death will be felt very much indeed.[47]

The rest of May 1916 saw little rest for the battalion. Holding positions in the La Gorgue, Fauquissart and Laventie areas, a steady trickle of casualties was inflicted by the Germans. Between 18 and 21 May two men were killed and six wounded whilst between 26 and 28 May a further two were killed and another four wounded. At about this time Private Ernest Beynon was wounded. He would be wounded on several other occasions before returning home safe, if not 100 per cent sound, at the end of the conflict.[48]

Having had sufficient time to find its active service feet, the battalion was now readied for more ambitious operations than merely holding a length of trench. Plans for raiding the German lines were being drawn up and elements of the battalion would play a full part in this dangerous enterprise.

Notes

1. SWDP, 18 December 1915.
2. IWM/Rees, op. cit.
3. SWDP, 28 December 1915.
4. SWDP, 31 December 1915.
5. SWDP, 4 January 1916.
6. SWDP, 29 December 1915.
7. WGAS, TC 26/3.
8. SWDP, 10 January 1916.
9. PRO/WO/339/47970.
10. SWDP, 20 January 1916.
11. SWDP, 20 January 1916.
12. SWDP, 25 January 1916.
13. SWDP, 1 January 1916.
14. SWDP, 20 January 1916.
15. PRO/WO/339/28828.
16. SWDP, 5 February 1916.
17. SWDP, 7 February 1916.
18. SWDP, 7 February 1916.
19. SWDP, 8 February 1916.
20. SWDP, 23 February 1916.
21. SWDP, 9 February 1916.
22. SWDP, 16 February 1916.
23. Thomas.
24. SWDP, 2 March 1916.
25. SWDP, 25 February 1916.
26. SWDP, 23 February 1916.
27. SWDP, 28 February 1916.
28. SWDP, 23 February 1916.
29. SWDP, 4 March 1916.
30. WGAS/Mew.
31. SWDP, 2 March 1916.
32. SWDP, 11 March 1916.
33. SWDP, 14 March 1916.
34. ibid.
35. SWDP, 24 March 1916.
36. SWDP, 7 April 1916.
37. SWDP, 11 March 1916.
38. SWDP, 8 March 1916.
39. SWDP, 11 March 1916.
40. SWDP, 24 March 1916.
41. SWDP, 30 March 1916.
42. SWDP, 13 July 1916.
43. SWDP, 11 September 1916.
44. PRO/WO/374/32090.
45. SWDP, 3 April 1916.
46. PRO/WO/339/15343.
47. SWDP, 1 May 1918.
48. Beynon.

CHAPTER SIX

Lieutenant Corker's Raid

If pitched battles were not being fought at this stage of the war there was still ample opportunity for engaging the enemy. Trench raids were seen as an important element of front line activity. Raids could be used to discover which enemy units occupied trenches on the other side of no man's land, as well as providing a chance to familiarize oneself with terrain over which an attack might eventually have to be made. They were also meant to improve confidence amongst the troops by showing that it was possible (under certain conditions, usually involving the cover of darkness) to move relatively freely between the lines. And, of course, they provided opportunities to simply kill or capture some of the enemy.

In preparing for a raid, a number of measures were taken to try and maximize the chances of success. Mock attacks might be staged over a model of the target area and careful study would be made of the likely weather conditions and the phases of the moon. Watches would be synchronized two days in advance of an attack, passwords would be learned and simple German phrases for 'hands up' or 'come out' would be memorized. The raiders would be kept and trained as a tight knit group so as to engender team spirit and would not be billeted on the local populace lest careless talk should let slip any details of the plan.

At the time of the raid faces would be blackened, identifications removed and some sort of recognition badge or mark substituted so as to aid the visual distinction between friend and foe. Weapons that could be used in reasonable silence, such as knobkerries and knives, would be issued so that perhaps a sleepy enemy sentry could be discreetly dispatched without alerting any of his comrades.[1]

On the night of the 4 June 1916 elements of the 10th (1st Rhondda) and 14th (Swansea) Battalions were detailed to launch separate bombing (hand grenade) attacks on the German trenches opposite them. An earlier bombardment by British trench mortars had been intended to cut the barbed wire guarding the approach to the German trenches before the raiders set off across no man's land, but this was not entirely successful. Indeed, in the area targeted by the fifty-seven man raiding party of the 10th Battalion, the wire was still largely intact and efforts to clear or bridge it using wire cutters and a mat proved ineffective. When it was realized that the Germans had been aroused by the British activity and were manning the trench parapet the raid was abandoned, but not before three men were killed and thirteen others (including all four officers) were wounded.

The raid carried out by 'C' company of the Swansea Battalion, their first, was more successful. The raiding party consisted of Lieutenants Strange, Wilson and Frank Corker together with thirty-nine other ranks. A two pronged approach was to be made to the German trench with Lieutenant Corker leading on the left, Wilson on the right and Strange holding back in the centre with two telephonists, two stretcher bearers and a nine man reserve.

At 11.02p.m. the left and right raiding parties crawled forward and then stood up upon reaching the German wire, which was damaged but still represented a considerable obstacle to the advance. After quietly threading their way carefully through the wire, an exercise that took five suspense-filled minutes, Corker and Wilson's parties immediately jumped into the German trench hoping to catch the enemy unprepared. Wilson's party, on the right, initially found no Germans but then stumbled upon five enemy soldiers who were promptly bombed with a mix of percussion and Mill's grenades.

On the left Corker's party, on entering the trench, had apparently come into immediate contact with the enemy who threw several bombs in the direction of the British party. Lieutenant Corker was wounded and, in the excitement and tension of the moment, many of his men threw their bombs in the general direction of the enemy, adding to the confusion that now prevailed and temporarily preventing the effective use of revolvers and rifles. Since a further advance into the trench system seemed too risky, a rather hasty evacuation commenced and this action uncovered the rear of Lieutenant Wilson's party, forcing him to also start withdrawing his men hurriedly from the trench.

Both raiding parties now joined with Lieutenant Strange's party in a nearby ditch before making their own way back to the British trenches. Once in the safety of their own trench it was realized that Lieutenant Corker had apparently not returned with his party.[2] Lieutenants Strange and Wilson, accompanied by Corporal O'Brien, wasted no time in commencing a search for Corker who, before the raid, had indicated a ditch that he would head towards in the event of his being wounded. No trace of Corker could be found there though the body of another man killed in the raid was discovered and brought in. This was Private William Williams of Lan Street, Morriston. Ironically, after being hit Williams had initially been assisted by Private J. Oswald Lewis, an old friend. As Lewis later told his parents:

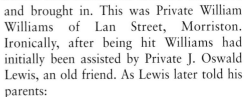

He died in my arms, poor chap. He was killed on the way back to our lines after one of the most daring bombing raids made. We were only 20 altogether, including officers. We crept up to their barbed wire and then made a dash into

Private Will Williams (right), of Lan Street, Swansea, with his brother Richard. Will was killed while raiding the German trenches in 1916 while Richard was killed in 1917. They came from a family of thirteen children. After their deaths their mother wore black for the rest of her life. Two other brothers (David and Edwin) also served and survived though both were wounded. Hedley Morris

their trenches and bombed... out of them. We were only there about five minutes and made a dash out again. Every man came out of the trenches and passed their barbed wire quite safely. I was the last but one to come out, so I knew Will was in front of me somewhere. I came back to a ditch which was running into our trench quite safe, and there I sat for about ten minutes until I saw their machine gunners playing on us. I crept along the ditch for about 20 yards when I came across poor Will. He had been shot through the head. I bandaged him the best I could, but I knew that he was practically dead then. I sat alongside him, and very soon afterwards he passed away. There was one consolation, he went quite peacefully, suffering no pain. He had done his duty and done it well. He was one of the most noble and fearless bombers we had.[3]

The next night Strange and Wilson again went out into no man's land with a small search party and came under heavy fire as they searched for the missing Lieutenant Corker. Private Austin, who accompanied them, was struck seventeen times by a burst of machine-gun fire but still managed to crawl back to the British lines and report no sign of Corker before expiring from his wounds.[4] Lieutenant Strange later wrote to Private Austin's widow, assuring her that:

...his death was as noble as his life. He was hit very badly when out with me on the following night searching for Lieut. Corker, and his mate was hit beside him. Though in pain he forced himself to keep quiet, and so enabled us to rescue both himself and his wounded mate. The last words I heard him say were 'Stick it Welsh'.[5]

The phrase 'stick it' has a somewhat different connotation today than that which applied during the Great War. At that time it had a particular resonance for members of the Welsh Regiment since it was associated with the death in action of one of its officers, Captain Mark Haggard. In an engagement with the enemy in September 1914 Captain Haggard, who was a nephew of the famous author Sir H. Rider Haggard, fell having been mortally wounded. With the battle still raging around him Captain Haggard, despite the severity of his wounds, still managed to occasionally encourage his men by calling out 'Stick it, Welsh, stick it'. The men, heartened by his example, did indeed stick it and continued fighting. Captain Haggard succumbed to his wounds later in the day, and even then his last words were 'Stick it Welsh'. Little wonder then that Private Austin should echo these brave and inspiring words thus encouraging his comrades even as his own life ebbed slowly away.[6]

Richard Williams, brother of Will. Richard was also killed later in the war while serving with the King's Liverpool Regiment. Hedley Morris

Strange again reached the area where Corker had indicated that he had hoped to shelter in the event of difficulty, but once more found it deserted. The search party was thus forced to return to its own trenches empty handed. Lieutenants Strange and Wilson were both subsequently awarded the Military Cross for their efforts in attempting to find Lieutenant Corker.

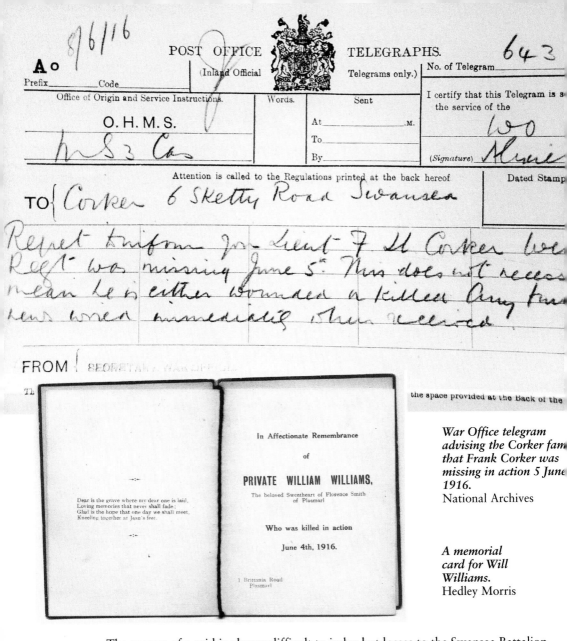

In Affectionate Remembrance

of

PRIVATE WILLIAM WILLIAMS,

The beloved Sweetheart of Florence Smith
of Plasmarl

Who was killed in action

June 4th, 1916.

1 Brittania Road
Plasmarl

Dear is the grave where my dear one is laid,
Loving memories that never shall fade;
Glad is the hope that one day we shall meet,
Kneeling together at Jesu's feet.

War Office telegram advising the Corker fam that Frank Corker was missing in action 5 June 1916.
National Archives

A memorial card for Will Williams.
Hedley Morris

The success of a raid is always difficult to judge but losses to the Swansea Battalion raiding party were quite light by the standards of the time with only two killed and a small number wounded. German losses were probably at least six killed or wounded. A battalion sniping officer reported seeing two Red Cross ambulances and eight laden stretchers behind the German trench some hours after the raid.[7]

Subsequent interviews with members of the raiding party revealed a confused picture, which is not surprising given the speed with which the skirmish developed once the German trench was entered. Several soldiers reported seeing Corker leaving the German trench, possibly with the assistance of others in the party. He seemed to have been wounded in the face and shoulder. He had apparently managed to reach the

Midnight, March 1st, 1916, marks the passing of the unattested el[...] bachelor into the ranks of the Army. A memorable St. David's Day.

The introduction of conscription draws the 'hangers-back' into the net of the military. South Wales Daily Post

German wire and was also seen sheltering in a shell hole in no man's land while the rest of the party retired. It was felt possible that, in a confused and possibly disorientated state, he had mistakenly re-entered the German trench and either been killed or taken prisoner.

Mrs Rosa Corker was still grieving following the sudden and untimely death of her husband, Alderman Corker, some three months earlier. Indeed, she had also recently lost her brother on active service, her father to old age, and would also lose George, her other son, who was only six years old, before 1916 was out. Thus the War Office telegram dated 8 June 1916 informing her that Frank was 'missing' must have come as a particularly heavy blow.[8]

By the 10 June 1916 the *South Wales Daily Post* was able to feature a letter from Lieutenant Colonel Hayes, Commanding Officer, 14th Welsh in which he advised Mrs Corker that:

I am afraid your boy has been killed in action. He will be officially put down as missing... he was slightly wounded... and I am afraid must have been hit by a machine-gun bullet on his way back... I was with him just before he went out and was very much struck by his calm cheerfulness. I have seen a good many boys and men go out on dangerous enterprises, but never one who went off to his death more bravely. You have every cause to be proud of such a son, who went down for his country with such a brave heart.

Despite this sad news the family understandably clung to the hope that, in the absence of a body, the possibility that Frank was a prisoner of war could not be fully discounted. Indeed, a letter from the Red Cross to Mrs Corker raised hopes somewhat. The letter quoted Second Lieutenant Lethaby (who was himself wounded in the raid) as saying:

No Man's Land...was here about 250 yards wide...the grass...had grown very long, and it is possible that the Germans got him before our search party went out.[9]

As Frank's name continually failed to appear on the lists of men captured by the Germans, the stark truth of his likely fate must have become more apparent despite the last hopes still clung to by his family. In February 1917 a letter, edged in black, from Mrs Corker to the War Office asking for further information about Frank's fate elicited the response that:

...the Army Council are in consequence regretfully constrained to conclude that this officer died on or since the 4th June 1916, and I am to express their sympathy with you in your bereavement.[10]

In respect of her son's service for King and country Mrs Corker subsequently received the sum of £68, being the gratuity due. Having no known grave, Frank Corker is commemorated on the Loos Memorial, Pas De Calais, Panels 77 and 78. His father, mother, brother and a sister all rest in a single grave at Oystermouth Cemetery, Swansea.

The remainder of June 1916 proved to be a quiet period for the battalion. On 5 June it moved into Brigade reserve at La Gorgue before moving to Busnes, then Rambert and Savy, where it underwent divisional training. On 26 June it was at Bouquemaison, moving to Bernevil and Septen Ville as the month drew to a close.

It marched from Septen Ville to Herissart on 1 July 1916, the first day of the Somme offensive, though the battalion was not involved in any fighting at this time. It relocated to Franvillers on the 3rd and Heilly on 4 July 1916, as it was positioned by the higher command to relieve the 7th Division near Fricourt. It was now being readied for what would be its first major engagement with the enemy.

Notes

1. Marden, Major General T.O., *The History of the Welch Regiment, Part II, 1914-1918*, p.378
2. PRO/WO/95/2559.
3. SWDP, 13 June 1916.
4. PRO/WO/339/15332.
5. SWDP, 24 June 1916.
6. SWDP, 7 October 1914.
7. PRO/WO/95/2557.
8. PRO/WO/339/15332.
9. SWDP, 22 June 1916.
10. PRO/WO/339/15332.

Citation for Temporary Lieutenant J. S. Strange for his part in the trench raid of 4-5 June in which Frank Corker was killed.
London Gazette

machine-gun and rifle fire. He has on all occasions shown himself to be a capable and brave leader.

Temp. Lt. John Stanley Strange, 14th Bn., Welsh R.

For conspicuous gallantry when reconnoitring the enemy's position prior to a raid, and later commanding the covering party to the raiders. He also displayed great courage when searching for a missing officer under machine-gun fire. Both the men with him were wounded, but he brought them both in after two hours under heavy fire.

Lt. (temp. Capt.) William Assheton Summers, 18th Hrs., and R.F.C.
Temp. Lt. William Owen Tudor Tudor-Hart, North'd Fus. and R.F.C.

CHAPTER SEVEN

The Assault on Mametz Wood

The 38th Welsh Division and, with it, the Swansea Battalion were spared the carnage of the first day of the Somme offensive. Launched at dawn on 1 July 1916, the attack has long been recognized as the blackest day in the long and distinguished history of the British Army. Almost 20,000 men were killed and a further 40,000 wounded whilst, with some notable exceptions, at the end of the day most of the objectives of the attack still remained firmly in German hands.

The Battle of the Somme was not, however, planned to be a mere one-day wonder though it had, in any event, failed spectacularly. Had the attack been successful it is very likely that the Welsh Division, and with it the Swansea Battalion, would soon have been engaged in exploiting the long awaited breakthrough and supporting the advance of the cavalry into open country, freed at last from the shackles of trench warfare. If that long-cherished dream remained painfully unfulfilled, there was still

A British soldier tends a grave near Mametz in the Summer of 1916. Taylor Library

other work that the division could usefully undertake as part of what was still an ongoing offensive. Steps were now taken to bring it speedily into play.

On 3 July 1916 the division formed part of the XV Corps reserve and was located about four miles south-west of Albert. By 6 July it had taken over the front line between Bottom Wood and Caterpillar Wood from the 7th Division, and Mametz Wood now lay to the north.

Sir Douglas Haig considered Mametz Wood to be an important objective. If it could be captured it could then be used as a jumping off point for a further attack northwards towards the German front between Contalmaison Villa and Bazentin le Petit Wood. If this proved successful, the attackers would then be able to swing eastward and advance on Longueval, while British artillery placed in the newly captured Mametz Wood could target the German defences which would then be in range.

The Germans would clearly be keen to retain control of the wood since it represented a considerable obstacle in the development of any future British attacks. The wood itself was not particularly well fortified. It did not need to be, since the naturally tangled nature of its undergrowth together with the shattered remnants of trees felled by artillery fire meant that the passage of troops was, in any event, very difficult. Fields of fire within the wood were obviously restricted due to the lack of lengthy and clear lines of sight. However, carefully sited machine guns placed near the edges had the advantage of a reasonable view of anyone advancing on the wood whilst the guns and their crews remained largely hidden from view.

The wood itself was defended by a mixed bag of German units, though they were not to be taken lightly. Elements of the Lehr Infantry Regiment (3rd Guards Division), the 16th Bavarian Regiment and the 184th Regiment were present, as was a battalion of the 122nd (Württemberg) Reserve Regiment. Indeed, the units of the Lehr Regiment had previously fought on the Russian Front and were well trained and battle hardened.

The approach to Mametz Wood lay down a slope and then a steep chalk bank towards Willow Stream. From the stream the ground then rose for more than a mile towards the ridge that runs from Pozieres through the two Bazentin woods (large and small), to Longueval. At this point lay the fortified trenches of the German second line. Troops attacking from the south, east or west would first have to descend the slope and chalk bank and then climb up to the ridge while, all the time, being exposed to the full attention of the enemy.

The wood was about a mile long and about three-quarters of a mile wide at its widest point. Not having been maintained since the outbreak of war it was now overgrown and the undergrowth was very dense, making the passage of troops extremely difficult. The trees were mainly oak and birch though there were also beech and ash. Some of the trees reached a girth of nine feet and a height of between thirty and forty-five feet. A 'ride' ran north to south through the centre of the wood whilst two other rides ran west to east. These, too, were partly overgrown and not always as clearly discernible to troops on the ground as might appear from a map. A notable feature of the wood was that its contours naturally formed the shape of a 'hammer head', similar to that of a claw hammer, at its eastern extremity.[1]

Operational map of Mametz Wood and its surrounds.
Swansea Battalion would advance from the area of W
Trench, near the bottom of the map. National Archiv

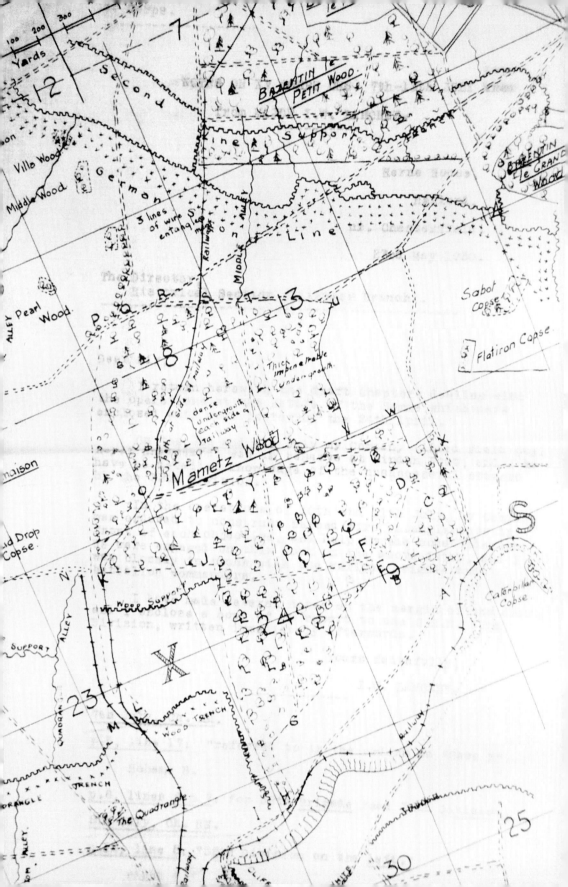

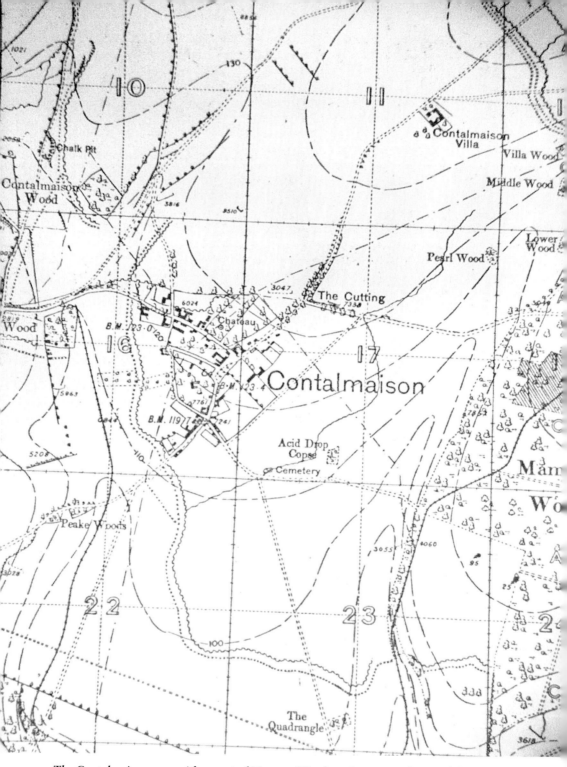

The Contalmaison area with a part of Mametz Wood on the eastern fringe of the map.
National Archives

98

On the night of 3-4 July 1916 a patrol of the 2nd Battalion, the Royal Irish Regiment, investigated with great caution the approaches to the wood before quietly entering it. The patrol found a tripwire at the edge of the wood, obviously placed there by the Germans, in the hope that it would give early warning were an attacker to stumble over it. A small trench inside the wood was examined but was, at the time, unmanned.

The patrol also reported that Strip Trench and Wood Trench were both well wired. The positions of a number of machine guns were classed as 'certain', 'practically certain', or 'suspected' and it was noted that the machine guns at Acid Drop Copse could fire directly down the valley, presenting great danger to any attacking troops.[2]

An attack by units of the 17th Division and units of the Welsh Division was planned for 7 July, with the Welsh troops attacking in the direction of the hammerhead. At 8.30 a.m. waves of troops from the 16th Welsh and the 11th South Wales Borderers moved off down the slope and into heavy German machine-gun fire that was soon augmented by an artillery bombardment.

The eastern edge of Mametz Wood with the Flatiron and Sabot Copses in close proximity.
National Archives

The attackers were promptly compelled to take cover due to the ferocity of the fire, with some being able to retire quickly back to the safety of their starting positions. Those troops left sheltering in no man's land now attracted the undivided attention of the Germans and suffered accordingly. A fresh attack, reinforced by the 10th South Wales Borderers, failed to make any real progress. A third attack, planned for 5.00 p.m., was called off when it was realized by higher command just how disorganized the attacking troops had become and how little disrupted the German defenders seemed to be. The 17th Division attack to the west of the Welsh Division had also ground to a halt. By the end of the day all the attacking troops had been withdrawn to their starting positions.

By 7 July the Swansea Battalion was in the vicinity of the Citadel, a wooded area near to the lines at Fricourt where it relieved the 7th Division. Here final training was undertaken as the men prepared for the further offensive action that was soon to take place. Training was of itself a risk filled activity and, following an accident, a Court of Enquiry was convened and heard from Second Lieutenant J.A. Wilson that:

> ...on the evening of July 7th 1916 at the Citadel lines, Fricourt, the four wounded officers with Captain A.H. Dagge, Lieut. J. Strange, and myself... were practising the throwing of (no.19) percussion bombs, undetonated bombs being used. The four injured officers formed one group, and the remainder of the party another, at about 30 yards distance. Undetonated bombs were being thrown from one group to the other. These bombs had previously been used for the same purpose in the forenoon... after throwing had been in progress for about a quarter of an hour there was an explosion.[3]

Aerial view of Mametz Wood showing the general line of attack taken by 13 and 14 Welsh. The fringe of the Hammerhead is just visible on the right, opposite the Dragon Memorial. Trevor Tasker

Another aerial view of Mametz Wood showing the general line of advance followed by the 13 and 14 Welsh from a different angle. The Hammerhead fills the bottom of the picture with the bulk of the wood off picture to the right. Trevor Tasker

The officers concerned were H. Jones-Willams, D.E. Evans, F. Roderick and A.F. H. Kelk. Luckily none of the wounds was serious and the enquiry finding was one of 'accident' since it seemed that all due precautions had been taken. Naturally, such an occurrence hardly helped preparations for the attack on Mametz Wood.

On 8 July the 17th Division made two further attacks on the wood but each assault was repelled by the defenders. On the Welsh Division sector, XV Corps Headquarters wanted a small scale raid to be carried out to further evaluate the defences during the night of 7-8 July, whilst its subordinate formation, the 113 Brigade was actually planning a larger attack of battalion strength. With the larger attack plan being overruled by the higher command, a planned night attack failed to occur at all, the orders arriving late and the trenches being too full of troops to permit the necessary movement into the line of the attacking units.

This confusion and, as Haig saw it, lack of decisive action with the troops not even entering the fringes of the wood, caused much consternation further up the command chain. Haig and Rawlinson together visited the headquarters of XV Corps on 9 July and left it in no doubt of their disappointment at the performance of the 17th and 38th Divisions. Both commanding officers were relieved of their commands, Major General Watts, the commander of the 7th Division, being given temporary control over the units of the Welsh Division, to use as 'he saw fit'. Ivor Phillips, commander of the Welsh Division and friend of Lloyd George, returned home to 'rest' with a shadow over his reputation. In its first major engagement elements of the Welsh Division had been judged wanting and it suffered an early blow to its prestige that would prove difficult to eradicate.

Also on 8 July 1916 a German deserter was questioned. The resultant report stated:

A deserter of the Lehr Regt, who has been in Mametz Wood for two days and came into our lines yesterday described it as a perfect Hell. A large number of dead and wounded are lying about and only one trench exists which the men have dug for themselves.[4]

Having been given a free hand with the Welsh Division Major General Watts was determined to use it in a further attack despite any of its perceived or alleged shortcomings. This attack was originally planned for 9 July but was postponed until 10 July. Using two brigades with the third close at hand, it would result in a much greater weight of attack than had hitherto been applied by the assaulting units to the wood's defences. It was to be very much a head on charge intended to simply overrun the German defenders due to the sheer weight of numbers in the attacking force. There would be no feints or diversionary attacks to distract the enemy. The operational order for the attack was suitably blunt stating unequivocally,

The Division will attack MAMETZ WOOD to-morrow with a view to capturing the whole of it.[5]

The attack was to be well supported by the artillery, with a mix of explosive and smoke shell, as well as assistance from the heavy and medium trench mortars. Royal Engineer and Pioneer detachments would be available to wire and fortify the ground gained. The men were to be carefully instructed in the compass direction of the advance since once inside the wood it was easy to lose one's sense of direction. As the rides or edges of the wood were reached a pause would be required for consolidation

Memorial plaque with the names of Phelps, Johnson, Smale and Beard. Jason Muxworthy

Memorial tablet featuring the names of W.H. Phelps, C.H. Johnson, Stanley Smale and D.J. Beard. Jason Muxworthy

and reorganization. Men were to follow the creeping barrage as closely as possible and would need to be warned in advance that artillery explosions would sound much louder within the cramped confines of the wood than they would outside it.

As far as the 114 Brigade was concerned, the Swansea Battalion would form the left of the Brigade advance with the 13th Welsh (2nd Rhondda) on the right. The 10th Welsh (1st Rhondda) would be in support in White Trench whilst the 15th Welsh (Carmarthenshire) would be in reserve in the Pommiers Redoubt. As the advance progressed the central ride would be marked by the placement of yellow flags to help with direction finding. Due to the tangled nature of the wood, exacerbated by the damage caused by shellfire, all units were to carry cutting tools in order that pathways could be cleared.

EX-SWANSEA BILLIARD MARKER.

Pte. Willie Durk, of 6, Earl-street, Hafod, killed in action in France. He was formerly employed as page-boy and billiard-marker at the Mackworth Hotel, High-street.

Private Willie Durk killed in action at Mametz Wood. He was formerly a billiard marker at the Mackworth Hotel, Swansea. South Wales Daily Post

Also attacking, but to the west of the 114 Brigade, would be the troops of the 113 Infantry Brigade under Brigadier Price-Davies. This Brigade consisted of the 13th, 14th, 15th, and 16th Battalions of the Royal Welsh Fusiliers. Units of the 115 Infantry Brigade had already suffered in the earlier attacks on the wood so were held back, for the moment, in support roles.

As the orders for the attack were received so the officers and platoon sergeants of the Swansea Battalion were instructed to report to the Commanding Officer. They found Lieutenant Colonel Hayes:

...staring across at the irregular shaped wood which was about 600 yards in front of our trench...he did not say a word until all

were together then he looked each of us over in a deliberate manner. He then pointed with his stick in the direction of the wood and I remember distinctly the words he made use of. 'Tomorrow at five minutes past four our battalion is going to take that wood, but' (then after a pause) 'we shall lose our battalion.'[6]

Lieutenant Colonel Carden, Commanding Officer of the 16th Royal Welsh Fusiliers, shared Hayes' concern, telling his men on the eve of the battle:

Boys make your peace with God! We are going to take that position and some of us won't come back. But we are going to take it.[7]

With every Welsh town and village having its quota of chapel, church and choral singers, and with this naturally being reflected among the waiting masses, it is not surprising that the men sang to relieve the tension of the long wait for night to pass into dawn. Amongst others, the hymn Jesu Lover of my Soul, sung in Welsh, was rendered in a manner that apparently gave great heart to those about to face their sternest test to date.

Sergeant Dick Lyons, the Irish-born former Swansea police constable, was somewhat surprised to hear that the battalion's objective was to be a wood. Battalion training had previously been concentrated on free movement

Dick Lyons 'somewhere in France'. Kae War.

over open ground, in stark contrast to the close-in fighting likely to be encountered in a dense area of woodland. No doubt the failure of the British Army to achieve a clear breakthrough on or after 1 July 1916 necessitated this change of plan. In any event 'going over the top' was Sergeant Lyons' preferred option if the alternative was to merely sit in a trench under enemy artillery fire.

At 3.00 a.m. on the morning of 10 July all troops were in position and the artillery bombardment commenced at 3.30 a.m. Almost 300 mortar bombs were also fired to good effect before the smoke barrage began at about 3.50 a.m. Sergeant Lyons recalled:

...it must not be assumed that all was peaceful and quiet prior to this stage. Gun firing was heavy for weeks previously. When we had the signal to advance, our guns lifted to targets further back, whilst the German guns which was firing on our trenches switched to 'No-

Dyson Brock Williams *whose post-war difficulties ended in tragedy* South Wales Daily Post

*Corporal Rowe,
killed in the attack
on Mametz Wood.*
South Wales Daily
Post

Man's-Land' and in particular to their own barbed wire.[8]

At 4.05 a.m. the 14th (Swansea) and 13th Welsh Battalions began moving forward in eight waves and in perfect walking order. Stanley J. C. Williams writing as 'Yelnats' recalled the scene some years later for the local newspaper:

...not even a rat could recover after such a 'strafe' and as it was going on our boys remained quietly waiting with fixed bayonets, five cartridges in the magazine, one in the breech and two bombs each...at 4.05 a.m. precisely our colonel, who was waiting about fifty yards in advance of our position took off his steel helmet and, as the artillery raised its fire to another part of the wood, he gave a movement with his helmet to get the first line to advance. There was not a moment's hesitation – each and every man moved off in perfect order and the colonel repeated the sweeping movement with his helmet each time the line was 100 yards in advance of those still lying down.[9]

Sergeant Lyons remembered the moment as the troops advanced into the German counter barrage:

Machine gun and rifle fire was trained on us as well. Words fail me to adequately describe this stage of the attack. We suffered a great many casualties particularly among our officers. The Germans were adept at picking them off. When we reached their positions we escaped a good deal of the gun fire in 'No Man's Land'. They would not fire on their own positions for fear of killing their own men, but they were still firing over our heads whilst our guns were also firing over our heads on to German targets. Many of the shells...hit the trees above us, detonated, and caused us more casualties.[10]

Indeed, during the day the Germans managed to wound the second in command, three company commanders and three junior officers out of a Swansea Battalion officer contingent of only seventeen that led its men towards the wood. Another officer was killed during the same period.[11]

Lieutenant Colonel Carden of the 16th Royal Welsh Fusiliers had earlier warned his men in a rousing address that the wood had to be taken regardless of cost. He now made a conspicuous target as he advanced across the exposed terrain while brandishing his swagger stick above his head and encouraging his men. He quickly fell wounded but managed to struggle on to the fringe of the wood. Still exhorting his men to even greater efforts he was struck again by enemy fire and killed. He had sadly become a victim of his own prediction.

Corporal G.H. Crick of 'D' Company, whose platoon sergeant was Dick Lyons recalled:

...spreading out across the field in front of the wood. I was close to my company officer Lieutenant Arnold

Frederick Bond, brother of William, killed at Mametz Wood while serving with the 10th Welsh. Ceri Rees-Powell

Wilson (the big fight promoter) in case he wanted any messages sent... when we got close to the wood some of the Germans came out. Lieut. Wilson had his revolver pointing at them, but they were more or less surrendering.[12]

Private Charles Henry Mew went across in the third wave even though his personal speciality was that of sniper. When he got to the fringe of the wood he could see no obvious signs of the first two waves. Some men he knew had fallen, and those he had passed. The others had presumably entered the wood and were now lost to sight. Mew found himself at first literally unable to enter the wood due to the tangled undergrowth and he had to move sideways before he found a point of entry. Once in the wood he quickly saw where some of the earlier waves had gone since he could see 'our fellows and the jerries lying pretty thick'.

As he pressed forward he fleetingly saw two Germans in the thick bushes and 'had a pot at them'. A German sniper had been hiding in the upper reaches of a tree. Shot by the attacking troops his body hung from the branches, as he had been strapped in to his position. Lieutenant Strange was in the wood and was barking out orders to men of his own unit as well as those of the Rhondda's, trying to impose some order on what was already a chaotic situation.[13]

As the officers of the Swansea Battalion led their men forward it was inevitable that they would, themselves, be in the forefront of the fighting. Lieutenant Wilson distinguished himself by:

Bayoneting in single combat at the head of his Company a burly German, and then bringing down a shot sniper in a tree. Lieutenant Hawkins, a Welsh International Rugby player, did equally good, if not better work, by charging down on two separate machine guns, both of which he captured, though unfortunately he was wounded the second time.[14]

As Major D. Brock Williams, second in command of the battalion, advanced across the open field a shell exploded nearby so that, as a subsequent medical board was informed:

...a splinter of shell entered the right chest in front...3˝ below the nipple. This passed round the chest and lay underneath the ribs but did not penetrate the lung.[15]

Another officer who was wounded in the fighting was Arthur Henry Dagge. An insurance manager, thirty-two years of age, he had attested in September 1914 at Cardiff. Fighting in the wood he was struck by small fragments of shrapnel that inflicted puncture wounds on the left upper arm, the right thigh and the right patella. These wounds would eventually require some sixteen months of treatment and three surgical operations plus regular massage and electrical treatment. Apparently undeterred by these experiences of active service Dagge was to offer his services again to his country at the outbreak of the Second World War. As he was by then in his mid fifties, his country decided, much as it appreciated the offer, that it would try and manage without him.[16]

By 4.50 a.m. the Swansea Battalion was reported as having reached its second objective. To Sergeant Lyons progress nevertheless seemed slow:

This was due mainly to the German machine gun fire but also to the density of the undergrowth in the wood. This also impeded visibility. In the

Ned Bevan (right) and Tom Bennett. A veteran of Mametz Wood, Ned was still alive in 1976.
Trevor Tasker

circumstances it was difficult to maintain our sense of direction. I was helped in this by being able to tell the difference between the sound of our guns and the Germans...the Germans offered stubborn resistance throughout but they were not over keen on close-quarter work. The machine gun and rifle were the main weapons of their infantry but when it came to 'Bayonet fighting' they did not show any enthusiasm.[17]

Private David John Rees made his way into one of the clearings in the wood where he was spotted by a German sniper. A well aimed bullet struck him in the face, causing the loss of an eye. Stunned, he fell into a shell hole and came around slowly to find himself still being targeted by the sniper. Shouted instructions from his concealed comrades led him to safety and he then assisted a non-walking case back to the dressing station.[18]

Private Colin Charles Thomas of Pontardulais, had already been wounded in February 1916, but had returned to service with the Swansea Battalion. He now found himself fighting in the wood where he was wounded again, this time more seriously. He was hit on the left side below his armpit. He was assisted by a stretcher bearer named Cled Walters, who coincidentally was from his local village. Being evacuated by field ambulance over the rough terrain proved more painful than the actual wound itself. At Number 12 General Hospital at Rouen he slipped in and out of consciousness, resting on a cot. In one of his more lucid moments he heard a comment that the cot cases were effectively 'no-hopers' but those on palliasses had some chance of survival. Suitably motivated by this stark judgement, he rallied and soon found himself moved onto a palliasse, so that a more serious case should benefit from the comfort of the cot. He was eventually evacuated to Britain via the Red Cross ship *Asturias*.[19]

By 5.10 a.m. the 10th Welsh had been unavoidably drawn into the fighting as reinforcements, due to the heavy casualties being suffered by the 13th Welsh. Despite its losses the 13th was able to report that it was through the wood, though it was then realized that having advanced so far both it and the Swansea Battalion were at risk of

Hospital ship Asturias *which brought Colin Charles Thomas back to Britain.*
Denzil Thomas

Hospital ward for wounded soldiers.
Denzil Thomas

running into their own pre-planned barrage. To avoid this the 14th and 13th Welsh were ordered to fall back out of the pre-arranged target area to the first objective line, and to wait until the barrage had passed before advancing again.

As 7.00 a.m. approached the 13th Welsh was again forced to call for reinforcements and some men could be seen leaving the wood and moving back towards the British lines. One company of the 15th Welsh was sent forward to assist but was counter-attacked by the enemy. A further two companies were dispatched and these succeeded in making contact with the Swansea Battalion. As these companies pushed further forward they were outflanked by the Germans who shot down two platoons before they were able to dig in. Shortly after 7.10 a.m. the 10th Welsh called for reinforcements and the last company of the 15th Welsh was committed. The 114 Infantry Brigade was now at full stretch with all its troops fighting in the wood and no reserves left.

Instances of men leaving the wood had also been observed by the 14th Battalion of the Royal Welsh Fusiliers sometime earlier. Supporting the attack of the 16th Battalion, the Royal Welsh Fusiliers, the 14th got to within 150 yards of the entrance to the wood by about 5.00 a.m. to be met by men of the earlier waves falling back to shouts of 'retire'. To compound the problem at this moment Major Gwyther, Commanding Officer of the 14th Royal Welsh Fusiliers was wounded and Major R. H. Mills was killed,

Colin Charles Thomas. Wounded several times he finished his war service with the King's Scottish Light Infantry. Post war he worked in the postal, coal and metal industries before having another pot at the Hun by making tank tracks during the Second World War. Denzil Thomas
Colin Charles Thomas in hospital after being wounded during the attack on Mametz Wood. Denzil Thomas

Alf Jackson in 1986. At Mametz Wood a bullet had removed several of his teeth and a piece of jaw bone. Trevor Tasker

adding to the men's confusion. Sterling work by Captain J. Glynn Jones steadied the men and they reformed in a hollow about 150 yards from the wood.[20]

If all the troops of 114 Brigade were now fully engaged in the wood, the ambulance services were not too far behind as they struggled to deal with the demands placed upon them. The War Diary of the Assistant Director of Medical Services, 38th Division recorded:

...large numbers of wounded had arrived at Minden Post during the morning from the renewed attack by the 113th and 114th Bde's in the early morning - additional ambs cars and some char-a-bancs were obtained...and these were busily employed all day. 50 additional Bearers were obtained....[21]

The extra bearers had come from the 131st Field Ambulance and had all volunteered for the duty, the War Diary of the 130th (St John) Field Ambulance recording that it was found necessary:

...to apply to O.C. 131 at Minden Post ADS for extra bearers, as 52 stretcher cases were then lying at TRIANGLE awaiting removal to ADS...the message was received...by Capt. A. Jones, RAMC, who paraded every man of the few left at Headquarters and asked for volunteers - every man volunteered, including a large number of men who had been up all the previous night dressing wounded at MORLANCOURT....[22]

By 4.00 a.m. on 11 July the men of the 130th (St John) Field Ambulance were reported as being 'extremely exhausted'. However, no relief being readily available, they manfully stuck to their tasks for a further thirteen hours.

Between 9.00 p.m. on 9 July and 6.00 a.m. on 10 July, thirty-nine casualties were dealt with by 130th Field Ambulance. In the six hours to noon on 10 July another seventy-four were received whilst from noon to 9 p.m. on the 10th a further 350 were dealt with, as the intensity of the fighting increased and the wounded were slowly gathered in.[23]

The medical work itself was not without its own dangers and one medical officer was killed and another wounded by enemy shell fire in the vicinity of Queens Nullah. Near to the advanced bearer post at Mametz, Lieutenant R.J. Jones of the RAMC was killed by machine-gun fire while going out to tend to the wounded.[24]

Where the fighting was at its most intense there was little time for the niceties of war. As the Swansea Battalion advanced through the wood, Dick Lyons noted:

Their casualties and ours were left behind for our stretcher bearers to deal with. Their cries of 'Mercy! Kamerad!' come to me vividly as I reflect on the scene. We were not encouraged to take prisoners and another factor was that owing to casualties and the enormous task confronting us, we could not afford to deplete our strength by using our men to take prisoners back to our support lines. There was little mercy shown by either side in this battle or in any other

Edward George Hughes (rear, left) with his father and brothers. Severely wounded, he was captured by the Germans, probably in the action at Mametz Wood. Sue Rouse

encounter we had with the Germans. They were fierce, ruthless warriors.[25]

Whilst the statement made by Sergeant Lyons is largely correct, the possibility of small numbers of men being taken prisoner and being quickly evacuated from the wood by their captors cannot be entirely ruled out. One such possibility concerns Private Edward George Hughes. Initially joining the Glamorgan Yeomanry, he later transferred to the Swansea Battalion.

It is possible that he was engaged in the attack on Mametz Wood though the records and family recollections are not clear on this point. What is known is that he suffered a severe wound, with a bullet entering his head just above his eye and exiting at the back of his ear. Miraculously he survived, but was captured and eventually taken to a prisoner of war camp in Germany.[26]

Lieutenant Colonel Hayes recalled the confusion in the wood:

In the wood itself direction was most difficult to maintain; it was almost impossible to read a map, and certain troops were found to be following the artillery, which proved to be the enemy's and not their own barrage. I personally found two platoons taking cover and firing towards the first ride...the 14th Welsh did gain their objectives, but they were only there in detached posts. I visited them and lost my way doing so two or three times. I saw a few dead Germans and some wounded, but on my own front there was no organised resistance, with the exception of the well placed machine guns, and all of them either had a dead man in the pit or were deserted...most of my own battalion's casualties were caused by machine-gun fire, a certain amount by both our own and hostile artillery fire; there was some hand to hand fighting at the edge of the wood, but very little.[27]

If the Germans were relatively few in number, a Royal Welsh Fusilier nevertheless recalled that those that were encountered in the wood were very determined men, despite the odds being heavily against them:

...every man of them was killed where he stood...they refused offers of quarter right to the last. They were very brave men, and we were sorry indeed to have to kill them, for we could not but admire them for their courage.[28]

At about 9.35 a.m. a British artillery observer reported seeing large groups of German troops entering the wood from the north, obviously intending to shore up the defence. As the precise position of British troops was not entirely clear at that time it was deemed prudent not to bombard this enemy movement for the moment, lest casualties

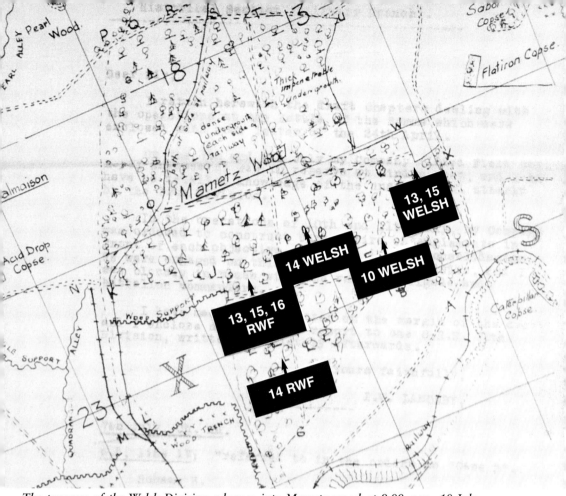

The progress of the Welsh Division advance into Mametz wood at 9.00 a.m., 10 July 1916. National Archives/Author

Aerial photograph of Mametz Wood. Trevor Tasker

Shattered trees at Mametz Wood. Imperial War Museum, Q860

be accidentally inflicted on friendly troops.[29]

To try and bring some order to a very difficult situation at 10.30 a.m. Lieutenant Colonel Hayes of the Swansea Battalion was placed in command of all 114 Brigade troops in the wood and was ordered to push on to the second objective. He first had to deal with German defenders who were making it very difficult for the supporting Pioneers by way of rifle fire, as well as an enemy counter-attack on the 15th Welsh position. These actions resulted in only partial success and the 15th Welsh Battalion was slowly forced back by the enemy. With Hayes now engaged in other duties and Brock Williams, the designated second in command, already having been wounded, the command of the Swansea Battalion devolved to Lieutenant Strange.

As he reached a clearing, Private Mew came across a British soldier guarding three German prisoners. As Mew took in the scene another German appeared from the undergrowth and raised his rifle in the direction of the guard. Mew was able to quickly fire a shot from the hip that struck the attacker and removed the threat. Pushing on to the central ride, Mew found a British machine-gun crew setting up their equipment in anticipation of a German counter-attack. At that instant a German shell landed in the midst of the party and exploded.

Mew was about ten or twelve yards from the centre of the explosion. As he recovered his senses he could see no sign of the machine gun or its crew. He was 'tingling all over and my eyes was filled with dirt'. As the tingling wore off and his sight cleared he realized that the sleeve on his right arm had been torn away at the elbow and there was also blood on his chest. Lieutenant Strange was quickly on the scene and applied a field dressing. Mew was ordered to retire despite his protestations that the wounds were minor. Lieutenant Strange remained in the wood until he was, himself, wounded at about 6.00 p.m., still fighting his way forward to its northern edge.

As Mew made his way out of the wood he encountered Henry Brown, a Harbour Trust employee, who lived at Lambert's Cottages in Swansea. He had also been hit in the arm. Both men had the use of their legs, however, and the stretcher bearers were waved away as the two casualties hurried on their way. A German machine gun targeted them but they were able to take refuge in a shell hole until the gunner paused to change his ammunition belt. During the temporary lull in firing they made good their escape from the wood.

Outside the wood they managed to find a field kitchen and savoured a much needed cup of tea. They parted at this point and Mew never saw Brown again. Mew was placed in hospital at Rouen where he was treated for flesh wounds and two broken bones. He was at first bemused to see the letters 'TB' placed above his bed but was then delighted to discover that this was not indicative of his having caught a serious disease. In fact it conveyed the very welcome news that he was off 'To Blighty!'[30]

Private O.B. Charles also found the wood to be an extremely dangerous place and the *South Wales Daily Post* later reported on Private Charles's experiences:

Charles Henry Mew who was wounded in the fighting at Mametz Wood.
Trevor Tasker

> *Pte. O.B. Charles... is now in hospital in this country, wounded in the left thigh, but is progressing very favourably, and expects to be able to get about in a day or two.*
>
> *We kept together all right until we came to a wood, when there was the difficulty of finding entrances before us. A few chaps and myself managed to find a way, however, and then picked up with a machine-gun section of ours, and together we pushed our way through. When we got through the wood we pushed forward on our own, the other chaps (machine-gunners) had not come up with us, so we took a position in shell holes. We had not been there very long when the Germans, who were in a redoubt 300 yards in front of us, spotted us, and turned a machine-gun on us.*
>
> *I got one in the arm as a result of that, and then got lower down in my hole until the Huns ceased firing. I took a peep to see how the other chaps got on; the sight that met my eyes was terrible. Poor fellows were lying about in all positions dead. They probably tried to fall back into the wood when the Germans opened fire on us, and thus got the full force of the machine-gun fire.*
>
> *When things quietened down a bit I decided to try and make my way back into the wood and from there to the dressing station. With this object in view I worked my way down out of the shell-hole gradually, but had only gone six yards when I heard 'bang, bang'. I felt them too, I can assure you, when I got another in my left hip and left shoulder. It was a good job there was another*

shell-hole just in front of me, or I might have had it even worse. I got into it quickly and stopped there, dressing my wounds the best way I could, and then lay down to await events.

About four hours afterwards our people began shelling the redoubt with lyddite shells - and there is a vast amount of smoke with them. The redoubt was completely obscured at times with this smoke, so I seized my chance of reaching safety and made a dash into the wood, and got there all right.

I came across a party... digging themselves in when I arrived, so I asked an officer to allow one of his men to help me down to the stretcher-bearers. This he did, and a young fellow carried me on his back for nearly a mile. When he left me I embraced him and wished him the best of luck. I went under an operation at the base hospital and it proved very successful.

I am very sorry to say that the little pair of opera glasses were smashed to atoms. I carried them in a little satchel by my side and the bullet that got me in the hip went through them. I was very sorry to lose them because they had been like an additional pair of eyes to me on my sentry-go in the nights, and also the fact that they were a wedding present of mother's. Never mind, I am thankful that I am alive.[31]

Brigadier General Marden then decided that he needed to find out at first hand exactly what was happening in the wood. He thus gained permission to enter the wood and, having assessed the position, speedily agreed that a concerted effort should be made to drive the enemy out, with an attack going in at 4.30 p.m. This attack was

German transport wagons destroyed at Mametz Wood. Imperial War Museum, Q874

successfully carried out though the advance was halted within about 100 yards of the northern edge of the wood due to enemy machine-gun fire coming from a trench outside its confines. An attack by the 14th Welsh and the 17th Royal Welsh Fusiliers failed to get through to deal with this resistance, partly due to the thickness of the undergrowth and fallen trees. A temporary withdrawal, while the northern edge of the wood was first bombarded and then attacked again, failed to significantly improve the position.

During this action Lieutenant Arthur Rosser of the Swansea Battalion bravely led a bombing team forward. Private George Britton, who had attended school with Rosser, witnessed part of the scene:

> *The lieut. was in charge of some bombers and saw that his men were going to be surrounded and told his men to dash for safety, while he himself stayed on. These bombers were new draft men. Rosser was no doubt killed during this second attack. I myself went right through the wood and the Germans would have no chance of taking prisoners, as we were driving them before us.*[32]

Second Lieutenant Arthur Rosser, killed in Mametz Wood. Swansea Library Service

Lieutenant Rosser was nineteen years old when he was killed. He had been a student at the Swansea Technical College prior to his enlisting. He was the son of William Rosser, an upholsterer, of Eaton Grove, Swansea. William Rosser himself died in 1931, having been one-time President of the Swansea West Liberal Association.[33]

Dick Lyons found it difficult to fully comprehend exactly what was happening as he and his comrades thrashed their way forward:

> *...the description which I have given of the scene falls far short of the true position and I wonder how I can rectify this. Such terms as 'Bedlam' 'Hell let loose' 'The World gone mad' occur to me...we were relieved sometime during the night greatly depleted in numbers. On our way back...one of my most vivid memories was the groans of the wounded and dying.*[34]

General Watts, meanwhile, may well have been running out of patience at what he apparently still saw as a lack of drive in some quarters of the attacking force. The record of a headquarters telephone message revealed that:

> *...the situation in Mametz Wood was now being investigated with a view to clearing it up and establishing a line on the northern edge of the wood. General Watts was of the opinion that if the 38th division were not in a condition to do so, he had better put one of the battalions of the 7th division in to do the job.*[35]

However, all the wood, except for its northern edge, was now in the possession of the British and some time later the Commanding Officer of 7th Division was able to report that between 9.30 and 10.30 p.m:

> *...our infantry are holding a line about 150 yards north of the Central Ride, and are apparently well dug in. The undergrowth of the Wood is very thick and many trees have fallen. Danger from German counter-attack is, therefore, not great, as they could only advance by the rides.*
>
> *The enemy placed, for several hours this evening, a very heavy barrage on the Rides in rear of the line held and on the road running round the south western side of the wood; shells of 5.9 and of heavier calibre were falling.*

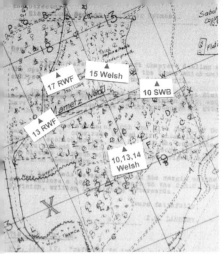

Mametz Wood at 9.00 p.m. 1916; the Swansea Battalion had earlier approached the northern edge of the wood but was driven back by machine gun fire from outside the wood.
National Archives

A postcard sold to raise funds for the 'Llandilo Soldiers & Sailors Fund'. It shows the Welsh dragon doing battle with the German eagle in Mametz Wood.
Trevor Tasker

This barrage caused many casualties to orderlies and communication has been very difficult and impossible in any other way than by runners; many runners had been casualties...the northern edge of the Wood is fairly strongly held by the enemy. Our own infantry of the 38th division were at that time evidently exhausted and jumpy.[36]

Sergeant Glanffrwd Buse was eighteen years of age and was apparently the youngest sergeant in the Corps. He had distinguished himself during the attack and was later awarded the Military Medal. His company commander had told him:

I think you behaved very well in the wood; in fact you did excellent work, being of the greatest assistance to your officers and in every way an example to your men. You acted just as an ideal NCO should do.[37]

At 5.00 a.m. on 11 July the 113 and 114 Brigades were relieved by the 115 Brigade, the Swansea Battalion being withdrawn to the Citadel. Though sporadic fighting in and around the wood would continue for two more days, the Swansea Battalion would play no further part in it.

The battalion, in its first major engagement and after almost two years of training, had advanced on the wood some 676 strong. By the end of the day it had lost over ninety men killed and almost 300 wounded (total casualties were recorded as being 376). No doubt others who had been wounded on 10 July 1916 would succumb to their injuries in the coming days and weeks making the real toll even higher.[38]

The other battalions in the 114 Infantry Brigade had also suffered heavily. The 10th Battalion (1st Rhondda) had lost 314 killed or wounded whilst the figure for the 15th Welsh (Carmarthenshire) was 245. The 13th Welsh (2nd Rhondda) arrived at the Citadel on 11 July where a roll call revealed that twelve officers and 350 other ranks were unaccounted for. It seems very likely that a number of stragglers and wounded from the 2nd Rhondda were later gathered in, since the regimental history records the casualty figure as being 290.[39]

The Brigade left the wood in a state of exhaustion from want of sleep, food and water but its men were reported as still being in great heart and able to sing as they marched. Many of them carried captured German helmets (Pickelhauben) as trophies of the struggle. The Germans had suffered heavily too. Max Borns had been captured by the

British in Mametz Wood early on the morning of 12 July. His interrogation, which should be read with caution since he might have been saying what he felt his captors wished to hear, revealed:

German losses as being very heavy – 4 divisions being practically out of action...of many companies only 15 to 20 men could be collected...prisoner described confusion behind German line as very bad. He states a number of men from various Coy's. and Regts. would be collected from stragglers in rear and pushed back into the fight. He says has heard that many officers had been shot by their own men.[40]

Another prisoner, Max Daebler, largely echoed the views of his comrade:

There are no trenches in Mametz Wood except what the men have dug for themselves, and that the wood is an indescribable scene of wreckage and confusion...food is almost unprocurable as owing to our artillery fire it is extremely difficult to get anything up at all.[41]

On the 13 July 1916 Brigadier General T.O. Marden, CMG, Officer Commanding of 114 Infantry Brigade issued a Special Order of the Day. In this he congratulated:

...all ranks on their achievements of the 10th July, when they firmly established the fighting reputation of the 114th Infantry Brigade by capturing that portion of the MAMETZ Wood allotted to them by the Divisional Commander, thereby gaining the thanks of the Commander-In-Chief for the performance of a task which called for special effort.

Wood fighting is recognised as the most difficult form of fighting and it reflects the greatest credit on all engaged, that at the end of the day all Units in the Brigade were under their own Commanders.

The advance to the attack was carried out in perfect order by the 13th and 14th Welsh, to whom fell the majority of the wood fighting, the severity of which is shown by the casualty lists.[42]

Lieutenant Colonel J. H. Hayes, of the Swansea Battalion was also praised for his 'splendid work throughout the day'.

Over the next few days a number of literary figures would, by chance, be very close to the wood. Indeed, some had actually taken part in the attack itself. Siegfried Sassoon had actually captured a German trench almost single handed on 4 July 1916. Exhausted, he had slumped temporarily on the fire step and counted

Brigadier General Marden's Order of the Day commending the efforts of 114 Brigade in the attack on Mametz Wood.
National Archives

114th INFANTRY BRIGADE

SPECIAL ORDER OF THE DAY

by

BRIGADIER GENERAL T.O.MARDEN C.M.G., COMMANDING 114th INFANTRY BD

The Brigadier General congratulates all ranks on their achievements of the 10th of July, when they firmly established the fighting reputation of the 114th Infantry Brigade by capturing that portion of the MAMETZ Wood allotted to them by the Divisional Commander, thereby gaining the thanks of the Commander-in-Chief for the performance of a task which called for a special effort.

Wood fighting is recognised as the most difficult form of fighting and it reflects the greatest credit on all engaged, that at the end of the day all Units in the Brigade were under their own Commanders.

The advance to the attack was carried out in perfect order by the 13th and 14th Welsh, to whom fell the majority of the wood fighting, the severity of which is shewn by the casualty Lists.

The 10th and 15th Welsh showed equal steadiness in the advance when called on to support. The thanks of the Brigadier are specially due to Lieutenant Colonel J.H.HAYES Commanding 14th Welsh for his splendid work throughout the day, and to Captain A.P.BOWEN, Brigade Major for his staff work and organising work in the Wood.

They are due to Lieutenant Colonel F.E.RICKETTS, Commanding 10th Welsh, to Major D.A.EDWARDS Commanding 13th Welsh, and to Major C.G.PHILLIPS Commanding 15th Welsh who all, unfortunately, became casualties during the action.

They are due, too, to those Officers and Non Commissioned Officers who assumed command of Battalions, Companies and Platoons, when their Leaders fell, and to others whose names have not yet been ascertained.

With such a splendid start, the 114th Infantry Brigade can look with confidence to the future, and with pride to the past.

July 13th 1916.   (Signed) T.O.MARDEN,
                                        Brigadier General,
                            Commanding 114th Infantry Brigade.

This order will be read on Parade to every man of the Brigade.

almost fifty abandoned German infantry packs. Unable to hold the position himself, he had eventually been forced to hurry back to the shelter of his own lines.

Wyn Griffith (author of *Up to Mametz*) was acting as a temporary brigade officer and was helping direct the fight for the wood on 10 July 1916. He had the terrible misfortune to send his younger brother, Watcyn, back into the wood with a message. On attempting to return to headquarters for further orders Watcyn was killed by shellfire and his body lost. Entering the wood later in search of his brother's body, Griffith recalled seeing several severed heads, torsos or other limbs lying around, as well as a leg that had been blown into the branches of a tree. This was stark testimony to the ferocity of the fighting in the wood and the awesome power of modern artillery.

David Jones (author of *In Parentheses* and later to become a distinguished artist) was wounded during the attack. He crawled out of the wood leaving behind the heavy burden that his rifle represented for, as he commented with amazing foresight, the future scrutiny of a Cook's Tour party.

Frank Richards (author of *Old Soldiers Never Die*), an old sweat of the Indian Army, had rejoined the 2nd Battalion of the Royal Welsh Fusiliers at the outbreak of war, and approached the wood some days after the fighting had moved on. He recalls having to sleep in a shell hole since the more suitable ground was still strewn with the dead of both sides.

Also with the 2nd Battalion, Royal Welsh Fusiliers, was Robert Graves (author of *Good-bye to All That* and *I, Claudius*) who entered the wood in search of a warming and, now to its late owner, surplus German greatcoat. He came across the macabre sight of a South Wales Borderer and a German who had simultaneously bayoneted each other and now stood transfixed and propped up against the support of a tree, side by side in death.

As the remnants of the Swansea Battalion moved away from the wood, the town of Swansea was naturally ignorant of the heavy blow its 'own' battalion had suffered. Censorship restrictions and the often snails' pace release of information meant that it was some time before it became clear that the battalion had been in its heaviest engagement to date and had suffered proportionately. But gradually the news seeped out, with the lengthening casualty lists, the War Office telegrams bringing terrible news of a loved one, and the gradual arrival home of the wounded, some of whom were fated not to recover:

> The military funeral took place at Danygraig Cemetery on Wednesday of Private Arthur Thomas Pillifant... who was wounded in action on the 10th of July and subsequently succumbed at Liverpool Hospital.[43]

The parents of Sergeant Jim Lloyd were informed:

> I am very sorry indeed to inform you that your son, Sergeant Lloyd, has been missing since July 10th. On that day...the battalion was very heavily engaged and your son was seen entering the wood which we had to capture. Since then we have heard nothing of him and we greatly fear that he may have been killed. He may be in one of the hospitals in France, and if we hear anything of him I shall let you know.[44]

On 2 September 1916 the *South Wales Daily Post* printed a list of 'recent' casualties that, the newspaper soberly commented, was the longest list yet, with many of those named having fallen at Mametz Wood. Still further snippets of information appeared over the coming weeks as families received or sought further information on loved ones. The body of Private Richard Henry Rowe had been found but identification, possibly due to the nature of his wounds, seemed to have been made only with some difficulty:

> He died bravely and gloriously, doing his duty to the last... After a big battle I found him in (Mametz) Wood, and I am sure it was him, because he was a corporal, and his small book confirms my belief.[45]

Samuel Thomas Gammon was from Mumbles, near Swansea, and was advancing through the wood when a German shell exploded nearby. One of his comrades fell wounded, and eventually had to have a leg amputated as a consequence of the injury.

Private J. Doran, captured by the Germans. South Wales Daily Post

Private W.C. Jerram who fell on 12 July 1916 and D.J. Pritchard who was killed in action at Mametz Wood. South Wales Daily Post

Lance Corporal Edmonds who left a wife and six children. South Wales Daily Post

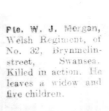

Private W.J. Morgan who left a wife and five children. South Wales Daily Post

Samuel Gammon, killed in action at Mametz Wood.
John Powell and Fred Gammon

The Gammon family. Fred is on his mother's lap. John Powell and Fred Gammon

In Ever Loving Memory

OF

SAMUEL GAMMON,

(Of the Mumbles, near Swansea).

The dearly beloved Husband of Gladys Gammon,

Who was killed at Mametz Wood, France, whilst serving his King and Country, July 10th, 1916.

AGED 29 YEARS.

———

INTERRED AT FRANCE.

Into the field of battle he bravely took his place,
And fought and died for England, honour, and his race ;
He sleeps not in his native land, but 'neath a foreign sky,
Far from Wife and Children dear, in a hero's grave he lies.
No one knows the silent heartache, only those can tell
Who have lost a Husband and Father dear, without saying farewell ! .

Front and reverse of Remembrance Card for Samuel Gammon.
John Powell and Fred Gammon

120

Samuel was killed instantly by the explosion. He left a widow, Gladys, and three children, the youngest of whom, Fred, was not yet one year old.

There is no record of Samuel being buried in a marked grave and it is possible that either his body was buried as unidentified or, after burial, the precise location was lost in the subsequent fighting and confusion. He was twenty-nine years of age. In early summer 1916 Gladys had received a crucifix from France, sent to her as a token of affection by Samuel. Mrs Gammon had promptly arranged to have her photograph taken together with her children, including Fred, then aged about ten months, at a commercial studio in Swansea. A copy was sent to Samuel at the front. Sadly, it is not known whether the photograph arrived before Samuel entered Mametz Wood. The crucifix remains a treasured possession of the Gammon family to this day.

Being so young Fred never really had the chance to get to know his father though he has never 'forgotten' him. Samuel's medals and remembrance plaque are still carefully retained and cherished. Fred did recall the hard times that the family saw in subsequent years as Gladys struggled to bring up three boys without the assistance of a father. As a young boy, summer treats involved being taken to the holiday homes at Llangennith on Gower, with other children who had also lost a father in the Great War. One striking memory is of Bernard Freyburg, the legendary New Zealand soldier, visiting Gower and being entertained by the young children singing and reciting poetry. He gave each a shilling in return. Flowers were regularly placed on the Cenotaph at Swansea by Mrs Gammon in proud, if sad, memory of Samuel and his comrades.

The Gammon family eventually moved to England but further tragedy was not very far away. First, brother Thomas was killed in an accident at the age of only twenty-three years. Fred's uncle, William, was later lost at sea with the other seven crew members of the Mumbles lifeboat *Edward, Prince of Wales*, while going to the aid of the stricken vessel, the *Samtampa*, off Sker Point, at the height of a ferocious storm. Fred was still alive in 1995, by then a sprightly octogenarian.[46]

Corporal Ernest Beynon had already been wounded while serving in the Laventie area in May 1916. Returning to the unit he was now wounded again in the fight for Mametz Wood and had to return home for rest and recuperation. He later returned to the front line though with a different Welsh Regiment battalion and was involved in the capture of Bourlon Wood by elements of the Welsh Division in 1918. The Germans either found Corporal Beynon an irresistible target or he believed in leading from the front since he was once again

Private Ernie Beynon as a young volunteer. Bill Benyon

Ernie Beynon (standing extreme right) while convalescing at the Birmingham home of the Chamberlain political dynasty following a wound.   Bill Beynon

wounded in action.[47]

For some, the news received of loved ones seemed to pose more questions than it answered. The family of Private Edmonds was told:

> *I have made many enquiries amongst the remaining members of the platoon, and the only news I can get is that he was wounded* (in the stomach) *and missing. The boys were unable to stop and assist him, and they all seem to think that he died immediately, otherwise the stretcher bearers would have brought him in, as he was one of the first to fall.*[48]

Private Edmonds was a married man with six children. Before the war he had run a fruit stall in Swansea Market.

Charles Henry Johnson had been born on 2 August 1884, the eldest of five children. Married in 1909 to Florence, he worked at the premises of Messrs. Vivian & Sons, at Landore, Swansea. He had joined the battalion with his younger brother, Bertie, and both had entered Mametz Wood on 10 July. Bertie was seriously wounded by the explosion of a bomb that was thrown at him at close range by a German officer. Shrapnel had entered his leg and his shoulder. It was the third time he had been wounded but he was to return to active service yet again after rest and recuperation. Charles was killed in the wood and his body lost in the subsequent fighting.[49]

If the effect on the town of a lengthy casualty list was hard, the surviving men of the battalion were obviously even more affected. The intensity of the fighting and the scale of their losses in what was their first major encounter with the enemy must have left a psychological scar on men who, until very recently, had been mere civilians. Despite this the men did not seem to have been unduly dejected by their experience and the satisfaction of fighting for what they largely saw as a just cause probably still shone through in their everyday demeanour.

For example, Private Richard Thomas worked in the battalion's transport section and had obviously witnessed, if not taken part, in the attack. In 1917 he put his thoughts on the engagement into an inspiring verse that emphasized the 'glory' rather than the 'sacrifice':

The 14th Welsh at Mametz Wood by Richard Thomas, Transport Section, 14th Welsh, in the field. 1/3/17.

It was on a Summer Morning on the 10th of last July,
When the order came to the Swansea boys, To take the wood or Die.

Steady and determined, as if on a morn's Parade,
Down the Slope – Across the ridge – like the Boys of the Old Brigade.

The Gallant lads of little Wales, and good old Swansea Town,
The Leading Battalion in the charge, and the order was laid down,

'To take the Woods at all costs', from that Warrior, Colonel Hayes,
Onward went the 'Swansea Boys', in the Good old British Ways,

Onward, onward went the boys through their Gruesome task,
Comrades falling all around – but the wood was reached at Last.

Into the wood we went, Sir, and met the German horde,
We showed them the way the Welshman fights, and stuck to his new abode.

Throughout the long hours of the night, Sir, we stuck like British Sons,
Faithful and true to that dear old flag, and our Pals behind at the Guns.

Counter attack at night, Sir, by Hun and Bavarian Creed,
But we were boys of the Good old Stock, boys of the Bull Dog Breed.

                                                            Pte. R. Thomas [50]

Another outcome of the attack on Mametz Wood was that the heavy losses in dead and wounded meant that if the battalion was to continue serving at the front then it would need to be urgently supplied with replacements. The designated reserve for the battalion was unable to cope with the numbers required in the short term. It was also becoming clearer to the senior commanders that having men from one locality concentrated in particular units was a problem in itself should heavy losses be sustained. The impact of high casualty numbers within single, locally raised units on the small and closely knit communities from whence they had come was enormous. Replacements subsequently tended to come from far and wide, thus seriously, but understandably, diluting the Swansea and district element of the unit.

Writing in 1936 on the twentieth anniversary of the battle the then Lieutenant Colonel Milbourne Bransby Williams, who had been a junior officer in 1916, paid the men of the 'original' battalion an eloquent tribute:

Charles and Bertie Johnson. Charles was killed and Bertie wounded in the fighting for Mametz Wood.
South Wales Evening Post

When I think of the Battalion as it was just before Mametz the impression it makes upon me is that it was a very good Battalion, that we had a very fine lot of officers and men and that though we may have gained in experience as the war progressed we never again had such good material. Most of us had been associated with the Battalion practically from its formation and the fact that so many actually came from Swansea increased our feeling of comradeship, and our pride in the fact that it was really a Town Battalion.[51]

On the evening of 11 July 1916, leaving the wood and its painful memories behind, the exhausted battalion arrived at Buire, setting out for Mericourt on foot the next day, before taking a train to Longpre, followed by a final foot slog on to Montfliers. It reached Gorenfloss on 14 July and, much to the relief of the men, was transported in the relative comfort of lorries to Covin on 15 July. Here it was inspected by the Commander of the 8th Corps, Lieutenant General Sir A. Hunter-Weston, or Hunter-Bunter, as he was irreverently known to the troops.[52]

The month ended with a spell of front line duty in the area of Hebuterne during which Temporary Lieutenant Noah John Gould was severely wounded by shrapnel in the foot, leg and abdomen on the night of 22-23 July 1916. He was subsequently evacuated to the Number 1 Southern Hospital at Birmingham and, with no possibility of a return to active service, was granted an honorary rank of Second Lieutenant in 1917. Indeed, he was still classified as being seventy per cent disabled until his death in 1967.[53]

The end of the month also saw an inspection by the Brigade Commander, Brigadier General T. O. Marden, and a move by train to Arques. Corporal Crick recalls his nervousness on the parade before Marden, as apparently he and a select few were allotted the task of demonstrating the art of:

...fixing and unfixing bayonets, the usual feature on 'Big Noise' parades. It's a wonder I didn't poke the bayonet through my trouser pocket. It's a bit of an ordeal when you have to step up in front of so many men.

Corporal Crick penned these remarks in 1974, with the full knowledge of what he went through at Mametz Wood and, later, in the Ypres salient. It almost seems as if parading before a 'big noise' was more of an ordeal for Crick than the test of battle itself. A remarkable man, indeed![54]

In August 1916, after training at Volkerinchove, the battalion spent some time at both Wormhoudt and Brandhoek before it was temporarily attached to the 29th Division. Probably adjudged as not having fully recovered from its traumatic experience at Mametz Wood, it was employed in pioneer-like work. It spent more than a week working at night on buried cable trenches to the north of Ypres. It was certainly not entirely immune to the unwanted attentions of the enemy whilst performing this task. Indeed, during this time two men were killed and six wounded as the Germans sought to disrupt the work.[55]

In the early part of September 1916 the battalion relieved the 17th Royal Welsh Fusiliers at Machine Gun Farm and on the Canal Bank. This was part of the Ypres salient and was a most inhospitable place. The Germans held the surrounding high ground, giving them a good view of British movements, each of which could be warmly welcomed with well-directed machine-gun or artillery fire. Corporal G. H. Crick had come through the trial of Mametz Wood physically unscathed. His platoon Sergeant in 'A' Company was Dick Lyons, another veteran of the wood encounter. Almost sixty years later Corporal Crick, by then approaching the age of eighty, recalled that after Mametz he was sent:

> ...up to the Ypres Salient, a worse place than ever. I still get nightmares thinking about it.

Where Mametz Wood had perhaps been the very epitome of the 'short, sharp shock' in terms of battle experience, the Ypres salient was an ongoing and bitterly fought war of attrition, undertaken in a clinging morass of mud. Corporal Crick remembered serving in the salient under Dick Lyons, the Irish born Swansea policeman:

> I was very impressed with him. He was a fine man as I have reason to testify that up at Ypres, Sgt. Lyons, myself and about 6 other men were holding an advanced post. There were no trenches but plenty of huge craters. The Germans were not very far away from us. In the nights they would come quite close, we could almost hear them talking. One day they sent over a heavy shell which wasn't meant for us, but dropped short. It exploded right at the back of us...none of us was hurt but one of my mates was mentally upset and jumped out of our post into no-mans-land and Dick Lyons went over and brought him back. Yes he was a good soldier, and a good friend also to have around.[56]

In September 1916 Corporal D. Arnold:

> ...was wounded on the 13th by the bursting of a shell...We shall all miss him very much as he was undoubtedly one of the best men in the battalion and the mainstay of No. 3 Platoon, of which he had been a member since the early days of the war. Quiet in his methods, yet fearless, he was ever ready to give a helping hand to new men. He has been a real soldier and man all through.[57]

During the month of October 1916 the battalion carried out the usual mix of front line, support and reserve duties. A draft of forty-one other ranks arrived on 15 October and casualties during this period were thankfully quite light. Lieutenant Colonel Hayes left to take temporary command of the 114 Infantry Brigade, Major Coote Brown briefly taking over command of the Swansea Battalion, before passing it on to Major J. Aubrey Smith.[58]

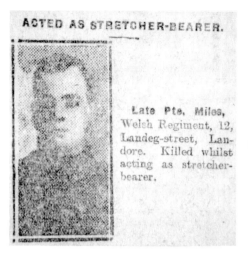

ACTED AS STRETCHER-BEARER.

Late Pte. Miles, Welsh Regiment, 12, Landeg-street, Landore. Killed whilst acting as stretcher-bearer.

Private Miles, killed while acting as a stretcher bearer. South Wales Daily Post

The battalion casualties continued to mount even in the absence of any large scale actions:

> *News has been received of the death in action of Private Wm. John Morgan (14th Welsh), of 32 Brynmelin-street, Swansea, who, in the letters home, is described as 'a man greatly liked in the company and a very good soldier.' Pte. Morgan was married and leaves five children. He was a blacksmith by trade, and Pte. James Morgan, a brother, was previously killed in action while a third brother, Pte. Charles Morgan, is still serving.*[59]

Private Miles had died remembering his family; seventy years later his family had not forgotten him. Trevor Tasker

During this time Ernest Miles was carrying out his usual stretcher bearer duties while yet again being under enemy fire:

> *...he was the stretcher bearer stationed at an advanced post when the artillery started a bombardment on the enemy trenches. I was about fifty yards from poor Ernest at the time, but I was told a shell burst very close to him, and a piece of it caught him in the neck, cutting one of the chief arteries. He was quite conscious for an hour after he was hit, and managed to walk around to where I was. I shall never forget his last words. They were, 'Tell the wife and children I thought of them until the last.'...He was without doubt the finest stretcher bearer we had. If anybody was wounded and the cry went up for bearers, poor Ernest would always be first on the spot...when I was wounded just over a month ago, although machine guns were firing and bullets dropping around us, poor Ernest came and bandaged me.*[60]

Also in October 1916 Private T.J. Dyer was assisting Second Lieutenant J. Garvin. Private Dyer was probably one of the better known men of the battalion, having won a Military Medal for his actions during the attack on Mametz Wood. In early

November Second Lieutenant Garvin had the difficult task of writing to Private Dyer's mother:

> *Your son was killed on the morning of October 22nd. As you probably know, he was my servant, and was in the act of preparing some meat when a high-explosive shell dropped practically in the trench and killed him instantaneously. When I saw him a few seconds later he was dead. He can have suffered nothing at all.*

The newspaper report continued:

> *...it is only about four weeks ago that Pte. Dyer was home on furlough, and he then received the news that he had been awarded the Military Medal for gallantry at Mametz Wood. His workmates took the opportunity of showing their appreciation of the honour bestowed upon young Dyer in the form of a presentation...Pte. Dyer, who was only 21 years of age, joined the army in 1914, and before the war worked at Messrs Baldwin's Works.[61]*

Private Thomas J. Dyer who gained the Military Medal before being killed by an exploding shell.
South Wales Daily Post

On 1 November 1916 Private John Charles Burr was reported as 'missing'. His body was found two days later, he having fallen victim, apparently, to a sniper.

On 4 November the battalion moved by train from Ypres to Brandhoek where it entered a reserve camp. It sent a concert party to entertain the 8th Corps school before moving once more into the front line trenches on the Canal Bank on 15 November 1916. Having had a period of relatively low level activity following its exertions at Mametz Wood, a modestly sized contingent of the battalion had, over recent weeks, been preparing for some minor offensive work. The plan, a raid on the German trenches, was about to be put into effect.[62]

Notes

1. Hughes, Colin, *Mametz: Lloyd George's 'Welsh Army' at the Battle of the Somme*, 2nd Ed. 1982,
2. PRO/WO/95/2539.
3. PRO/WO/339/4638.
4. PRO/WO/157/468.
5. PRO/WO/95/2539.
6. SWDP, 10 July 1926.
7. Hughes, op. cit.
8. Warr.
9. SWDP, 10 July 1926.
10. Warr.
11. PRO/WO/95/2559.
12. Information provided to Colin Hughes by Corporal G.H. Trick, hereafter Crick/Hughes.
13. WGAS/Mew.
14. Marden, op. cit., p.387.
15. PRO/WO/339/15328.
16. PRO/WO/339/13521.
17. Warr.
18. Information supplied by Mr Danny Rees of Swansea.
19. Thomas.
20. Information provided by the Royal Welch Fusiliers Museum, Caernarvon.
21. PRO/WO/95/2543.
22. PRO/WO/95/2549.
23. ibid.
24. PRO/WO/95/2543.
25. Warr.
26. Information supplied by Mrs Sue Rouse.
27. PRO/CAB/45/189.
28. SWDP, 10 July 1930.
29. PRO/WO/158/322.
30. WGAS/Mew.
31. SWDP, 31 July 1916.
32. PRO/WO/339/25990.
33. SWDP, 17 July 1916.
34. Warr.
35. PRO/WO/95/921.
36. ibid.
37. SWDP, 21 August 1916.
38. PRO/WO/95/2559.
39. Westlake, Ray, *British Battalions on the Somme*, 1998.
40. PRO/WO/157/468.
41. ibid.

42. PRO/WO/95/2559.
43. SWDP, 10 August 1916.
44. SWDP, 19 August 1916.
45. SWDP, 12 October 1916.
46. Powell/Gammon.
47. Information provided by Mr Bill Beynon of Swansea, hereafter Beynon.
48. SWDP, 19 October 1916.
49. *South Wales Evening Post*, 8 July 1996, article by Mrs Cora Warner.
50. NAM, 2000-99-05.
51. SWDP, 10 July 1936.

52. PRO/WO/95/2559.
53. Warren.
54. Crick/Hughes.
55. PRO/WO/95/2559.
56. Crick/Hughes.
57. SWDP, 21 September 1916.
58. PRO/WO/95/2559.
59. SWDP, 6 October 1916.
60. ibid.
61. SWDP, 2 November 1916.
62. PRO/WO/95/2559.

Artillery entering Mametz Wood. Taylor Library

CHAPTER EIGHT

The Raid on the High Command Redoubt

In the winter of 1916 the Welsh Division position was in the area of the Canal Bank, in the Ypres salient. The terrain favoured the enemy, who had the advantage of the higher ground, overlooking the British positions and providing several advantageous sites for artillery observation posts. One of these German posts was located at the point where the Ypres-Langemarck road crossed the line.

Here the enemy constructed a particularly strong fortification known to the British as the High Command Redoubt. Due to the terrain the Germans were able to relieve or reinforce the redoubt out of sight of the British and it could not be approached by an attacker without first running a gauntlet of machine-gun fire from both flanks. Whilst the British strove to improve the canal crossing points and communication trenches, as well as strengthening the few natural strong points, the German artillery wreaked havoc on the work, their fire being well directed from the redoubt itself.

To resolve this difficulty it was decided to mount a raid on the position, the planning being undertaken by Lieutenant Colonel J.H. Hayes, commanding officer of the Swansea Battalion. Given the strength of the enemy position an unusually large number of men of the Swansea Battalion comprised the raiding party, some 158 in all including a small number of Royal Engineers, especially skilled in demolition work.

Nothing was left to chance in the planning of the raid. Indeed, the raiding party spent six weeks out of the front line rehearsing the attack on specially dug trenches in the reserve area that replicated the German positions. At the front line small parties went out every night to gain familiarity with the ground and to confirm the positions of enemy posts and machine guns. British artillery made a point of damaging the German wire on a wide front so as to make the enemy unsure of exactly where the focus of any future attack might fall. The Swansea Battalion men chosen to take part in the attack were also specially prepared:

> ...every detail was thought out minutely. Beyond the ordinary raid precautions such as blackened faces, removal of badges, dirtied buttons, use of knobkerries, etc., luminous discs were carried to be planted at the points of exit from the enemy trenches, mats were taken in case the barbed wire was not sufficiently cut, dugout searchers were provided with electric torches and sandbags to collect documents, officers had horns instead of whistles to sound signals, policemen were stationed in No Man's Land to bring back prisoners, our own front trenches were cleared to escape the retaliatory bombardment, and special duckboard trenches were laid for the three columns as the ordinary communication trenches were too waterlogged to admit of their being used by so many men.[1]

Indeed, little was left to chance and great thought was given to the equipment that would need to be taken out to help ensure the raid's success. The officers, for example, carried a revolver, a shunters' horn, a torch and one percussion bomb each. The central assault troops were equipped with the usual rifles and bayonets as well as a forty round bandolier, with one man in three carrying wire cutters so that access to the enemy line would not be impeded unduly by uncut wire.

There were blocking parties on the right and left of the central assault troops. Their role was to prevent interference from German soldiers moving down the trench on the flanks of the attacking force. As well as the usual riflemen these groups also included bombers, who each carried twelve bombs, a body shield and a knobkerrie (a wooden club, often spiked with nails and capable of inflicting great harm, without undue noise, on a surprised foe). Bomb carriers were also present, each carrying a bucket with eighteen bombs as well as a knobkerrie.

Clearing parties contained a mix of riflemen and bombers and also carried mats that might be useful when draped over uncut wire. Various other men were also present. There was a small reserve as well as a team tasked with the job of tying up and bringing in any captured Germans. Lewis gun teams were available to provide rapid fire support if required and a number of runners were present so that messages on progress and difficulties could be relayed to the higher command.

To aid identification of friend and foe in the darkness and to reduce possible confusion during the raid, all the raiders wore large white waistbands while the

A British Lewis gun team poised for action and anticipating an enemy gas attack. Taylor Library

blocking teams wore white bands on the right or left arm. Shrapnel helmets were worn, torches and wire cutters were carried on lanyards and old tunics and trousers were worn, presumably in the hope that their drabness would further hinder enemy observation a little.[2]

Prisoners interrogated after the raid revealed that the Germans had expected an attack on 16 November 1916 and when it failed to materialize they were convinced that it would take place on 17 November instead. They were, therefore, in a state of heightened awareness even before the raid commenced. The raid plan had allowed for this eventuality. A heavy bombardment commenced at 6 p.m. on 17 November, intended to lead the Germans into thinking that the attack was imminent. However, the bombardment was deliberately not followed up at once.

At the cessation of the bombardment the opportunity was taken for a final five-man general reconnaissance of the ground and wire and especially to confirm if a suspected 'borrow pit' actually existed. This pit, depending on its depth and width, would possibly hamper the raiders and prior examination would allow suitable lengths of plank to be provided if it proved necessary to bridge it. No pit was found and the patrol then superintended the laying of tapes and boards behind the British front line to help guide the raiding party. Gaps were also cut in the British wire so that the raiders could clear the trench area with minimal difficulty.

Finally, on 17 November 1916, on a pre arranged signal at about 11.00 p.m., a terrific three minute artillery barrage hit the German defences. The German counter-fire fell harmlessly onto British trenches that had already been temporarily evacuated in anticipation of just such a response. The raiding party had already been guided out into no man's land and now moved forward a mere fifty yards behind the advancing barrage.

After the initial three minutes of intense shelling, the bombardment was switched to the German support lines and the first wave of raiders swept over the German position and made for the support trenches themselves, in order to prevent the early movement of enemy reserves. The second wave of raiders attacked the redoubt itself.

Surprisingly, the front line trenches were in the main earthworks with some concrete machine-gun emplacements. The second line defences were found to be concrete dugouts with steel doors rather than the more usual simple trench works that had been expected. In most cases these dugouts were about nine feet by nine feet with a height of about six feet. Some of them were comfortably furnished with beds and fires. The trenches themselves were about six feet and six inches deep with a width of about four feet.

German dugouts could be surprisingly comfortable.
Taylor Library

Footways were either concrete or duckboard and were dry except where shelling had blown in the sides of the trench. However, the artillery fire had already damaged some of the installations and further explosions arranged by the Royal Engineer contingent helped to complete the work.[3] Lieutenant Gundry, who commanded the raiders, left an account of the action in which he stated:

> Like fish from shells the Germans were hauled forth on steel points from their hiding places. They were presented with the alternative of surrendering or being blown to pieces by hand grenades. Most of them chose the former, some of them suffered the latter. On the right flank of the attack there was a little hand-to-hand fighting, the result being that the German casualty list of dead was that night increased by a few names.[4]

The raiding party remained in the enemy trenches for forty minutes which, at that time, was almost a record for a raid. Many prisoners, a machine gun, a hundred-weight of 'plunder' and much information was brought back to the British lines for the loss of two men killed by a trench mortar bomb and eight others wounded.

The withdrawal from the enemy lines was carried out with minimal confusion even though the horns that were meant to signal the withdrawal proved inaudible to the right flank parties. In the apparent absence of the expected signal these parties were withdrawn carefully by their officers by using their synchronized watches and moving at the previously expected times despite the apparent absence of a definite signal. A minor German attempt to disrupt matters was broken up by Lewis gun fire with one dead German yielding a unit identification.[5]

Second Lieutenants Vaughan and Kelk were awarded the Military Cross, whilst four other ranks were awarded the Military Medal. The press coverage of the time stated:

> Some little time ago 170 of them went across No Man's Land on one of these raids. It had been rehearsed beforehand and was led by a captain of the Welsh Regiment reported by his general as a leader of men 'far above the average'. It seems as if each man among them had resolved to do a special act of gallantry.
>
> A young second lieutenant was first into the enemy's trenches and last out, and carried a wounded man across No Man's Land. A private...brought his Lewis gun into action and, in spite of heavy rifle fire, which swept around him, served his weapon very coolly until the withdrawal was ordered. One young Welshman captured seven Germans in a dug-out and stayed to clear up their papers, which might contain useful information. Attacked by two Germans, a Welsh corporal killed them both, and would not leave the trenches until his comrades were safely out again. Then he picked up a wounded man and trudged back with him across No Man's Land, where the ground was alive with machine-gun bullets.[6]

One of the other ranks who gained a Military Medal for his actions that night was Lance Corporal Haydn David of Taibach. Lance Corporal David was credited with capturing a German trench, complete with several German soldiers and their officer. Not content with this, the prisoners were presumably passed back, and he continued to search the trench. This was a risky business since the potential occupants of any enemy dugouts would understandably have been less than pleased to see him.

Undaunted by this prospect he commenced searching and recovered some useful documents, maps and a machine gun before falling victim to the attentions of the enemy, resulting in his being wounded in the left shoulder and back. This led to his eventual evacuation to Torquay for convalescence, though he was to return to action later in the war.[7]

The raid had clearly been a great success and the congratulations received included a message from General Plumer, in command of the Second Army. Indeed, the raid was subsequently often referred to in the Second Army as 'a perfect example of discipline, forethought, and *espirit de corps*'.[8] While the raiding party regrouped and were debriefed, the rest of the battalion had already been withdrawn into the support position at Canal Bank. The raiders were then entrained with a view to rejoining the battalion. The journey was not without incident:

Sergeant Haydn David wearing his Military Medal ribbon. Connie Evans

> *The raiding party of the 17th inst. were proceeding by train from BRANDHOEK to rejoin the battalion on the CANAL BANK. The train collided with a light engine coming down on the same line. Front carriage telescoped. 2Lt England, 2Lt W.N. Lewis and 10 O.R. ranks admitted to hospital suffering from injuries and shock as a result of this collision.*[9]

Councillor David Davies had played a prominent part in the formation of the battalion and had seen them both at Rhyl and Winchester. Even a trip to dangers of the front line was not beyond his capabilities and in November 1916 he visited the battalion at the front, reporting back to a Swansea meeting that also saw Major Dyson Brock Williams attending. Councillor Davies reported that:

> *(Major Dyson Williams) had been many months in the firing line, and they could, he thought, see in him an example of what surgical science could do nowadays. A few years ago a man shot through the lungs would be regarded as good as dead. Major Dyson Williams had not only been shot through the lungs but also operated upon, and was now so well recovered that he hoped to being back with the Swansea Batt. about Xmas...(he) received his wound in the fighting round Mametz Wood...The Mayor described his visit to the trenches 'with a tin hat on'. All that could be seen above was a narrow strip of sky, whilst the noise of the firing was hideous. At first the sensation was a little disturbing,*

but they got accustomed to it...the cheeriness of the Swansea boys was commented upon, and the war, said the Mayor in conclusion, was going to bring absolutely a new world with new ideals. The boys who had fallen were going to live in the memories of those who survived, because they gave up their lives so that progress and liberty should continue in the world.[10]

As November 1916 drew to a close, the village of Clydach, near Swansea, received sad news of one of its sons who had joined the battalion:

Pte. Ll. Williams, Welsh Regiment, who some time ago was suffering from typhoid, following trench fever, has, after a lingering illness, succumbed to his many ailments. Pte. Williams, who was the only son of Mr George Williams, Woollen Mills, Clydach, was an ardent worker at Hebron Congregational Chapel. He had played football and cricket for the Clydach clubs, and was well-known among the billiard-playing fraternity of the district, being one of the most successful cueists among the members of the Clydach Institute.[11]

At the end of November 1916 the battalion was in the front line on the Canal Bank where Machine Gun Farm and Hilltop Farm were familiar locations as the usual rotation of reserve, support and front line duties were undertaken. Casualties continued to occur regularly if, thankfully, in low numbers.

A party working on the Atlas Trench came under enemy fire on 2 December 1916 resulting in the death of Sergeant Thomas Henry Shute and the wounding of four other men. Two men were accidentally shot on 5 December before the battalion moved into Divisional reserve. As Christmas approached, Brigadier General T. O.

Trench map showing Atlas Trench where Sergeant Thomas Henry Shute was killed and four others wounded in December 1916. National Archives

Dugouts on the Yser Canal bank, Ypres salient. IWM Q17470

Marden inspected the troops while Lieutenant General Hunter-Weston attended a Christmas Eve non-conformist service and inspected the camp. Christmas dinner was duly enjoyed before a concert party was staged in the YMCA hut. A concert was also given by members of the 130th Field Ambulance unit. With the Christmas and New Year festivities fading in the memory, the battalion was back in the front line on the Canal Bank by 18 January 1917. It was warmly welcomed by the Germans who inflicted casualties at the rate of one man killed and seven wounded in the first three days of front line duty.[12]

Meanwhile, back in Swansea, the Battalion Committee sanctioned the purchase of eighteen telescopes at thirty-five shillings each as well as a further six for the use of the snipers at a cost of seventy shillings each. It was later noted that they had 'proved of great service to the Battalion'.[13]

On 8 February 1917 Private Stan Dymond was killed and another man wounded while in the reserve positions. In September 1916 Private Dymond's brother was also serving in the armed forces, albeit in a different unit, and Stan had written to him at that time:

> ...hoping this will find Emily quite well as it leaves me at present. Dear Brother I am glad to hear you are not out here as I think it is safer to be at home, for I don't think it will end very quick. I suppose you have had your share of the war. Dear Brother I am glad to hear you are writing to mother, as we know it

must worry her at such times as these, for her not to have any news of her sons. Dear Brother I have come out to do my bit but God knows whether I should return again, as I know it must be a worry to mother and father, not knowing whether she is going to see her sons again or not...I am glad that you have got a photo of me it will be a remembrance of me...I have not had much chance of doing any Germans in.[14]

Stan Dymond was twenty-six years old when he died and was buried near Ypres. His parents lived at Devonport.

Private William Robert Pearson had worked at the Swansea Gasworks before the war and was also a member of the Salvation Army Band. He had joined the battalion in September 1914 and served as a stretcher bearer. Indeed, such was his enthusiasm and commitment to this often dangerous role that he was awarded the Croix de Guerre in early 1917. As the local newspaper and Private Pearson commented:

Pte. Pearson...has repeatedly brought in wounded under heavy gunfire... I have done my best and stopped at nothing when the boys have been wounded. Bullets or no bullets I have gone on, and I give all honour to God, Who has preserved me all the way.[15]

On 9 March 1917 Second Lieutenant Arthur Frederick Hastings Kelk was killed in action in the front line trenches near Lancashire Farm. He had been born in Beirut, Syria (now Lebanon), but was registered as a British citizen by his father, the Reverend A. H. Kelk, lately of Leeds. In June 1919 the Reverend Kelk received a communication from the War Office explaining that it was the King's wish that:

...the next of kin of all officers and men who have fallen in the defence of their country should receive a plaque and scroll bearing the name and regiment, as a memorial of their patriotism and sacrifice.[16]

Private Pearson, awarded the Croix Du Guerre for his bravery. South Wales Daily Post

On 18 March 1917 Second Lieutenant John David Vaughan was wounded while in the front line trenches near Lancashire Farm. He was taken to the 130th Field Ambulance station but died shortly afterwards. He was thirty years of age and had lived at Burry Port, Carmarthenshire.[17] He had earlier won a Military Cross:

...for conspicuous gallantry in action. He carried out a daring reconnaissance with great courage and determination, obtaining most valuable information.

In April 1917 the battalion's activities were spread over the Esquelbecq, Millain and Wormhoudt area, with front line duties being undertaken near Lancashire Farm. On 10 April Second Lieutenant

Sergeant R.A. Simpson (left) and pals at Wormhoudt. Brian Simpson

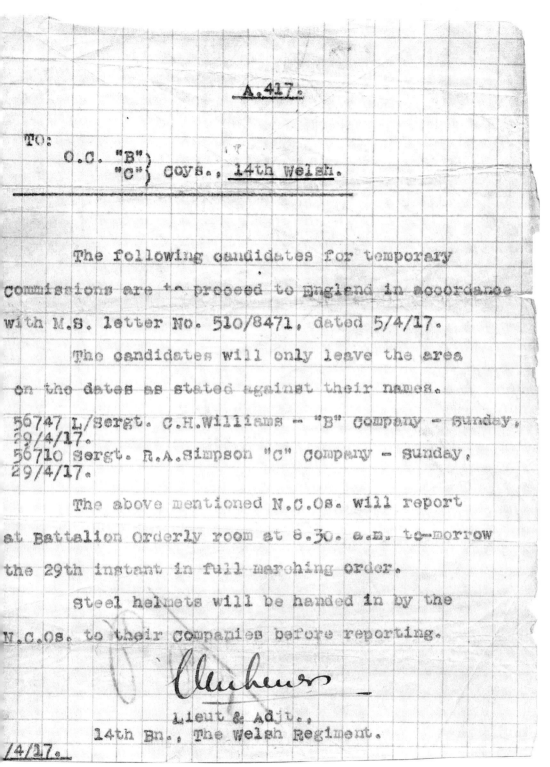

A.417.

TO:

O.C. "B")
    "C"} Coys., 14th Welsh.

The following candidates for temporary commissions are to proceed to England in accordance with M.S. letter No. 510/8471, dated 5/4/17.

The candidates will only leave the area on the dates as stated against their names.

56747 L/Sergt. C.H.Williams - "B" Company - Sunday, 29/4/17.
56710 Sergt. R.A.Simpson "C" Company - Sunday, 29/4/17.

The above mentioned N.C.Os. will report at Battalion Orderly room at 8.30. a.m. to-morrow the 29th instant in full marching order.

Steel helmets will be handed in by the N.C.Os. to their companies before reporting.

Lieut & Adjt.,
14th Bn., The Welsh Regiment.

/4/17.

Sergeant R.A. Simpson is ordered to proceed to England as a candidate for a commission.
He was subsequently appointed to the rank of Second Lieutenant.
Brian Simpson

Second Lieutenant
William Morley Williams.
Swansea Library Service

R. P. Evans and one other rank were wounded as a result of a bomb practice accident. Robert Prichard Evans was thirty-two years of age and died of his wounds on 11 April 1917. He was the son of Elizabeth Evans of Felin Llecheiddior, Garn Dolbenmaen, Caernarvonshire and the late William Evans. He had entered University College at Bangor in 1904 and had served in the Bangor Volunteer Company of the 1st Caernarvonshire Royal Garrison Artillery, before joining the Welsh Regiment.[18]

On 1 May Lieutenant Colonel Hayes returned after hospitalization but then went on leave on 11 May, resulting in Captain Chamberlain being in temporary command of the battalion. John Chamberlain had served with the 3rd Battalion of the South Wales Borderers but was now attached to the Swansea Battalion. He was thirty-five years of age and was the son of Arthur Chamberlain, JP of Birmingham. Sadly, Captain Chamberlain was killed within three days of taking command and he was succeeded in turn by Captain J. C. Partridge. Towards the end of the month Captain Wilson and Dyson Brock Williams also commanded the battalion for short periods of time.[19]

Commemoration of
Second Lieutenant
W.M. Williams.
Simon Peter Lee

Private George H. Parkin was from the St Thomas area of the town and had been with the battalion since its early days. In the summer of 1917 he was seriously injured by a gunshot wound to the left thigh. He had worked for Hughes and Morgan, Sawyers, of Swansea prior to joining the battalion.

On 7 June 1917 a fighting patrol on the Canal Bank encountered the enemy and Second Lieutenant William Morley Williams, a Swansea Grammar School old boy, was killed in the ensuing action. He was twenty-one years old and was the son of John and Ann Williams of Brunswick Place, Swansea.[20]

With a major British offensive in the offing, from 14 June onwards the battalion undertook several periods of training. It moved from Poperinghe to Stomer before route marching to Esquerdes. It spent a week there before moving to Wismes and Boyaval, then reached Estree Blanche on 27 June 1917, where further 'training for offensive action' was undertaken over the next two weeks. For the first time since Mametz Wood, more than a year earlier, the battalion was about to be deployed in its entirety in a major offensive action.[21]

Notes

1. Marden, op.cit., p.404.
2. PRO/WO/2557.
3. ibid.
4. Marden, op. cit., p.405.
5. PRO/WO/2557.
6. SWDP, 25 June 1917.
7. Evans.
8. Marden, op. cit., p.404.
9. PRO/WO/95/2559.
10. SWDP, 27 November 1916.
11. SWDP, 24 November 1916.

12. PRO/WO/95/2559.
13. WGAS, TC 26/3.
14. NAM, Dymond.
15. SWDP, 20 February 1917.
16. PRO/WO/339/4638.
17. PRO/WO/339/46515.
18. Warren.
19. PRO/WO/95/2559.
20. Marden, op.cit., p.413.
21. PRO/WO/95/2559.

CHAPTER NINE

Pilckem Ridge

At the end of May 1917 the 38th Welsh Division was holding the line from the Ypres-Pilckem Road to Boesinghe. At some points on this line the German trenches were about 500 yards away, meaning that any attackers would be likely to be exposed to enemy artillery and machine-gun fire for a considerable length of time. To reduce this risk, and with future offensive operations in mind, the division was advised that it should start to reduce this distance by running out saps and constructing assembly trenches closer to the German line than had hitherto been the case.

This was done during late May and early June 1917, taking advantage of the distraction caused to the Germans by a Second Army attack on their lines on the Messines-Wytschaete Ridge. The result was that in parts the distance between the Welsh Division line and that of the enemy was reduced to only about 200 yards. This shorter distance was much more conducive to the likelihood of a successful infantry attack. Happily, the Germans paid little attention to the work while it was in progress, possibly thinking it was a ruse designed to divert their attention from the attack with which they were already dealing.

At the end of June the 38th Welsh Division, and with it the Swansea Battalion, left the line and travelled to St Hilaire where it would rehearse its role in the planned offensive over specially prepared terrain. Indeed, a replica of the German system of trenches and strong points had been laid out on the ground so that the attacking units should become intimately familiar with the terrain to be fought over.

On 19 and 20 July 1917 the Division returned to its allotted sector of the line and waited for the commencement of the offensive. This was planned for 31 July. In the intervening period, now close to the enemy again, the Division suffered a number of casualties from German gas and explosive shells.

Obviously suspecting that an attack was imminent, and understandably wishing to avoid a heavy bombardment of its troops, the Germans took the precaution of evacuating their front line trench by 27 July, this fact being confirmed by a British aerial reconnaissance. Patrols were sent forward from the British lines and these found that although the Germans had indeed abandoned their front line trenches they were still holding the support, reserve and second line systems in considerable strength.

The Swansea Battalion, as part of 114 Brigade, was detailed to form the right flank of the attack with 113 Brigade on the left and 115 Brigade in reserve. Key objectives for the assault were to be the village of Pilckem and the Pilckem Ridge up to halfway between the Steenbeek River and the village itself. Once this point had been reached, the attacking battalions were to consolidate while the reserve battalions pushed through them with a view to capturing the river and its crossings.

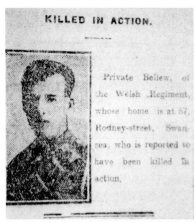

Ernie Bellew killed in action on 31 July 1917. South Wales Daily Post

The objectives were given colour codes to aid coordination and the reporting on the progress of attacks. The Blue Line ran to the north of the Mackensen and Hindenburg farms whilst the Black Line ran north of Pilckem Village and Jolie Farm. The Green Line was about 300 yards beyond a strongpoint known as the Iron Cross. Beyond this lay the Steenbeek River. Zero hour was set for 3.50 a.m. on 31 July 1917.[1]

As the hour of attack drew near it was natural that many men would turn their thoughts to the possibility that they might suffer injury or death in the forthcoming action. This was an opportunity for preparing final letters home in the event that their worst fears were, in fact, realized. Such thoughts were evidently in the mind of Captain Aubrey Sandbrook, and he set himself to addressing them fully before he was called upon to lead his men into the fray.

He first wrote a letter for the benefit of his brother that was purely businesslike in its intent. The responsibility for administering the company mess account had naturally devolved to Captain Sandbrook since his appointment as company

Moving forward on Pilckem Ridge. Imperial War Museum Q6049

commander. In reality he had had little to do with it, meeting several minor expenses from his own resources with the intention of, at some stage, merely reclaiming his outlay. It had subsequently transpired that the mess account was several hundred francs short of what it should have been and Aubrey Sandbrook found himself viewed with some suspicion by those in authority.

Captain Sandbrook was entirely sure of his own innocence, the discrepancies clearly having arisen while the fund was in the charge of another officer, since invalided home. He had made this point cogently to the authorities on several occasions but still the matter rumbled on. In the letter, he instructed his brother to robustly reject any claim from the War Office in the matter should he himself 'stop one' in the forthcoming attack. He had the document witnessed by his batman.[2] That matter dealt with, Captain Sandbrook turned his thoughts to his mother, and drafted her a letter that he clearly hoped would provide her with some comfort in the event of his death in action. He wrote:

At dawn we go over the parapet to fight for all that is worth fighting for. When I travelled from Southampton to London in September 1914, in the perfect golden calm of a St. Martin's summer evening, and looked out of the windows at the gracious southland of England, the quiet villages and poppy-studded cornfields, the green pastures dotted with cattle – the perfect picture of England as I had always dreamed of her – I felt a sudden flush of anger of the idea that Germany had for one moment imagined that the owners of so fair a heritage would lay it down at the bidding of a military autonomy.

To-morrow I have a chance of translating the emotions I then felt into deeds and if anything happens to me please do not grieve but rather be glad that my best thoughts of the England I may die for are so very bright.

Ever since I was a little child I have always thought that no man could die more proudly than for England, and tomorrow when I have my men over the top, their thoughts, mingled with thoughts of you, will inspire me more than anything I can say to you.

My colonel, when he said 'Good-bye' to me last night, said 'I know you will lead them well, and I know they will fight for you.' ...So darling, if I die, I die proud and happy. I dedicate my life to the England I have always loved, and my soul to Jesus Christ, Who died for all the world, and whose example England, as a nation, is trying to follow.

Wherefore mourn not for me, and please don't allow anyone to wear mourning for me.

With all my love, darling.

Your affectionate son,

Aubrey.[3]

These tasks having been carefully attended to, Captain Sandbrook waited patiently for zero hour and the trials that would undoubtedly come with its arrival.

Very heavy rain had started on the night of 31 July and was to continue for many days to come. The attack that was about to commence has been called 'Third Ypres' but is better known to the modern reader as the Passchendaele Offensive, renowned

Summary of Event and Information

The Battalion moved up to its assembly trenches on the night of 30th/31st July without casualties, due to careful preparation and also to a hostile relief going on at the same time. The following Officers went into action. MAJOR D. BROCK WILLIAMS - in command. LIEUT VH LEWIS - asst. M.B. WILLIAMS - signalling officer. LIEUT T.D. THOMAS - transport officer

Lieut R.K. BELLINGHAM
" R.B. SHEPPARD
2. " V.L. HOWELLS
" C.W. FERMSTON
} = A Coy

Capt D. YORKE M.C.
2 Lieut JA DYEN
" E.H. BALSOM
" W.R. FULLEYLOVE
} = B Coy

CAPT J.I. STRANGE
2 Lt A.D. ROBERTS
" F.N.W. FOX
} = C Coy

Capt D.A. SANDBROOK
Lieut F. RODERICK
2 Lieut JH ENGLAND
" A.N. MONSON

Operation order attached

Zero was fixed at 3.50 a.m. on the 31st July. The Battalion advanced at 4.0 a.m. behind the 13th Welch who took the German front lines. The Battalion then passed through, and advanced to the "Black line" on the PILCKEM RIDGE, "B" & "C" Coys leading. All ranks went very close

1875 Wt. W593/826 1,000,000 4/15 J.B.C. & A. A.D.S.S./Forms/C. 2118.

Battalion War Diary entry for the first day of the Passchendaele offensive, 31 July 1917.
National Archives

today for mud, blood and, after a promising start, futility.

As was usual, the start of the attack was heralded with a tremendous barrage of the enemy positions. This included discharges of thermite and oil drums. The 10th and 13th Welsh Battalions made the initial attack on the German positions and the Swansea Battalion soon caught up with, and then passed through, those units in completing the capture of the Blue Line. So far little effective opposition had been encountered.

During this action the German 23rd Division had the misfortune to be caught in the process of being relieved by the 3rd Guards Reserve Division, one of whose regiments was the 3rd Guards Fusiliers, the famous 'Berlin Cockchafers', and reported to be the Prussian Army's crack troops. It was thought that this much vaunted unit had been brought up especially to hold Candle Trench.[4] Notwithstanding their illustrious record, the Cockchafers were given a very rough time by the men of the Welsh Division and this was commented on in the press coverage of the time:

Starting at 3.50 a.m., the first point was taken with very little trouble and insignificant loss. Leaping out of their trenches, almost waist deep in mud, the

Celts were over the top, and with sheer impetuosity hurled back the enemy opposed to them. So complete was their success that at 4.15 a.m. a halt was called for concentration. Pilckem Ridge was then assaulted and taken. Here again these sturdy little Welshmen fought with rare doggedness, and took a huge toll of the Germans...

Throughout the whole engagement the casualties were exceedingly moderate. Most of the losses were occasioned after the taking of Pilckem Ridge itself. This is all the more remarkable when it is taken into account that they were opposed by the German Guards, the Berlin Cockchafers, who were caught in the process of relief which the British guns made more difficult by an excellent barrage. They were also opposed by the 3rd Lehr and the 9th Grenadiers...over 600 prisoners of the Cockchafers were taken. When an officer of that regiment was acquainted with the fact, he refused to believe it, and replied that the 'Cockchafers never surrendered'.[5]

Another account of the action paid further tribute to the skill of the devastating artillery support:

It was still dark when the men went over the top. They declare that our barrage was wonderful in its precision, and that it was a great experience to stride forward in the wake of such a perfectly-ruled curtain of creeping fire.

The ascent of the ridge proved to be less difficult than had been apprehended. The intensity of our artillery fire drove the Huns to cover, and our men were upon them so quickly when the deadly rain of shells had passed over their heads that they were unable in many cases to put up a show of defence at all, and either surrendered or broke away in a dazed fashion to seek fresh concealment.

When the total count was completed it was found that the Welshmen had taken seven officers and 622 other ranks as the result of their attack.[6]

Pushing past the Black Line, the Swansea Battalion now moved towards Iron Cross and the Green Line, a position that was particularly strongly held. Two German machine guns inflicted a number of casualties before they were first outflanked, and then rushed with the bayonet, an action that resulted in twenty Germans being killed and forty taken prisoner.[7]

A weak German counter-attack at the junction of the Welsh Division and the French First Army was driven off though a German strong point at Colonel's Farm proved stubborn in holding out until about 4.00 p.m.[8] As the battalion surged onwards it:

...took part in the hard fighting near Caesar's Nose, and subsequently captured Pilckem Mill and a portion of the village. They suffered considerable casualties later in the engagement in the neighbourhood of Iron Cross. It was

T./Capt. John Stanley Strange, M.C. Welsh R.:

For conspicuous gallantry and devotion to duty. Having led his company with great ability and determination to its final objective, he took over command of the front line, and held it for three days until relieved. He personally reconnoitred his whole front, and sent back very valuable information, setting a very fine example throughout to all ranks under most trying circumstances.

Citation for Temporary Captain J.S. Strange for his actions in the attack of 31 July 1917. London Gazette

here that Lieut. Jack England, the only son of Mr and Mrs T. H. England was killed while acquitting himself with great bravery. Beyond Iron Cross, on the Langemarck road another well-known officer of the Battalion, Capt. R.K. Bellingham...was wounded.[9]

As regards Lieutenant England, who died aged twenty years, it was reported that his death was:

> *...a great loss. He was a fine brave boy, and always did his work well. (His) company had fought their way to the final objective before he was killed.*[10]

Mr T.H. England was the distraught father of Lieutenant England. If losing his son was not, in itself, a terrible enough blow it was made all the harder by the fact that:

> *...the whole of his equipment has been lost, including a pair of very valuable glasses, which were lent to him privately. The only things returned to me were his clothes. Is there no compensation payable in respect of this loss?*[11]

The War Office was unable to help, noting that in the abnormal conditions currently appertaining to active service, it was impossible to guard against the sort of losses of personal equipment that sometimes occurred in a rapidly changing situation.

The Green Line was now reached and Captain Sandbrook was particularly conspicuous capturing, in concert with Sergeant White and six men, a house used by

Trench map showing Pilckem village and Stray Farm where Captain Sandbrook was killed in action. National Archives

the Germans as a dressing station. This produced a haul of twenty-two unwounded, and sixteen wounded prisoners.[12] If Captain Sandbrook's courage and offensive spirit were showing no signs of exhaustion his luck sadly was.

A little later on he was killed while fighting in the area of Stray Farm. Captain Yorke was wounded in the same action.

At the outbreak of war Aubrey Sandbrook had returned to his homeland by working his passage from South Africa, intent on rendering his country what services he could. His service with the battalion had been exemplary and his country could ask no more of him. It would, however, be a further year before the War Office would accept, at the insistence of his brother, that any Company Mess Fund deficiency was not the responsibility of the late Captain Sandbrook.

Other units now pressed on and reached the Steenbeek itself, attacking the pill-boxes and effecting a crossing of the river despite suffering heavy casualties. A massed German counter-attack was successfully repulsed before the weather worsened and heavy rain made conditions extremely difficult for both defender and attacker. The unavoidable lull caused by the deteriorating ground conditions prevented the Germans from exerting their full weight on the British positions over the next few days. On 6 August 1917 the Welsh Division was relieved after suffering a daily bombardment of its defence lines that were, in reality, little more than a series of water-filled shell holes. The Swansea Battalion had gone into action with nineteen officers and 470 other ranks. Casualties over the week amounted to some eighty-five killed and 145 wounded.[13]

Among those killed was Captain L. P. Godfrey, who died of wounds received in action. He had also been wounded in the encounter at Mametz Wood. An assayer by profession, he had joined the battalion as a private. He was twenty-six years old. His possessions were itemized as being a cigarette case, a clasp knife, one whistle and strap, three pencils, some letters, a receipt and a gold signet ring.[14]

Another to die was Temporary Lieutenant Francis Roderick. Born at Cross Hands in 1893 he was a schoolteacher before joining up. He had served in the Aberystwyth Officer Training Corps before joining the Swansea Battalion in January 1915. He had been wounded along with three other officers in a bombing accident just prior to the attack on Mametz Wood. Wounded again in the attack on 31 July 1917, he died later in the day. In August 1917 his widow was in communication with the War Office:

> (his) *account with Messrs Cox & Co. is overdrawn £7-12s-9d. This I will certainly pay, as soon as I have a settlement. If there are any other claims I shall be glad if you will let me know, then I shall know better what to do as I have no private means of my own. My late husband is insured for £50, but until I receive the packet from Messrs Cox & Co., said to contain his will etc., I don't know how his affairs are left. As I am about to become a mother I shall be glad if you will tell me what to do as regards my pension.*[15]

Francis Nevil Wilson Fox was the son of Denise Fox, a widow, from the village of Gownhill, Devon. A Second Lieutenant aged twenty-three years he had joined the Swansea Battalion after first serving in the 21st Reserve Battalion, the Welsh Regiment. He was another officer who fell during the 31 July attack.[16]

The War Diary records as being wounded officers Yorke, Bellingham, W.L. Howells, Furmston and O. K. Morgan. It was noted that rain had fallen heavily during the day and the state of the ground, already churned up by heavy shelling, became increasingly difficult.[17]

Happily, not all of the casualties sustained in the attack were human. Major D. Brock Williams was soon in contact with the Battalion Committee in Swansea, telling it that during the recent fighting many of the band instruments had been destroyed, having had the misfortune of a shell landing on their storage area. Urgently required were two tenor drums, two bugles and a small bass drum. The battalion's portable piano, which was very popular for sing-alongs, had already been bruised and battered over the last two years and was practically destroyed in the recent big push. Happily, the committee's answer was almost literally music to the ears, with both requests being acceded to at a cost of just over £40.[18]

'H.B.D.', a Welsh Division soldier whose precise unit is unknown, took a somewhat sombre view of the Pilckem Ridge action that appeared as a poem in the Welsh Division magazine in 1918:

Pilkem, 1917.
On Pilkem Ridge's battered clay
  In Hell's own fury –
The victors and their trophies stay
  To tell the story;
But those that lie, their conflict done,
  Took Death a captive;
To them the honour, for they won
  Life's Grand Objective.[19]

On 17 August 1917 Lieutenant Colonel Hayes, commanding the Swansea Battalion, had a very lucky escape. The 114 Infantry Brigade was due to relieve the 61 Infantry Brigade, whose headquarters were at Periscope House, on the top of Pilckem Ridge. As was customary, Brigadier General Marden took his battalion commanders with him to meet and be briefed by the officers they were about to replace. Also present were Captains Wilson and Jones-Williams, company commanders of the Swansea Battalion, as well as Major E.E. Helme, second in command of the 15th Welsh (Carmarthen) Battalion.

Periscope House was a small, two room cottage that had been heavily fortified by the Germans on what had previously been the British side, but was only lightly concreted on the side that now faced the recently driven back German lines. There were two doors on the German side. At the conclusion of the meeting Captain Parry, Lieutenant Caskie and two runners went out one door while the 114 Brigade party left by the other. As the groups congregated outside a shrapnel shell burst nearby with deadly effect. Both runners were killed and every other officer was seriously wounded with the exception of Hayes, who was amazingly untouched.[20]

At the end of August the battalion was deployed in the Langemarck area, rotating as usual between the reserve, support and front line positions. While in support positions to the west of Langemarck Captain H. Jones-Williams, the battalion sniping officer was:

...seriously wounded on the 19th inst., gunshot wounds in left elbow and head; admitted in hospital in France. He was formerly manager of Messrs David Jones and Co, Strand.[21]

On 22 August 1917 Lance Corporal D. J. Beresford died of his wounds. He had earlier been hit by shell fragments. The local newspaper reported that he was only eighteen years old, having possibly misled the enlisting authorities over his true age.[22]

Some sharp battlefield practices on the part of the Germans had been detected and, at the end of August 1917, an order was issued by Lieutenant Colonel H. E. Price, General Staff of the 38th Welsh Division, in order to deal with the problem. The order read:

The Germans have been noticed lately using stretchers in the day time; on one occasion under cover of a white flag.

It should be remembered that as the Germans often shift Machine Guns on stretchers under pretence of shifting wounded, that such parties are to be fired on.

In the case of a white flag, one warning shot near the party may first be fired, after that the party will be fired at.[23]

Also at this time Brigadier General T.O. Marden, Officer Commanding 114 Infantry

German stretcher bearers, some of whose comrades earned the mistrust of the Welsh Division. Taylor Library

Brigade, found time to reflect on the performance of his troops in a Special Order of the Day:

The Brigadier General congratulates all ranks...in the capture of PILCKEM RIDGE, which for the past year has dominated their trenches and communications. Though the artillery made the attack easy, yet it was the determination and closeness with which the Infantry followed the barrage that convinced some of the finest troops in Germany that resistance was hopeless. It will be a matter of proud remembrance to the 114th Infantry Brigade that they had the honour of meeting and defeating the 3rd Guard Fusiliers Regiment – the renowned 'BERLIN COCKCHAFERS'. These troops were fresh from reserve and had not experienced a quarter of the shelling to which (our) Battalions were subjected in turn during the fortnight preceding the battle. The Brigadier has remarked with pride and pleasure the high spirit of confidence which animates all ranks of this brigade and the cheerfulness with which they underwent the extreme discomfort of the days after the 31st July.[24]

Private S.J. Richards had been the late Captain Sandbrook's runner. He had already been wounded in the action at Mametz Wood, but had returned to the battalion after his recovery. While serving in the front line in the Cardonnerie sector on 28 September he again proved an inviting target for the Germans when:

...he was called upon to carry despatches under heavy fire, at the imminent risk of his life. Whilst doing so he was severely wounded, but 'carried on' and delivered his message...he was again wounded, after his recovery, this time so severely that he has had to resign from the Army.[25]

As the British offensive gradually ground to a halt the months of September and October 1917 proved relatively quiet for the battalion. Working in the area of Langemarck the battalion became familiar with both Talana Farm and Malakoff Farm as well as Steenvorde, Morbecque and Robermetz. It held the front line in the Cordonnerie sector at the end of September where it had a Portuguese unit as neighbours. On one occasion the Portuguese troops relieved those of the Swansea Battalion in the front lines. As Captain Milbourne Williams recalled:

The relief by the Portuguese must have been like a nightmare to the Company commanders. The 'dugout' accommodation in the line was limited, and the Portuguese Companies were much stronger than those of the Battalion. A seemingly unending stream of men arrived. There was only one interpreter and no one else spoke English. The night was dark and the men sat down anywhere, as if they did not care what happened to them. As for the noise they made, it was enough to announce their arrival to every German within a radius of a mile.[26]

The battalion then spent most of October in the area of Fleurbaix where it engaged in a programme of regular patrol activity intended to reconnoitre the enemy positions and gather information. For example, on the night of 1-2 October 1917, a patrol went out under the command of Second Lieutenant B. J. Griffiths. This provided useful information on the state of the enemy trenches and wire. Great care had to be exercised in the shadows of no man's land during such patrols, however. This one

Portuguese troops. Taylor Library

observed a German working party a short way off, whilst enemy sentries could be heard talking and whistling in the enemy support lines.

On the same night another patrol under Second Lieutenant Wilfred G. Rose moved out to observe an enemy post. The patrol also discovered a large German working party, revealed by the moonlight. The patrol retired carefully and, on reaching safety, fired a number of rifle grenades at the targets with supporting fire from a Lewis gun. The fire was seen to be accurate though the precise results could not be clearly determined.

Two patrols on the night of 13-14 October failed to make much headway with one finding little of interest to report, whilst the other went out just as a German patrol was coming in to the British lines. The enemy threw two bombs before retiring. As the British patrol followed the now withdrawing Germans it came under machine-gun fire from the area of Delangre farm. After waiting for half an hour the patrol was fired on again as it attempted to move forward. It then retired to the British lines.

On 16 October Second Lieutenant I. Williams took out a patrol at 7.00 p.m. Its object was to reconnoitre Orchard Farm, which was believed to have an enemy post

'By the guttering light of a candle...' A letter sent from France by Will Williams. Hedley Morris

in its vicinity. As the patrol crept forward via a ditch into no man's land:

> ...*about 9 of the enemy were observed walking towards patrol. Enemy eventually established a post about 50 yds. east of old dugout at junction of two ditches and front line. Patrol finding it impossible to take post by surprise owing to water and wire decided to fire on post. The two Officers threw a Mills bomb each, while the men each fired one round. Patrol then tried to rush post but failed owing to wire and water. Enemy retaliated by throwing bombs.*

Happily, no casualties were suffered and the patrol withdrew to safety. Second Lieutenant W.G. Rose was out again with a patrol on the night of 17 October 1917. The objective this time was to discover exactly where the enemy positions were located. The patrol left the British lines at 5.50 p.m. and approached the suspected German positions, which seemed poorly protected by barbed wire. Indeed, the Germans were also conscious of this and, as Rose later reported, the enemy:

> ...*was moving about with wire in four places, and also working with a spade could be heard. Enemy was wearing equipment judging from the rattle. I then proceeded to advance with my five bombers on the right and five riflemen on the left. When within 20yds. of the stream, enemy was silent, evidently suspicious, so I immediately pushed forward to the edge of the water, through a volley of bombs, and opened rifle fire. Enemy retaliated with two or three bombs, which dropped in the water a few feet in front, splashing the water over us. We immediately threw another five bombs supported by rifle fire and withdrew about 30 yards. One man was heard to groan and another coughed, so I think some damage was done. We waited for nearly an hour but heard nothing more. The enemy had the advantage of being behind a stream with only two or three crossings and also having plenty of cover in the old trench so that it was not wise to rush him as I had intended doing.*[27]

Naturally, not all of the battalion's time was spent on such potentially hazardous activities. The routine army rhythm of front line duty, followed by a hopefully quieter period in the support lines, and then the relative luxury of some time in reserve, allowed for some relaxation. Especially while in reserve, there were opportunities for rest and recreation.

When not engaged on fatigue duties much of this time could be spent in any one of a number of local estaminets, essentially cafés where food and drink could be obtained and some peaceful pastimes pursued. As regards alcoholic drinks, there were three main options. The staple was vin blanc or vin rouge with champagne on offer for those with a taste for it. Quality may not have been high, but what was offered filled a need, assisted relaxation and was therefore very welcome.

Warmth, crowded rooms, dense cigarette smoke, card games and noisy conversation all helped to take the soldiers' minds off the trials and troubles of life on active service, even if only for a brief interlude. Whilst glasses would usually be available, some of the poorer quality establishments resorted to using Nestlé milk tins instead of glasses, which had long been 'captured' by visiting troops, or broken by constant rough handling. The milk tins had had the lids cut off and the edges smoothed but were understandably viewed with some disdain by those on whom they were foisted.

After a reasonable meal, often the ever popular egg or omelette and chips, a few glasses of the local brew and perhaps a raucous sing-song alongside an out of tune piano, the troops would eventually make their way back to camp, still singing as they went. The songs were usually of a nostalgic or maudlin nature and tended to gradually subdue the recent high spirits, as some over indulged comrades were helped to bed and the thoughts of others began to turn to the uncertainties of the morrow and the dangers it might bring.

For those who preferred a quieter time and no alcohol then there was always the option of remaining in whatever quarters had been allocated to the unit. These might be houses, barns, bakeries, breweries or other buildings that had been abandoned or damaged. Tented camps were another possibility. Here men could be found quietly reading a book or a letter from home. Others would be penning a few words in pencil by the guttering light of a candle or taper. The usual chores of darning socks, sewing on buttons and cleaning boots or rifles could also be attended to; in itself a form of relaxation after the tension of front line or support trench duty. While some men slept, others might sing quietly the songs of their homeland and youth, no doubt bringing back memories of far happier times that it was fervently hoped would soon be experienced again.[28]

In November and December 1917 the battalion remained in the Cordonnerie sector, which seemed to be a relatively quiet part of the front. The 4th Battalion of the Canadian Expeditionary Force was given instruction during this period. An officer and four other ranks holding the Elbow Post were injured following a gas shell bombardment on 5 December.[29]

At the beginning of 1918 the Allied armies in France and Flanders braced themselves for an anticipated German onslaught. The transfer of troops from the Russian front presented the Germans with perhaps one final chance to break the deadlock on the Western Front by unleashing these extra forces in an all-out offensive. The Allies, aware of the huge German build up in men and material, waited for the blow but were unsure exactly where it would fall. Defensive measures were, however, taken and the battalion found itself, for the time being, used in a largely labouring, rather than a fighting, capacity.

At the start of February 1918 the Swansea Battalion was employed in assisting the Royal Engineers in preparing a defensive line on high ground to the west of the River Lys, between Erquinghem and Armentieres. A special correspondent for the local newspaper found the men enjoying what was no doubt a well-earned rest from their daily exertions:

> *I was subsequently escorted by the adjutant...Lieut. V.M. Lewis... to a large three-storey building further along the street. Before the war it was a brewery. When I visited it was the temporary home of this Swansea battalion. It had been admirably adapted to the purpose. It was evening, and the lanterns arranged round the walls lit up the scene to weird effects of light and shadow. Some of the men were lying asleep on their mattresses, some were grouped around the lamps writing letters home, others sat in little groups singing as only Celts can sing, the songs of the old homeland so that the rafters reverberated with the harmonies...These quarters are well ventilated and located, and special facilities have been made for speedy escape in case of fire. Here, as elsewhere, all seemed bright and cheerful. There was no room for the 'grouser.' This battalion has changed very considerably in its personnel since it came out, and of the original 750 only about 120 are now included in the strength.*[30]

In February 1918 Lieutenant Colonel G.F. Brooke assumed command of the Swansea Battalion, replacing Lieutenant Colonel J.H. Hayes, who had been promoted. Hayes had been with the battalion from its early days though he had, at that time, never actually visited Swansea, joining the battalion after it had left the town to complete its training at Rhyl and Winchester.

George Frank Brooke was born in 1878 in Brookeborough, County Fermanagh, the eldest son of Frank T. Brooke, of Ardeen, Shilleagh, County Wicklow. The family was well versed in the ways of the military. George Brooke's father had been a Royal Navy lieutenant, whilst his uncle, Colonel Lionel Godolphin Brooke, had commanded the 1st Battalion of the Connaught Rangers in the South African campaign. Indeed, George himself had seen action in South Africa. He had been appointed Second Lieutenant in the 1st Battalion, the Connaught Rangers, in 1897 when he was nineteen years old. He was promoted to Lieutenant in October 1899 and had left Cork for Cape Town in the November of the same year.

On 15 December 1899 he was wounded in action at the Tugela River, two of the wounds (to the chest and knee) being described as 'severe'. He had subsequently received the Queen's Medal and clasp. In December 1902, having recovered somewhat from his wounds, he was posted to Poona, India. Reaching the rank of Captain in 1904, he had retired in 1907 only to be re-appointed as Captain in October 1914 following the outbreak of hostilities. He was posted to the 6th Service Battalion of the Connaught Rangers in February 1915 and saw service at Cork and Aldershot before leaving Southampton for Le Havre in December 1915.

In February 1916 he had taken over the 9th Battalion, the Royal Dublin Fusiliers, before rejoining the Connaught Rangers a month later. On 13 July 1916, a few days after the Mametz Wood engagement, Brooke was appointed to the command of the 10th Battalion of the Welsh Regiment, being further promoted to Lieutenant Colonel

G.F. Brooke (on the left) with a group of Connaught Rangers in France. Brooke took command of the Battalion in 1918. Hugo Brooke

in August 1916.

His younger brother, Henry Hastings Brooke, was born in 1882 and, in due course, followed what must have been to the family a well-worn path to the door of military service. He was commissioned in 1899 and served as a lieutenant with the Imperial Yeomanry in South Africa, being awarded the Queen's Medal and gaining promotion to Captain in 1903. In September 1914 he joined the 2nd Battalion of the Connaught Rangers, having spent some time in the 4th Battalion.

He commanded D company and was severely wounded by a shot to the head while serving near Ypres in November 1914. He was permanently blinded and was retired in January 1916. Sadly, having moved to the Isle of Wight, he died at the age of thirty-seven in 1920, his demise apparently being accelerated by the severity of his wound.[31]

Viv Walters was born in Cardiff and attended Severn Road School before leaving at the age of fourteen years. He worked in the insurance business before joining the Swansea Battalion as a replacement after the losses suffered in the Passchendaele offensive. Now a private, his brother Howard also served with the battalion but as a sergeant. During their service Viv was wounded in the back by shrapnel whilst Howard won a Military Medal for action in a trench raid.

On one occasion Sergeant Thomas Thomas, of the Royal Engineers, found himself in the area occupied by the Swansea Battalion and decided to pay a courtesy call on Viv Walters, who was courting his younger sister. Approaching the lines he stopped the first man he met and asked 'Do you know Private Viv Walters?' The reply was short and to the point. 'I do - he's my brother' said Howard Walters. The odds against such a happening must have been about 800 to 1! Viv Walters later married the young Miss Thomas and thus gained an erstwhile Royal Engineer as a brother-in-law.[32]

The long anticipated last major German offensive of the war was launched on 21 March 1918. At first the British Army reeled under the weight of the blow and commenced a widespread retreat, trading space for time, the better organization of

German infantry on the advance. The failure of their 1918 offensive, increasing American strength and civilian discontent in Germany undoubtedly affected morale. Taylor Library

resistance and the arrival of reinforcements. The Swansea Battalion was not caught up directly in this heavy fighting though it was being placed in position to meet the German advance just as it finally ran out of steam, some months later.

During this time it is likely that Sir Douglas Haig's famous 'Backs to the Wall' letter would have been read out to the men by their officers. The letter emphasized the importance of halting the German drive and asked that each man be prepared to defend his position to the death, with no question of retreat or surrender. It was certainly read to some men of the 15th Welsh (Carmarthen) Battalion and presumably to the Swansea Battalion as well, though there is no direct mention of it in the records. One group of 15th Welsh soldiers is reported as patiently listening to the address and then with notable soldierly indifference immediately declaring what was to be trumps in the next hand of cards![33]

Thus March 1918 saw the Swansea Battalion in the trenches, in what had now become a relatively 'quiet' sector, given the heavy fighting that was raging elsewhere. Even in these conditions of trench warfare, with little movement of any meaningful distance, the familiar routine of rotating the troops through front line, support and reserve duties continued. This, in itself, was no easy task since, especially when changing troops in the front line area, the job had to be completed without unduly alerting the enemy and giving him a chance to interfere in the process. For example, on 27 March 1918 the Swansea Battalion was in the trenches in the area of Houplines. It was due to be relieved by the 16th Battalion, the Royal Welsh Fusiliers, before moving back to billets at Erquinghem. The Relief Order was, of necessity, quite detailed. It specified precisely which individual company of the Royal Welsh Fusiliers would relieve which individual company of the Swansea Battalion. It indicated which trenches were to be used for getting both into, and out of, the line, a vital prerequisite if congestion and unwelcome noise were to be avoided. Guides were to be provided at key points to ensure that the new troops reached their positions with the minimum of delay. The Lewis guns were to come in by day, to ensure that in the event of any enemy action, concentrated firepower would be readily available to beat off any threat. Signallers were also to be replaced during the hours of daylight. Trolleys would be supplied for the easier movement of company stores, officers' kits and other items. Handcarts and transport limbers would also be provided for moving equipment and the Lewis guns themselves. Wherever possible, gum boots were to be returned to the gum boot store before the commencement of the relief operation.

On arrival at the billets, those relieved would be supplied with a hot meal and other rations; packs and blankets would also be sent over. On completion of the relief each company was to transmit by wire a pre-arranged sentence to the headquarters' staff. These signals would indicate the success of the operation, whilst not alerting the enemy to what had happened.

The pre-arranged sentences on this occasion were suitably cryptic and indicative of a subtle sense of humour. For 'A' Company it was 'All vacancies for leave taken'. For 'B' Company the sentence was 'Both men have returned'. 'Could we have more candles' was the supposed request from 'C' Company, whilst 'D' Company was to send the probably forlorn request of 'Don't forget my leave'![34]

The inevitable result of rain, mass movement and artillery. The battlefield becomes a loathsome quagmire. Taylor Library

In the middle of April 1918 the battalion was in the front line near Hennencourt where officers Howell, Smith and Dann were all wounded; Dann on two occasions. On 22 April 1918 Captain Richard Bellamy Sheppard was killed and the battalion moved to Brigade Reserve. Captain Sheppard's widow was informed that he had been:

> ...*buried in Contay British cemetery, west of Albert. The grave has been registered in this office, and is marked by a durable wooden cross with an inscription bearing full particulars.*[35]

In the area of Fleurbaix, the apple, pear and walnut trees were heavy with fruit. The 15th Welsh (Carmarthen) Battalion certainly used this to their initial advantage and it is likely that the Swansea Battalion would have done the same. Thus it was that stewed apples and stewed pears became regular features of the daily diet of the troops. It is not clear whether the men's enthusiasm, for what was at first a novelty but soon became monotonous, waned before the fruit supply was exhausted.

With the fruit being eventually exhausted it was simply back to the more traditional form of army cooking. Large portable 'dixies' would be filled with maybe four or five gallons of water and, when piping hot, would have added to them perhaps a dozen tins of the regular Maconachie ration. This tin contained cooked beef together with potatos, peas and gravy. Once heated through and thoroughly stirred in, dinner was ready.

If rationing was a problem perhaps due to enemy activity interrupting the normal flow of supplies, then recourse would have to be made to other options. Shredded dried vegetables would on occasion be added to the dixies and, in the probable absence of beef joints, corned beef would be thrown into the mix. This gave a passable stew once the soldier got used to the thick film of yellow grease that floated on the surface. Depending on trench conditions, hot tea or soup would be brought to the men by way of portable containers designed to retain heat and strapped to the carrier's back. The tops were fastened down by butterfly screw nuts and the containers were about two feet in height.

In extreme circumstances, such as might have applied on the Somme or in the Ypres salient, it might not be possible to make such supply trips on a regular enough basis for the troops. Effectively trapped in trenches that were frequently in a very poor state of repair, desperate measures might have to be taken. The trenches, of course, were usually surrounded by a large number of shell holes. Over time, depending on ground composition and the weather conditions, these holes would naturally fill with water. They also naturally filled with all the flotsam and jetsam that accompanied front line warfare.

It was not impossible for the shell holes to contain the gradually decaying remains of horses or even men as well as any number of other objectionable items. Indeed, given the depth and often impenetrable surface of these ponds, it was usually impossible to tell exactly what lay within the murky waters. However, if the supply run failed and thirst became a real issue then the men would occasionally, as a last resort, use these fetid pools as a source for a brew up. This would involve carefully parting the top coating of green algae in order to disturb the underlying water as little as possible. The dixies would then be filled and a makeshift wick would be made from a strip of sandbag. This would then be wound around a candle. Lit and placed in a depression in the floor of the trench (when dry enough) or a raised step, this would eventually boil the water allowing the 'tea' to be made.[36]

As April 1918 drew to a close the battalion was in the area of Aveluy Wood. Plans were soon being made to use elements of the Swansea Battalion, in conjunction with another battalion of the same brigade, in an offensive action against the wood and its defenders.

Notes

1. PRO/WO/95/2540.
2. PRO/WO/339/13576.
3. SWDP, 8 August 1917.
4. PRO/WO/95/520.
5. SWDP, 6 February 1918.
6. SWDP, 9 August 1917.
7. Marden, op. cit., p.416
8. PRO/WO/95/520.
9. SWDP, 9 February 1918.
10. Warren.
11. PRO/WO/339/39865.
12. Marden, op. cit., p.416.
13. PRO/WO/95/2559.
14. PRO/WO/339/15339.
15. PRO/WO/339/24857.
16. PRO/WO/339/15393.
17. PRO/WO/95/2559.
18. WGAS TC 26/3.
19. The 38th Welsh Division magazine, 1918.
20. Marden, op. cit., p.418-419.
21. SWDP, 25 August 1917.
22. SWDP, 31 August 1917.
23. PRO/WO/95/2540.
24. SWDP, 27 August 1917.
25. SWDP, 25 January 1918.
26. Marden, op. cit., p.437.
27. PRO/WO/95/2558.
28. IWM/97/16/1 War Memories of W.D. Shanahan.
29. PRO/WO/95/2559.
30. SWDP, 9 February 1918.
31. Information provided by Mr Oliver Fallon and Oliver and Hugo Brooke.
32. Information supplied by Mr H.T. Walters.
33. Shanahan, op. cit.
34. PRO/WO/95/2559.
35. PRO/WO/339/27879.
36. Shanahan, op. cit.

CHAPTER TEN

Aveluy Wood and the Advance
to Victory

On 10 May 1918 units of the 114 Infantry Brigade planned to attack Aveluy Wood with a view to improving the British position, by advancing its lines and clearing the southern edge of the wood. The attack was to be spearheaded by the 15th Welsh under Lieutenant Colonel Parkinson, supported by one company from the Swansea Battalion, led by Captain Strange. Two companies of the 19th Welsh Pioneers were to be responsible for consolidating any captured positions. Artillery, mortar and machine-gun support would also be provided and the Sappers were to use Bangalore Torpedoes should the opportunity arise.

The Pioneers were to cut lanes in the wood to aid the concentration of troops. Frequent stops would be necessary so that the attacking troops could regain their correct orientation. As at Mametz Wood, there were a number of rides, or paths, running through the wood. As these were reached the troops would have to pause while a scout crossed the ride first, to check the state of any barbed wire. If satisfactory, the rest of the wave would, on a given signal, rush across the ride, thus minimizing the potential exposure to hostile fire. A creeping barrage would be laid down fifty yards in front of the leading wave and the infantry would take care not to outrun it.

Each 'other rank' would carry 120 rounds of small arms ammunition, whilst the rifle bombers were to take six rifle grenades each. Lewis gunners would have twenty drums per gun. Every man would be given a four-feet long strip of white calico, to be held at arms length or placed along a parapet when called for by a contact patrol aeroplane to signal the position of the troops. Before the attack every man would be given a hot breakfast.[1]

Though the attack began encouragingly enough, it soon became apparent that something was going badly awry:

...at 9 a.m. the artillery barrage opened and the attackers moved forward. The hostile reply to our barrage was slow in developing and when it did develop consisted of a light barrage...

...owing to the mist and fog, the contact aeroplane had been unable to see anything from a very low altitude at 9.35 a.m.

2/Lieut. Thomas returned at 10.50 a.m., with a message from O.C. 'A' Company giving his position, and at 10.55 a.m. I received a message verbally through the Signal Office at Forward Battalion Headquarters, from the O.C. 'C' Company, 15th Welsh Regt., that our artillery was firing short and holding up our advance.

Several more messages to this effect were received and at 11.20 a.m., I received a message from Captain Sampson commanding 'D' Company that the attack had failed, also one from O.C. 'A' Company that our artillery was still falling short and had held up our advance...I found that the Battalion was, except on the extreme right of the attack, back in our original Front Line, and all the companies very much mixed up, having suffered considerable casualties from our own Artillery fire.[2]

Second Lieutenant Archibald Simpson in 1917. After promotion Archie left the Swansea Battalion and served with the 15th Welsh. He was wounded in action at Aveluy Wood, 10 May 1918. Brian Simpson

With the British artillery fire playing havoc with its own troops, the attack disintegrated in some confusion and the advance was abandoned. Brigadier General A. Harman commanded the 114 Infantry Brigade and was thus in overall charge of the operation. Having dispatched the Brigade Major, Captain Bucknell, and the Artillery Liaison Officer, Captain Phillips, forward to check on the progress of the attack, the disquieting nature of their preliminary report compelled him to head for the wood himself.

He first went to Parkinson's Command Post but found that he had, himself, left to visit the position and evaluate the situation at first hand. Moving towards the wood, Harman encountered Parkinson on his way back. He acquainted Harman with the steps he had taken to stabilize the situation. In response to a question asking what he attributed the failure of the attack to, he pointedly placed in Harman's hand the fuse from a British 18-pound gun. The clear implication was that the British artillery fire had been misdirected and had, in fact, fallen on its own troops.[3]

Captain Strange had led the Swansea Battalion company that supported the attack and was initially reported as being missing in the action. Brigadier General Harman had no doubts as to Captain Stranges's leadership qualities reporting:

The captain of the left flank company is missing and I have every confidence in saying that had it been possible for that company to go forward CAPTAIN STRANGE would have done it.

Happily, Captain Strange had been captured rather than killed, and just over a month later he was able to advise his wife by postcard, of his unavoidable detention as a guest of the Kaiser.[4]

It was obvious that the circumstances of such an unhappy operation would merit a full and urgent investigation. Reports were soon being filed as the search for answers began. The final explanation for the apparent inaccurate firing of the artillery was as simple as it was deadly for those caught underneath it:

...one battery of 18-pdrs which was engaged in the creeping barrage was undoubtedly shooting short. The reason was...some batteries have been supplied

with arcs and rulers which are fixed on to the Battery boards with drawing pins. The arcs are graduated into 1/2 degree Divisions, and there is no further mark on the arc except that '1/2 degrees' is marked on the edge. The Major of the Battery in question had fixed the arc on the board with drawing pins with handles and the handle of one of the pins was folded down over the '1/2'.

On the 8th instant the Major of the Battery was relieved by the Captain, who worked out the switches for the barrage and, in error, ordered the preliminary barrage line 'so many degrees' left of the Zero point instead of 'so many half degrees'.

The Battery therefore opened fire on a line well in rear of our front line and measurements show that it would catch the third wave of the infantry at the time when the advance to the second objective was due...

Finally, may I, on behalf of the whole of the Artillery of the V Corps, express my deep regret that mistakes on our part should have caused so many casualties to the 114th Infantry Brigade, and should have undoubtedly prevented them from succeeding in the operation in which they were engaged. I can assure them that every step will be taken to prevent a recurrence of such mistakes and I trust that they will not lose that confidence in the support of the artillery which these events have naturally shaken.[5]

This disastrous incident had cost the Swansea Battalion alone, twelve men killed and thirty wounded. Among those who fell was Sergeant David Howell Evans, who was twenty-seven years of age. The eldest of nine children, his mother had died at an early age in the first decade of the twentieth century, leaving his father to bring up the family alone. David had worked before the war as a miner in the Fforestfach area of Swansea, following in the footsteps of his father, William, who was also a collier.

William was a much-respected deacon at the Calfaria Welsh Baptist Chapel on Carmarthen Road, Swansea. Indeed, when David was home on leave after coming through the attack on Mametz Wood, the congregation had presented him with a Bible, while his father looked on with pride. Sergeant Evans' brother, Sergeant T.J. Evans, was also serving, but with the Welsh Guards. In action at Pilckem Ridge on 31 July 1917 his brave actions had earned him a *Croix de Guerre*.

Unlike many relatives of the fallen, David's father and brother were able to visit his grave in France during the 1920s. The photographs still show the pain that they had

Sergeant David Howell Evans killed in the disastrous attack on Aveluy Wood. Jason Muxworthy

suffered at his loss, etched on their faces. A specially made plaque to his memory still remains with the family to this day, the following words appearing beneath his portrait:

> *The path of duty*
> *Was the path to glory*[6]

Between the middle of May and early August 1918 the Swansea Battalion again went through the routine of front line, support and reserve duty. Locations included Varennes, Toutencourt Wood Camp, Mesnil and Forceville. Some time was spent in being instructed by the Royal Engineers in the art of 'proper' trench digging.

In the first week of August 1918 the British Army launched a series of attacks that met with unprecedented success. Indeed, such was the damage done to the German forces that Ludendorff later stated that 8 August 1918 was the 'Black Day of the German Army'.

The father and brother of David Howell Evans at his graveside. His brother won a bravery award at Pilckem Ridge while serving with the Welsh Guards.
Jason Muxworthy

Commemorative plaque to D.H. Evans.
Jason Muxworthy

General Eric Ludendorff.
Taylor Librar

On this date the Swansea Battalion was holding the front line at Aveluy Wood. With it in the trenches was a battalion of the 318th American Infantry Regiment, which was undergoing instruction from its more experienced comrades. This was not a particularly quiet sector and the Americans had to learn fast or suffer the consequences. The Swansea Battalion lost one man killed and one wounded while getting a patrol across the River Ancre on 8 August. A day later, unusually, it suffered one man killed and two men wounded by a bomb dropped from a German aeroplane. Two more men were wounded by shellfire before the battalion was moved to Brigade reserve.[7]

After a week's training for forthcoming offensive operations, the battalion relieved units of the Wiltshire's and the Leicester's and took up front line positions in the Hamel sector. On 22 August 1918 a twelve man patrol under Lieutenant I. Williams attempted to ford the River Ancre but found it impassable and covered by heavy machine-gun fire. Undaunted by this failure, Williams promptly tried again and this time succeeded in crossing the river and found that a part of the German defence system was currently unoccupied. Fording the river for a third time he brought with him six rifle sections of 'A' Company and occupied the deserted German position.

The German response was immediate and a number of rifle grenades were fired at the British party, causing several casualties. As the wounded were being evacuated back across the river, the party was caught by machine-gun fire causing even more casualties. Given this setback the evacuation attempt was abandoned. Seeing the plight of their 'A' Company comrades, Second Lieutenant L.O. Griffiths and Private A. Crocombe, attempted to wade the river from the British-held side while under heavy fire. On the third attempt they got across and succeeded in bringing back all the wounded.

At 10.30 p.m. on 23 August the rest of the battalion moved across the river, in some cases the water being literally neck-high, and consolidated the former German positions. The battalion was assisted in this task by Lieutenant Williams and Second Lieutenant Griffiths, who were still on the German side of the river, and now helped guide the rest of the troops over.

A scene during the British advance in the Somme area. A first aid post is visible in the background. Taylor Library

Further attacks by the reorganized battalion met with little concerted German opposition, so that by 5.00 p.m. on 24 August a position to the west of Pozieres had been attained. At battalion headquarters, having caught up with the attackers, Lieutenant Colonel Brooke then resumed command of the battalion.

In an effort to keep the enemy off balance another attack was quickly developed by the battalion, commencing at 4 a.m. on 25 August, and advancing 2,000 yards in the area of Bazentin-le-Petit before heavy machine-gun fire slowed the advance. A defensive line was quickly established in order to consolidate the ground gained from enemy counter-attack. The enemy, however, seemed to have had quite enough fighting for the moment and withdrew voluntarily at 4.00 p.m.[8]

On 26 August 1918 Temporary Second Lieutenant William Noel Hazard was killed in action. He was born in Norfolk in 1893 and had been employed as an Articled Clerk to a solicitor, following in the footsteps of his father, who was also a solicitor. Living in Putney, he voluntarily gave up a relatively safe commission in a Home Service battalion in order to get out to the front and see some action. He was granted a temporary commission in the Welsh Regiment in September 1917.[9]

With the German defence now apparently crumbling, it was important to maintain the pressure of the British advance. The Swansea Battalion therefore formed up in shell holes, in attack order, at 4.00 a.m. on 27 August 1918, under a bank at High Wood, the scene of very heavy fighting in 1916, before moving to the attack at 6.00 a.m. It followed the advance of the 13th and 15th Welsh Battalions that had attacked earlier. It soon came under heavy machine-gun fire. However, despite this unwelcome attention from the enemy it still managed to reach its objective, a trench to the north-east of Delville Wood. This wood was well known to the South African troops who had assaulted it in 1916 and encountered ferocious German resistance. Indeed, it had subsequently been nicknamed 'Devil's Wood'.[10]

The battalion now found that it had outrun any supporting troops and had no contact with friendly forces on either its left flank or its front. Despite the exposed nature of its newly captured position it was decided to remain in the trench in a defensive posture. Enemy machine guns opened fire from a flanking position, causing many casualties, and several German attempts to bomb the trench also had to be driven off. One of those wounded in this action was:

> *Pte. Chas. Mortimer Gustavus... wounded in France on the 27th ult...Pte. Gustavus was wounded in the thigh, back and wrist and had been removed to a base hospital. On Tuesday morning a postcard from the nurse contained the reassuring words 'Don't worry; progressing most satisfactorily'. Pte. Gustavus has been two years at the front, and he has two brothers serving - one in Salonika and the other at Chatham.*[11]

Among those killed was George Outram Smith. A native of Cheetham, Manchester, he enlisted at Cardiff, having probably found work in the area. His home was at Spath Lane, Cheadle Hulme, where he lived with his wife, Elizabeth. He was forty years old at the time of his death and the intensity of the fighting on this day is starkly illustrated by the fact that twenty-eight of his comrades died with him.[12]

As the afternoon developed the enemy, obviously desperate to regain his former

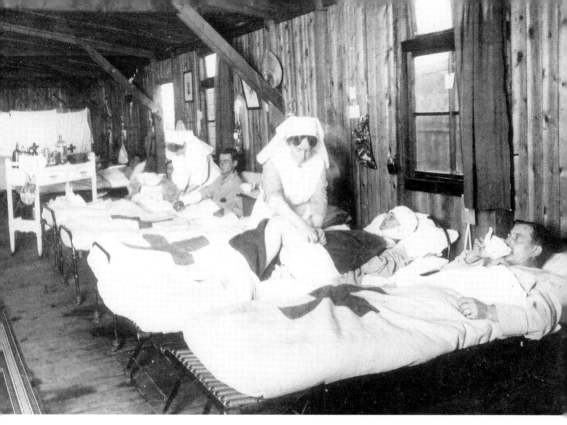

Private Gustavus was treated at a base hospital similiar to this one. Taylor Library

trench, began to work troops around both flanks of the Swansea Battalion, which now held an exposed position with no support to its right or left. With it becoming increasingly difficult to maintain this position Brigade Headquarters issued an order that required the battalion to retire to safer ground. This being accomplished after dark, the battalion was then deployed in defending the main Flers to Bazentin-le-Petit road before, on 28 August, it relocated to the cover of High Wood.[13]

At dawn on 30 August 1918 the battalion was in action yet again. This time the objective was Morval. The 13th Welsh were late in starting to advance which meant that, once again, a Swansea Battalion flank was exposed to the enemy. Nevertheless the battalion was soon approaching Morval, where it was held up by stiffening German resistance. The casualties suffered in a determined attack, included several fatalities amongst its officers as well as a number of other ranks. One of these officers was Second Lieutenant John Y.P. Jones ('Jyp') who had been:

> *...educated at the Cathedral School, Llandaff, being awarded a scholarship of £50 a year at the age of 10, finally rising to the highest position in the choir. From Llandaff he proceeded to Blundell's, Tiverton, in 1913, where he was a school prefect and head of his house, and played in the school XI. While still at school he had volunteered for the flying corps, but was rejected on account of 'slightly imperfect vision in one eye'. On leaving Blundell's, being intended for the medical profession, he successfully passed his preliminary examination, but never went into residence. In January 1917, he entered a cadet battalion at Cambridge, and was gazetted to the Welsh Regiment in the following April. He*

proceeded to the Western Front, and was posted to the 14th (or Swansea) Battalion, and saw much fighting during the summer of 1917, remaining continuously in the line until December 26th, when he was invalided home with severe trench nephritis. It is characteristic of the boy that, although extremely ill, he refused to leave the line until on a peremptory order from his C.O. (Colonel Hayes.)

After several months in hospital he returned to the depot of his regiment, on April 3rd, and remained there until July 17th, returning to the Western Front for a second time on July 31st.[14]

In September 1919 the family of J.Y.P. Jones was present in St Mary's Church, Clydach, near Swansea, when a memorial window to his memory was unveiled.[15]

Ernest Henry Balsom was born at Porth in 1893. Living at Caerphilly and employed as a clerk, he had attested at Cardiff on 5 September 1914. He had served with the 9th and 12th Battalions of the Welsh Regiment before being discharged to a commission in October 1916. He had subsequently joined the Swansea Battalion and was another of the officers who died in the attack on Morval. The payment made to his estate for his war service as both an other rank and an officer amounted to less than £100. It was hoped that the death duty normally due on this sum would not be payable as he had been killed in action.[16]

Despite these losses the attack was resumed at 4.45 a.m. on 1 September and the objectives of the Sunken Road and the railway were both reached with many Germans being killed.

After a short rest on 2 September the battalion was once more on the move. At noon on 4 September the Canal du Nord was forced at Manancourt and, with the assistance of the artillery, after some hard fighting the nearby ridge was gained. A German counter-attack was repulsed. Further small gains were made the following day before the battalion was relieved by the 2nd Battalion, the Lincolnshire Regiment. During this period the Williams family back in Swansea received some worrying news:

Mrs. Edith Williams, 19 Neath Road, Swansea, has received news that her

Britsh troops rest on the banks of the Canal du Nord. Taylor Library

David Lloyd George addresses a large crowd at Morriston, Swansea, in 1918.
Bernard Mitchell

son, Sergt. Glyn Williams (Swansea's Own) has been wounded in the head and is now lying at a base hospital in France. Sergt. Williams is one of four brothers serving; one Bdr. Aubrey Williams, RFA., is now in hospital at Newcastle, having been gassed, and another son, Sergt. Stan. Williams, has been discharged through wounds received at Mametz Wood with Swansea's Own; while there is still another son Pte. Jack Williams, S.W.B., serving in France.[17]

At Le Transloy on 5 September the battalion rested and cleaned up after its recent strenuous exertions. It had lost almost eighty men killed and nearly 400 wounded. In the following days both the Commanding Officer, Lieutenant Colonel G.F. Brooke, and the Brigadier General, T.R.G. Price, inspected the troops and no doubt passed on their compliments for the hard fighting that had been so successfully completed of late. On 18 September 1918 a further attack was made and a German trench captured. This had not been an easy task as Lieutenant Colonel Brooke reported:

Indifferent resistance was encountered at the first objective, but from there to the second objective, machine-gun fire was very heavy and the enemy put up a stout fight, many being killed. Owing to the troops on our left not having reached the Green Line as soon as our attack, intense machine-gun fire was opened from the left, and from Gouzeaucourt, on the ground round and behind our new front line, making any movement practically impossible.[18]

On 20 September 1918, the Commanding Officer of the 38th Welsh Division, Major General T. A. Cubitt, CMG, DSO, published the following telegram for the benefit of

167

the men of the 38th Welsh Division:

From His Royal Highness the Prince of Wales, K.C., G.C.M.G., C.B.E., M.C.,

To the General Officer Commanding the 38th Division

19.9.18

Please convey to all ranks of the Welsh Division my most sincere congratulations on their magnificent successes in the recent offensive on the Western Front. These I have followed with the greatest interest, particularly in view of my close connection with the Division during the Battle in Belgium last year.[19]

After such a hectic spell of action the remainder of September must have come as a very welcome anti-climax for the battalion. Rest, the cleaning of equipment, the holding of a church parade and a reorganization were all completed, if not without incident. The training area was harassed by German shellfire, Major General Cubitt visited and presented awards, and 'D' Company was subjected to a gas shell attack that caused twenty-two casualties; four officers and eighteen other ranks. To round off the month, the battalion, after spending thirty-four months in France and Flanders, finally adopted continental time![20]

The start of October 1918 found the battalion in trenches on the Fins Ridge. By the end of the first week it was in the staging trenches ready to launch an attack on Malincourt. This commenced early on the morning of 8 October and, by about dawn, Mortho Wood was being approached. The Swansea Battalion was marching in fours, with fifty yards between platoons, when German gunfire from the wood halted the advance. An attempt to clear the wood failed and Lieutenant Colonel Brooke undertook a personal reconnaissance, finding very strong German wire along and inside the wood. He recalled:

I remember saying to myself 'I wish to goodness I had a couple of tanks'. I never expected any, but at that moment I heard a noise and turned round, and there they were. I've never had a wish gratified so promptly or appreciated it more. I hailed the tanks and they soon made short work of the wire and machine guns, thus enabling us to continue our advance. I saw both these tanks knocked out a little later, one quite close to me. They were hit by a Boche field gun, in a well sited and hidden forward position, which gun we got when we advanced. It was under a tree in some bushes and quite invisible from the front, and so placed that any tank coming over the ridge was 'easy meat' for it.[21]

Lieutenant Colonel Brooke found the new fangled tanks much to his liking. Taylor Library

By 3.00 p.m. the battalion had entered the village of Malincourt. Here it captured many machine guns, howitzers and two heavy trench mortars, complete with limbers. During this attack Captain Evan Francis Arthur was wounded by a bullet in the right shoulder.

Captain Arthur was thirty-one years of age. He had been born in

Llangadfan, and was a Supplementary Clerk with the Post Office London telephone service, living in Highgate, London. The bullet wound was not his first active service injury. In April 1917 he had suffered the ignominy of slipping off a trench fire step while observing an artillery barrage, with the result that his injured right knee had had to have a cartilage removed.[22]

Between 18-20 October the battalion, in conjunction with elements of the 13th and 15th Welsh, moved towards the high ground running from Amerval and overlooking Forest. Two fighting patrols were sent across the River Selle to capture enemy positions that were situated in a quarry and a house. Whilst the house was taken, it was only possible to establish a presence in a trench that ran in front of the quarry. Another attempt was again frustrated by the defenders, the officer leading the attack being killed and several men wounded.

The next plan saw the 13th Welsh stealthily crossing the river by a single footbridge and assembling undetected within 150 yards of the enemy. The Swansea Battalion, meanwhile, managed to cross the river at about 2.00 a.m. and catch up with the pre-planned barrage, which fell on the railway line. The 13th Welsh were then able to charge the defenders before they had recovered from the barrage. The Swansea Battalion was also able to advance at this time and, approaching from a different angle, they happily discovered that the German machine-gun fire passed harmlessly over their heads, rendered ineffective by the steepness of the railway embankment.

Despite heavy fighting around the railway line, where about thirty Germans were killed and sixty taken prisoner, all objectives for the attack were achieved. Overall, the Division escorted one German officer and 211 other ranks into the prison cages whilst a further 225 German dead were also accounted for. Four field guns, three trench mortars and about forty machine guns completed the haul.[23]

One of the casualties on the 20 October 1918 was Lieutenant George Stanley Williams of Brynglas, Coity Road, Bridgend. He was a well-known Cardiff rugby player, playing for the first team at fly-half during the 1912-13 season, and also playing for the Athletic. Lieutenant Williams had attested for service with the Glamorgan Yeomanry in August 1914. Following his initial posting with the Yeomanry he had been transferred to the 16th Battalion, the Welsh Regiment in 1915, and saw some service with the Machine Gun Corps before joining the Swansea Battalion.[24]

The Battalion now enjoyed a well earned rest and spent some time in billets in Bertry and divisional reserve at Troisvilles and Croix, before re-entering the front line on 29 October 1918. After resting at Croix for two further days, the battalion then prepared to attack German positions at Mormal Wood on 4 November. While in the assembly positions, the 114 Brigade came under fairly heavy shelling and suffered a number of casualties.

The Swansea Battalion then advanced with two companies in front and two in support. A British creeping barrage consisting of high explosive and thermite; smoke and shrapnel, and howitzer shells added to the enemy's discomfort. Attacking troops were warned in advance not to follow the barrage too closely (300 yards minimum was suggested) lest shells exploding in the tree tops cause casualties. The opposition was found to be slight, with some small outposts of enemy infantry and the occasional machine-gun post.

By 2.00 p.m. advanced elements of the battalion had reached the outskirts of Locquignol where they took shelter in the surrounding orchards, while a few German defenders fired at them from the nearby houses. By 10.30 p.m. the patrols of the 13th Welsh reported the village to be no longer occupied by the enemy. As the troops advanced through and beyond the village, they captured about forty of the enemy and then overran a German field ambulance, capturing ten medical staff, and over thirty wounded Germans. They also freed a captured and wounded Royal Welsh Fusilier. The village of Berlaimont was then captured with a further tally of sixty prisoners.[25]

One of those killed during this engagement was Private William Samuel Bond.

Private Bond had lived at Cardiff Road, Treforest. He had enlisted for the duration of the war at Pontypridd on 11 December 1915. Initially assigned to the 3rd Battalion, the Welsh Regiment, he appeared to be of an independent mind and did not simply disappear into the ranks. In July 1918 he was subjected to ninety-six hours detention for making improper remarks to a Non-Commissioned Officer whilst the following month he was fined six days' pay for overstaying his final home leave before departing for the front. Transferred to the Swansea Battalion he was, however, at his post and in the thick of the action on 4 November 1918 when he paid the ultimate price, just a week before the war ended. His body was lost or remained unidentified when buried.

His elder brother, Frederick, had served with the 10th Battalion, the Welsh Regiment, and had fought alongside the Swansea Battalion at Mametz Wood in 1916. He had been killed in the wood on 10 July 1916 and his body was also lost or unidentified on burial. The home they both left when joining the forces, never to see again, remains in family hands to this day.[26]

William Bond who was killed just a week before the armistice.
Ceri Rees-Powell

The battalion remained in occupation of Les Grandes Patmes before moving to Petit Mauberge and then continuing its advance.[27] German resistance was now crumbling rapidly as rumours of an armistice began to circulate.

Notes

1. PRO/WO/95/2559.
2. PRO/WO/95/2559.
3. PRO/WO/95/2540.
4. SWDP, 14 June 1918.
5. PRO/WO/95/2558.
6. Information provided by Jason Muxworthy.
7. PRO/WO/95/2559.
8. ibid.
9. PRO/WO/339/111278.
10. PRO/WO/95/2559.
11. SWDP, 4 September 1918.
12. Information provided by John Hartley of Stockport.
13. PRO/WO/95/2559.
14. SWDP, 9 September 1918.

15. *Herald of Wales* 6 September 1919.
16. PRO/WO/339/67305.
17. SWDP, 6 September 1918.
18. Marden, op.cit., p.470.
19. PRO/WO/95/2559.
20. ibid.
21. Marden, op. cit., p.478.
22. PRO/WO/339/4495.
23. PRO/WO/95/2558.
24. Warren.
25. PRO/WO/95/2558.
26. Information supplied by Mrs Ceri Rees-Powell.
27. PRO/WO/95/2559.

CHAPTER ELEVEN

Swansea Remembers,
Swansea Forgets

On 11 November 1918 a special, illustrated edition of the *South Wales Daily Post* was published to mark the signing of the Armistice. In Swansea there was:

...such a demand for copies that the resources of the publishing department were taxed to the utmost, joyous cheers being raised and bunting appearing as if by magic, the din of every available hooter and siren at the docks and works swelling the chorus...the 'Daily Post' staff joined in the general celebration and there was no edition after 2 p.m.

As the news spread throughout the town almost all work ceased at once and joyous celebrations began. In the town, Major A.A. Perkins, commanding the Swansea Garrison, announced that a naval and military parade would take place in the afternoon, whilst the Mayor of Swansea stated that he intended to declare 12 November a public holiday. The attendant crowd sang the National Anthem with great fervour and the military authorities discharged a gun on the beach at 11.00 a.m. to mark the formal cessation of hostilities.

Fireworks were much in evidence in all parts of the town. A request by representatives of the Temperance Movement to close the public houses for the day was declined by the Mayor, probably anxious to avert a possible riot if the general public were denied this outlet for their celebrations. Instead the Mayor was able to assure the delegation that he had no doubt that the Swansea public would act with their usual due restraint.

In France the battalion was located in billets at Ecuelin, where it still underwent training, presumably on the off chance that the Armistice might not hold. In an inter-battalion rugby match the Swansea Battalion defeated the 2nd Rhonddas by six points to nil.[1] The battalion remained at Ecuelin and continued training until the end of December 1918, briefly celebrating Christmas, before moving to Berlaimont, Vendegies-au-Bois, Inchy and finally Molliens-au-Bois. Here it still trained but now, thankfully, leavened the work with daily recreation periods as well. On 16 January 1919 the battalion was presented with the King's Colours at Allonville and proceeded to parade them proudly through the town.[2]

Though the main body of the battalion was not yet able to return home, some contingents were able to make the trip, albeit in most cases for a short visit only. One of these was the battalion concert group fondly referred to as the 'Swans', a nickname it shared with the local football club, Swansea Town AFC. There appears to have been some local misunderstanding over the precise purpose of this visit, so much so that

Lieutenant Dyson Brock Williams, at that time commanding the battalion, advised the local newspaper that:

...the Swans' concert tour in Swansea and district...is being made for two purposes. We thought it only right that those generous Swansea people who...have subscribed money to provide comforts and amusements for their battalion at the front, should have a sample of what we were able to do to try and enliven the evenings of our men whenever possible...

Secondly, when you and others with you took your stand with us at all our recruiting meetings...and used your eloquence to persuade men to join us, promises were made that the dependants of those who fell in the fight should be cared for, and that the disabled men should be looked after by the town of Swansea.

The time has come for those promises to be made good, and I hope this tour will result in a substantial sum being made to start a large fund for the disabled soldiers and dependants of our battalion.

There will (before we return to France) be only two more opportunities of Swansea proper seeing the Swans – once at the Royal Theatre on Wednesday night next,...and at the Empire on March 1st, when Mr Richardson is organising a great farewell matinee for us.

...every penny taken at the doors will go direct to the treasurer...without any deduction for expenses...

Swansea has become a very rich town during the war, but for every few pounds anyone has made, someone in France has given life or lost a limb on the battlefield of Flanders, and I know that the generosity of Swansea people will not be appealed to in vain, and that I have been right in telling my men, not once, but many times, that though many of them do not live in Swansea, Swansea claims them as her own as members of the real Greater Swansea they have brought into existence. We want peoples' personal support at our shows, and we want their money to help us.[3]

Grave of Thomas B. Snow who died of wounds 7 December 1918. Simon Peter Lee

During this time men began to be gradually released for transport home and on 27 February two officers and 100 other ranks were provided to the 2nd Battalion, the Welsh Regiment, for Army of Occupation duties. Whether these men were volunteers or were simply selected is unclear. It is difficult to imagine a further round of duty in a foreign country being a very popular option at that time. By the end of March, the battalion was still at Allonville, before moving to Blangy Tromville where it remained until 1 May 1919, by which time it was happily down to cadre strength, the bulk of the men having been released. On 23 May 1919 this last remnant of the battalion finally left France via Le Havre and sailed for Southampton.[4]

In a relatively short space of time, everyday life for the bulk of the population of

Swansea appeared to revert to what must have appeared, on the surface at least, to be near normality. Distant echoes of the war could still be heard, however, in the occasional newspaper articles or 'Letters to the Editor' on some aspect or other of the recent struggle. For example, in February 1919 'Citizen' wrote to the newspaper stating:

I see that it is suggested that a suitable war memorial for Port Talbot, Aberavon and district would be a commanding column erected on Penycae Mountain...would not some such sort of monument appeal to Greater Swansea, instead of the various district efforts being mooted, and which tend to disperse energy, instead of concentrating on one grand scheme for the whole area?

'Citizen' considered Kilvey Hill, or that part of the Mumbles cliff that overlooks the lighthouse, as being eminently suitable for such a memorial.[5]

In April 1919 a reunion of those who had served with the Swansea Battalion was fittingly held at the Mond Buildings, Union Street, the one-time recruiting office where many had signed up in 1914. Around 300 men attended and many old friendships were renewed and common experiences and hardships remembered. Milbourne Williams, late Major of the battalion, presided in the absence of Colonel Dyson Brock Williams who was still in France with elements of the battalion. Milbourne Williams explained that the purpose of the reunion was to assist in forming:

...some sort of an association, not in competition to the other soldier associations in the town, but to keep all members of the battalion together in peace as they had in war.

Amidst some humorous banter about a future reunion, a more serious note was struck with the suggestion:

...that we hold this reunion on July 10th, three years after the battalion's heroic and costly deeds at Mametz Wood.

This date being a Thursday it was realized that time off from work would be an issue for those lucky enough to have gained employment on their return and 12 July, a Saturday, was agreed instead. It was also noted that steps were in hand to write the history of the battalion as it was felt that 'the public of Swansea hardly appreciated the work the Battalion had done in the 4 years of war'.[6]

In late May 1919 several cadres of Welsh battalion units, including that of the Swansea Battalion and its colours, arrived at Southampton from France where they were met by David Lloyd George, who praised the work they had done. The units then proceeded to Newmarket, from where they were to be dispersed.[7]

On 2 June 1919 the Swansea Battalion colours were received in Swansea with all due ceremony. Having arrived at the train station, the colours were escorted through the town to the Guildhall, where the Mayor, Mr W.H. Miles, and the civic party waited. A large gathering was present and included Council representatives, Officers and former Officers of the battalion, a contingent of those who had served, as well as members of the public.

Lieutenant Colonel Dyson Brock Williams said:

...it was his duty to hand over the colours that had been presented to the Battalion by His Majesty the King. They stood to them as an emblem of the brave deeds of the living and the dead that had been performed in the war they

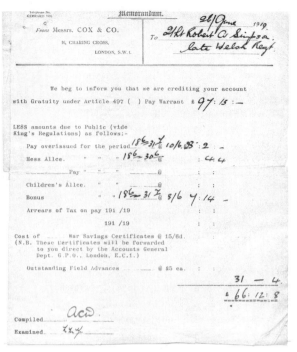

War gratuity for Second Lieutenant R.A. Simpson. Brian Simpson

1919 letter releasing Archie Simpson from military duty. Brian Simpson

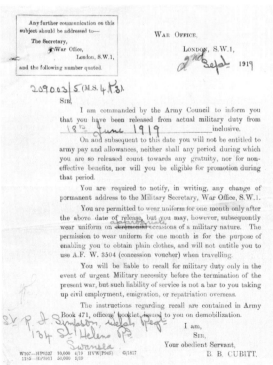

had just brought to a successful conclusion against the King's enemies, and he hoped the Mayor would treasure the colours as a reminder to the citizens of Swansea of the noble sacrifices that had been made by the Swansea Battalion, and that those who came after them would also remain faithful to those great principles of right and justice for which their comrades in France and Flanders fought and died.

Ex-Alderman David Davies had proposed the resolution to form the battalion almost five years earlier. He had seen the battalion at work in Swansea, Rhyl, and Winchester and had also visited it at the front, and under fire, in France. He was proud to be associated with it and paid it a fulsome tribute:

...he was thinking of those who were living today, and he was also thinking of the men who were dead in France, having left an imperishable glory as a heritage for Swansea – a source of inspiration to the generations that were coming after them...he was proud to be associated with Swansea and the Swansea Battalion, and he wanted, as one who realised the responsibility attaching to the raising of the Battalion to say: 'We told the men that if they enlisted in this battalion – and the men were the cream of our manhood of Swansea, for they were the men who came willingly, and not the men who came under compulsion – we told them 'go and fight for Britain and for human liberty, and we shall never forget you'.

The *South Wales Daily Post* editorial of 3 June 1919 praised the Mayor for the part he had played in what had been a very successful ceremony and further opined that:

...this should encourage the Mayor to take the lead in turning this feeling whilst

it runs in full flood into a useful and permanent channel. Neglect of ex-service men and their families may not be a present danger, but we have to provide for the future, when the great war will have receded into the distance and become merely a thrilling chapter in human history...(Swansea) should create a permanent committee...to deal promptly and sympathetically with the hard cases which are the inevitable aftermath of war. Its mission should comprehend not only the guardianship of war widows and orphans, but also the surviving ex-fighters themselves who must be convinced that the spokesmen for the people meant what they said when promising that the war services of our splendid manhood would never be forgotten by the country saved by them.[8]

Others in Swansea had also assisted in a number of ways during the conflict and a meeting of the Mayor's Comfort Fund held in October 1918 had noted the efforts made to keep the battalion, and other Swansea lads who were serving with the colours, supplied with 'treats':

The balance sheet for the period April 1916 to date showed that the total receipts amounted to £6,125, and of this £500 has been invested in War Loans, whilst a fairly substantial balance in hand will all be required to meet the needs of the local lads.

The articles despatched include 945,000 cigarettes, 1,150 lbs of tobacco, 9,783 shirts, 13,842 pairs of socks, 1,743 pants, 1,646 vests, 470 handkerchiefs, and smaller quantities of scarves, woollen gloves, writing pads, shaving soaps and outfits, footballs (21), musical instruments, boxes of chocolate, mouth organs, boxing gloves etc.

...in her report, Mrs Corker stated that for the past year applications had been received from about 2,000 soldiers and sailors, and parcels had been despatched to each one. From letters to hand, it was very gratifying to learn that the parcels were most acceptable, and that the recipients very highly appreciated the efforts made on their behalf.[9]

In a touching link with the fairly recent past, the Comfort Fund Committee was still chaired by Mrs Rosa Corker, widow of the late Alderman Corker, who himself had done so much to help form the battalion in 1914. Their son, Frank Corker, had, of course, himself been killed in 1916 while serving with the battalion.

Other members of the Corker family had also been active in supporting Swansea servicemen generally, though on occasion the response of a Swansea public apparently assailed by war related appeals from all quarters, was not all that was hoped for. In September 1914 the *South Wales Daily Post* had featured a letter:

Miss Winifred Corker, daughter of the Mayor of Swansea writes:

'A few weeks ago I opened this fund with the earnest hope that it would have a hearty response from the children of Swansea. We have not achieved anything like the success we ought to. All that has been collected to date is £7 15s 3d.

'If only children could think for a minute what a good and glorious object they would be subscribing their pennies to, I feel sure that there would be a much greater response. It is pleasant for us to think of our home life and the joys which we as a community participate in, more especially the children.

'The stress of war has hardly touched the major portion of the children of

Swansea, yet, on the other hand, we have numbers who in their young lives are suffering as much as those who are grown up. This should not be. I am sure you will all agree that the life of a child should be as joyful as it is possible to be, and, therefore, I appeal most strongly to the children of Swansea, who are in a position to contribute to my fund, to send their pennies, and to show that they can do their part, even if in a small way, to alleviate the suffering of those in distress.'[10]

Other local organizations had also been enthusiastic in doing what they could to help swell the funds of a number of appeals during the war years. For example, the girls of Oxford Street School had staged a 'war masque' entitled 'The Empire's Honour' whilst a football match held at the Vetch Field (home of Swansea Town AFC) between the Swans and a mid-Rhondda side saw the proceeds donated to the local war funds.

Similarly, those who preferred the oval ball to the round, supported a match at the St Helen's Ground (home of Swansea Cricket and Football Club) between a West Wales XV and the Australians. On the cultural scene, the Swansea Amateur Operatic Society no doubt hit the right note by donating part of the proceeds of its performance of H.M.S. Pinafore to the Prisoner of War Fund.[11]

A small number of prominent local dignitaries had also made their own homes or other properties available for the treatment of wounded soldiers and these medical facilities were kept busy as the casualty rolls lengthened during the war. The *South Wales Daily Post* had found Christmas Day 1916 a notable day as regards the treatment of the wounded heroes:

At Danycoed Hospital the day opened by a visit from Father Xmas, at 6.00 a.m. The men rubbed their eyes and wondered whether they were in Fairyland, but found that it was Father Xmas, accompanied by one of the nursing staff, disguised as a wounded 'Tommy,' each carrying a sack with a stocking for each man, containing numerous presents which were a great joy to all. The soldiers had been busily engaged for weeks past in making the paper flowers and decorations, and vying with each other as to who would have the prettiest and most artistic ward...a good old English Xmas dinner, consisting of turkeys, plum puddings, mince pies etc., was partaken of, ample justice being done to the same. Numerous toasts were then proposed and drunk.

Similar scenes were played out at the YMCA Military Hospital:

The happiest men in Swansea on Monday were apparently the war heroes in hospital uniform. They seemed to forget their wounds and lost limbs, and threw themselves whole-heartedly into the observance of the Yuletide season. At the Y.M.C.A. the patients fared very well. The various wards had been prettily decorated, and happy scenes were witnessed throughout the day. Men in bed played draughts and dominoes, whilst their more fortunate comrades, who were able to get to the recreation rooms, interested themselves in games of billiards, bagatelle, etc.

At the Parc Wern Red Cross Hospital it seemed that even the ward furniture would require medical treatment as there seemed to be a real risk of table legs soon fracturing:

...the tables at midday groaned under the weight of Xmas fare and

176

supplementary dainties, as was the just due to the many brave fellows for their self-sacrifice.[12]

By 1917 the pressure on the existing medical facilities had proven excessive and the Mayor and Council were compelled to consider the provision of additional accommodation for the reception of the wounded:

The Mayor said he had been asked by Mr. Bertie Perkins and Mr. Stanley Cook to say that they had been requested to provide...extra beds in Swansea for the wounded. The Y.M.C.A. building had been wholly secured...other accommodation was wanted and of all the buildings they had considered the new Brynmill Infants School was the most suitable.

The Mayor...observed that, if necessary, he would close all the schools for a year, as surely they owed a great debt to the wounded soldiers...it was resolved to hand over the Brynmill Infants School on Monday week next.[13]

The Red Cross Society had also been under pressure to devote more resources to the problem of housing the wounded as a 1917 press advertisement revealed:

Beds for our Wounded

A Swansea Obligation – which will be met

The Red Cross Society in the Swansea Area is being urgently called upon by the War Office to provide 200 Beds, supplementing the 230 now in use. This in anticipation of the saddening harvest of maimed men expected to be yielded by the Spring and Summer Campaign. Swansea, which has failed in nothing yet connected with the Great War, is asked to provide £2,500 at once so that the necessary additional accommodation and equipment may be furnished.[14]

The difficulties were eventually overcome, however, and a grateful hospital official was able to formally record his thanks in relation to one property by way of a letter that was published in the local press in 1919:

Commandant W. Cann, of the Parc Wern Red Cross Hospital, writes:

Sir – Parc Wern Soldiers Hospital closes this week. Please permit me to thank the Press for their kindly help during the long war. We are all greatly indebted to Miss Dulcie Vivian, Clyne Castle, for this mansion, and I know Miss Vivian is delighted with the loyal support of the citizens of Swansea for gifts of food and subscriptions for the maintenance in this hospital of 437 officers and 622 soldiers. The Castle Steam Trawlers Co. have sent a big weekly gift of fish throughout the war. Mr. David James has given free fares on the Mumbles Railway, and a nominal fare for the town trams, which has been tremendously appreciated by the patients.[15]

On 12 July 1919 at the St Helens Sports ground the long awaited Swansea Battalion field day was held. This was a successor to earlier such days that had been held at Rhyl and on the Continent, when the fighting allowed, at places such as Estrees, Blanche, Blembaise and Ecevelin. A goodly number of ex-officers and men attended and the officials were Lieutenant Colonel H. W. Benson (President), Lieutenant Colonel J. H. Hayes (Referee) with the judges including Messrs. Wilson, Bellingham, Strange, M. B. Williams and others. A variety of races were staged under Amateur Athletic Association rules.[16]

With the passing of time it was inevitable that the memory of the war and the part played in it by the Swansea Battalion would gradually recede in the public memory. On 10 July 1920, the fourth anniversary of the attack on Mametz Wood, the following poem by an apparently disillusioned 'Jack Point' appeared in the *South Wales Daily Post*:

> *The Tenth of July*
> *The anniversary this of Mametz Wood,*
> *That very name should stir old Gwalia's blood;*
> *And Swansea's in particular, for then*
> *Her sons proved they were heroes, aye, and men*
> *Of whom the British nation should be proud,*
> *Alas! Forgetfulness their deeds enshroud.*
>
> *   'Over the top' – a full battalion strong,*
> *Where hissing bullets sang their hailstone song;*
> *On, on, right through that fiery barrage dense,*
> *Where bursting shell and death's grim incidence*
> *Thinned out those gallant ranks – old 'Swansea's Own,'*
> *And just one company pulled through alone.*
>
> *   Old Swansea and the nation may forget*
> *Those whom for us the grim old reaper met,*
> *Who died that we might live – in Mametz Wood*
> *Fought, bled and died, all for the common good;*
> *Does Swansea and the nation heed their fate*
> *On that black day or even know the date?*

In the same edition a list of the officers and men who had died in the attack was published, presumably by the old comrades association, whilst the 'In Memoriam' column contained numerous remembrances of men of the battalion placed there by their still grieving families. Efforts were in hand to erect a Swansea War Memorial via a fund raising committee though the going appeared to be tougher than might have been anticipated:

CSM J. Boland who was awarded the DCM. He died in 1921, apparently as a result of wounds received during the war.
South Wales Daily Post

> *The Chairman said money had not come in as expected, only £6,132 13s having been collected. The original intention was to allocate £3,000 for a memorial, whilst £3,000 was ear-marked for the education of children; a third object being to relieve distress.*

As the local newspaper commented:

> *Alderman Sinclair failed, however, to put through the movement for a memorial to the town's fallen sons, and within two days of the anniversary of the armistice it is painful to have to record that the effort to commemorate the dead has reached*

apparent sterility, far short of the desired and needed sum, after months of stagnation. Primarily, however, the blame rests on the people of the town, who have shown a discreditable and utter lack of interest in the fund for the above object – not the few who are the mainstay of every public appeal, but the many who have neglected to contribute the mite that would have rendered a monument truly representative.[17]

Despite these difficulties, however, events had moved on sufficiently by July 1922 to enable an advertisement to be placed in the local press. In this the Mayor requested relatives, or those with pertinent knowledge of those from Swansea who had died on active service, to forward details to the Borough Architect. Such names as met the criteria could then be inscribed on the bronze plaques of the war memorial that was currently being erected despite the Appeal Fund still being some £2,500 short of the sum required. Local employers and other associations were asked to display details of the scheme at their places of work. This was a one-off opportunity since it was planned that the list of eligible names would be closed at the end of July.[18]

On 23 July 1923 a crowd of 20,000 thronged around Swansea's new memorial to her 'Glorious Dead' that was sited on the promenade overlooking the broad sweep of Swansea Bay and the Mumbles. The memorial took the form of a cenotaph surrounded by a Court of Memory that would eventually contain the bronze plaques on which would be inscribed the names of some 2,274 of Swansea's war dead. The number was set to rise even further since names were still coming in. The foundation stone had been laid a year earlier by the Earl Haig, victor of the Western Front, at the same time that he had been granted the freedom of the Borough of Swansea by a grateful Corporation and populace.

The bronze plaques were to be split into the various services such as the Army, Navy, Royal Flying Corps and a multitude of smaller units. The Army was further sub-divided into regiments and then into individual battalions within a regiment. In the case of the Welsh Regiment the spelling of the regimental name had been changed from 'Welsh' to the older style of 'Welch' in the 1920s and this was reflected on the plaques.

The plaques for the 14th Welch (the Swansea Battalion) contained the names of 187 men who fell while in its service. During the war, however, the battalion actually lost some 600 men killed and several times that number wounded. Some of these men were not from Swansea, but rather came from the surrounding area, including the towns of Neath, Port Talbot and Llanelli, amongst others. No doubt these men were remembered on the local war memorials in their own home towns.

Another factor was that after Mametz Wood, replacements and reinforcements for the battalion tended to come from further afield. This was partly due to the authorities rather belatedly recognizing the risks of committing large numbers of men from close knit communities in a single action. Additionally, relatives of the deceased had to apply for a name to be added to the plaques. In some cases, through oversight or other, possibly more personal reasons, it is possible that some eligible names were simply not put forward.

The unveiling of the cenotaph was performed by a hero of the Battle of the Falklands, Admiral Sir F.C. Doveton Sturdee who, the local newspaper reported, told the throng that:

> *...they were there to recognise the great services rendered by the men of Swansea to the Empire. It was a most solemn occasion, the unveiling of a memorial like that. It did not mean merely stone or marble, but it represented the hearts of the people...referring to those who had lost their near and dear ones, he hoped that time had by now somewhat alleviated the pain. In any case they could observe a sense of proportion. The loss to the Empire during the war was 900,000, and a million and a half would carry the marks of it to their graves. But the future was theirs.*

Following prayers and a benediction, Alderman Owen, on behalf of the War Memorial Committee, asked the Mayor (Alderman D.J. Davies) to formally accept the memorial into the care of the Council. The Welsh national anthem was sung and a large wreath was laid by the Mayor at the foot of the cenotaph, with other wreaths then being laid in succession.

Though the proceedings were generally deemed as being suitably impressive, there were several matters that nevertheless caused concern. The promised seating for thirty-one disabled or limbless ex-servicemen was not, in fact, provided, meaning that twenty-eight of them were forced to stand throughout the ceremony. As the memorial was thronged at the end of the service, thirty female wreath layers had great difficulty in getting to the cenotaph in order that they could lay their wreaths. Indeed, having finally completed their task with some difficulty, such was the crush that several tributes were accidentally

Mumbles Pier and the Mumbles train. The dedication of the Cenotaph (left) was disturbed by the train adhering noisily to its usual timetable.
Dave Westron

trodden underfoot. The quiet solemnity of the proceedings was also broken as the Mumbles train rumbled noisily past on its usual route, and following its usual timetable.[19]

The unveiling of the war memorial also reminded local officials and the public that the colours of the Swansea Battalion were still held by the Council and were in fact hung behind the Mayor's chair in the Council Chamber. Men of the Swansea Battalion had gathered at St Gabriel's church for refreshments after the cenotaph ceremony and, after some discussion, it was agreed that a more fitting resting place for the colours would be in the local parish church of the town. If placed in St Mary's church there would be the added benefit of their being more readily viewable by the citizens of Swansea. Lieutenant Colonel J. H. Hayes, former commanding officer of the battalion, wrote to the Council setting out this view. The Council decided to refer to their files on the matter and deferred a decision for a considerable length of time.[20]

St Mary's Church, Swansea, where the battalion colours were eventually placed after a lengthy sojourn in the Guildhall. West Glamorgan Archive Service

By the tenth anniversary of the attack on Mametz Wood it is apparent that the local press, and presumably the public of Swansea, were somewhat unsure as to whether the achievements of the local men were, in fact, fully worthy of the praise that had previously been afforded them. In an editorial on 12 July 1926 the *South Wales Daily Post* reviewed the facts, such as they were known. It saw some significance in the fact that the Earl Haig, in his foreword to the history of the Welsh Division, ignored the capture of the wood in July 1916 and focussed instead on the actions at Pilckem Ridge in 1917 and the advance to victory in 1918. Any such doubts did not, however, prevent the anniversary being marked in Swansea by a British Legion organized Mametz Memorial Service at the Albert Hall, held before a huge crowd.

On 10 July 1930, seven years after Lieutenant Colonel Hayes had requested that the Council place the battalion colours in the parish church of St Mary's, the handing over ceremony finally took place. The Mayor of Swansea, Councillor A. Lovell, handed the colours to Lieutenant Colonel Hayes who, in turn, presented them to the Reverend W.T. Havard, vicar of Swansea. A good smattering of former officers of the battalion was present at the gathering, including Messrs Milbourne Williams, Bellingham, Strange and R.P. Williams.

The colours had been hung in the Council Chamber for eleven years and, it was stated, the Council Chamber would be the poorer without them. Mr David Davies was reported as saying that 10 July:

> ...should be sacred in the town for all time; it should be sacred because they reached a higher point in their career historically than ever before. These colours should be reverenced by the present generation as a symbol of the bravery and sacrifice of the men who fell in France and other countries...he knew what

The laying up of the Colours. South Wales Daily Post

> *Swansea did and what Mametz meant to the future, and children born and unborn would look back remembering that their fathers or grandfathers fought at Mametz Wood.*[21]

At the church Hayes recalled that it was at about this time (6.00 p.m.), fourteen years earlier that the Swansea Battalion had finished the biggest thing it ever did. It did many things afterwards he said, but the capture of Mametz Wood was its biggest challenge. The Reverend Havard stated that:

> *...there were those who would criticise the ceremony in which they were taking part, those who were only too ready to ascribe to them on an occasion like that militaristic motives. But they recalled with pride and thanksgiving that the borough of Swansea supplied so many men, who rallied voluntarily to the colours, and many of whom never returned. They were inclined to forget the memory of those men to whom they owed so much.*

Reverend Havard was well qualified to speak on such matters. He had actually been at Mametz Wood with the Welsh Division and had been awarded a Military Cross for his service during the war. At a 'deeply impressive' service in commemoration of the battle held a few days after the handing over of the colours, he commented:

> *I take great pride in the fact that I was there myself...(the division) was the cream of Welsh manhood and represented something very real and an integral*

part of the life of Wales...I remember that at the time of war there was the impression at home that all soldiers on the battlefield were angels. We are not angels. Neither are we, on the other hand, the vilified creatures that we are made to appear in many recent books. Every sensible man knows that soldiers were neither angels nor brutes, but just ordinary men, who, in the hour of need offered their service, hoping that providence would bring them home again to a land of peace.[22]

If, even as soon as 1930, some veterans felt that the specific deeds of Swansea's own battalion were being gradually forgotten, the memory of the war in general still appeared strong in the town. This is evidenced by the 'In Memoriam' column of the *South Wales Daily Post* for 11 November 1930. This contained over twenty entries from local businesses and other organizations in remembrance of their members who had fallen in the conflict. The names included the GPO, Swansea, the Graigola Merthyr Company, the Midland Bank, the Swansea Gas Light Company, the British Mannesman Tube Company, Weaver & Co., David Evans & Co., and the Old Boys of the National School. Other entries related to individual servicemen who had died in various theatres of war during the conflict.

The Swansea Battalion had been a 'service battalion' in that it had been raised essentially for the duration of the war and once that task was successfully concluded, the unit was soon disbanded. This appears to have had an adverse effect on its ability to re-muster its old comrades for post war reunions. Indeed, February 1931 saw only the third annual reunion dinner. This was held at the Central Hotel, Swansea and was presided over by Lieutenant Colonel Milbourne Williams who told the gathering:

It appears to me...that the younger generation which is growing up treats all connected with war time with a sort of contemptuous indifference, is rather inclined to look upon those who took part in the war as suffering from a rather lower mentality than theirs.

He went on:

To talk of the monotony of the trench life, its routine broken by brief attacks, its pleasures looked forward to with delight – a decent meal, a warm bath, a few hours unbroken sleep...these and the never ceasing work carried out in extreme danger, and great nervous tension, and absolutely unbelievable physical discomforts, were really war...it was a marvellous exhibition of gallantry and 'sticking it out'.[23]

Others attending included A.V. Sinclair, J.S. Strange, W.H. Fisher and H.F. Strawford, who acted as Honorary Secretary and organized this and other events. Strawford worked in the family business of George Williams and Co., book and newspaper distributors. A sometime member of Swansea County Borough Council he had the misfortune to lose an election in the year that he would have become Mayor, thus missing out on the honour. He worked tirelessly on behalf of his old comrades.

The fifth reunion dinner was held at the Central Hotel, Swansea and was attended by a contingent of former officers and men that included J.H. Hayes, Milbourne Williams, A.V. Sinclair, R.K. Bellingham and S.G. Johns. Also among the gathering was Sergeant William Callaghan MM who, no doubt, enjoyed the main course of pork or beef and especially the 'Old Boys' ' pudding. Toasts were made to 'The King', 'The

Officers and guests at the 1931 dinner. South Wales Daily Post
Old times remembered. Attendees at the 1931 dinner. South Wales Daily Post

...... down to the reunion dinner at the Central

The Swansea Battalion.

14th (Service) Battalion

The Welsh Regiment.

"Gwell Angau na Chywilydd."

FIFTH ANNUAL

RE-UNION DINNER

HELD AT THE

CENTRAL HOTEL

ON

Thursday, February 9th, 1933.

... Menu ...

CLEAR JULIENNE

THICK MOCK TURTLE

FRIED FILLET SOLE — TARTARE SAUCE

ROAST PORK & APPLE SAUCE
OR
ROAST SIRLOIN & YORKSHIRE PUDDING

VEGETABLES IN SEASON

FRUIT SALAD & CREAM

APPLE PIE & CUSTARD

"OLD BOYS" PUDDING

CHEESE & BISCUITS

COFFEE

30 Seconds Silence

"They shall not grow old, as we that are left grow old.
Age shall not weary them, nor the years condemn.
At the going down of the Sun and in the morning
We will remember them."

... Toasts ...

"THE KING."

"THE SWANSEA BATTALION"

Proposed by Lieut. Col. E. Helme
Response by Lieut. Col. J. H. Hay

"THE VISITORS"

Proposed by Mr. W. E. Hodges
Response by His Worship the Mayor of Swansea
Councillor Dan Evans.
S. G. Johns, Esq.

*Menu card for the 1933
Battalion reunion dinner.*
Shirley Ferguson

William Joseph Callaghan pictured outside Aberdare Police Station (c.1939) in his 'Specials' police uniform. Shirley Ferguson

William Joseph Callaghan pictured in 1959. Shirley Ferguson

Visitors' and, of course, 'The Swansea Battalion'.

William Callaghan had been born in Merthyr Tydfil on 18 May 1891. His mother had died in childbirth and William and his older brother Cornelius spent some time at a children's home at Aberdare. His father having remarried, Cornelius eventually rejoined the family whilst William decided to stay at the orphanage. At the age of twelve he began to work underground in the mining industry near Aberdare.

He enlisted in the army following the outbreak of war and was eventually posted to the Swansea Battalion. He served at Mametz Wood and also saw service in the Ypres salient. He received shrapnel wounds for his trouble in 1918, earned the Military Medal and was eventually discharged to resume working in the mining industry. He became a mine fireman and leader of the mine rescue party. During the Second World War he enlisted as a Special Constable and reached the rank of Inspector. Leaving the mines, he pursued a career in the insurance industry with the Co-operative Wholesale Society and retired in 1956. Married with three children he died in his ninetieth year.[24]

The 1934 reunion dinner was staged at the Mackworth Hotel, Swansea. The event was presided over by Captain R.K. Bellingham, the principal guest of honour being Lieutenant Colonel E.E. Helme, DSO. A minute's silence was observed and 'For the

Fallen' by Laurence Binyon was solemnly intoned. Helme expressed regret that both Brigadier General T.O. Marden and Lieutenant Colonel Hayes were unable to attend, due to illness, but was pleased to report on Colonel Benson, who was still in good health despite his advancing years. Indeed, he told the gathering, they had dined together on Christmas night 1933. Captain Bellingham referred to the difficulties that many former battalion members were experiencing in finding employment. He felt that the spirit of comradeship evident at the gathering would help see them all through what were very difficult times.

Harold Frank Strawford (centre) with his brother Arthur (left) and Stanley (right). Another brother, Ralph, was killed in action in 1918. Peter Wright

He added that the next generation should not forget the sacrifices undertaken by those present on their behalf. To this end he hoped that the history of the battalion could be compiled and, given the cost implications, that Councillor W. D. Rees, Deputy Mayor of Swansea, would have a word with his council colleagues on the matter. He also thanked Lieutenant H.F. Strawford, an old comrade, who had again arranged the event, acted as secretary and who was generally indefatigable in his efforts to keep the Old Comrades Association vibrant.[25]

Following the dinner Milbourne Bransby Williams wrote to the local newspaper from the south of France, where he was staying. He praised T.O. Marden's history of the Welsh Regiment but noted that a battalion history must, of necessity, be more detailed than that of an entire regiment. He was in possession of a number of papers and records relating to the Swansea Battalion's activities and would be pleased to hear from individuals who held other items with a view to future publication. He echoed Captain Bellingham's view that the council, as the 'father' of the battalion should, perhaps, take the lead in what he was sure would be a very worthy enterprise.[26]

The Mackworth Hotel was again the venue for the 1935 reunion dinner and on that occasion both T.O. Marden and J.H. Hayes were able to be present, their attendance prompting a record turnout. Tickets were priced at three shillings each, though a number of 'free' tickets had been made available to unemployed old comrades through the generosity of a number of donors.

Marden commented that it was a great pleasure to come down among the men alongside whom he had fought, adding that:

186

...the 14th Welsh was a splendid battalion and they had a splendid commanding officer in Colonel Hayes. As the Swansea Battalion, they had a great advantage in being drawn from one place. They felt that they had the honour of Swansea in their hands. They were not going to let Swansea down – and they never did.

Colonel Hayes added that when he joined the battalion he felt that it was the best in the brigade and he thought that it still retained that distinction when he eventually left it for a higher command. He noted that many old comrades were not present due to the cost of attendance at a time of high unemployment. He wanted those men to be encouraged to attend future events. If they could not afford it themselves he stated that they could come as his guests. His generous offer was greeted with warm applause.[27]

By 1936 the memory of what the Swansea Battalion had endured at Mametz Wood still remained vivid in the minds of some. On the twentieth anniversary of the attack the 'In Memoriam' column of the *South Wales Evening Post* contained the following entry, placed by the Old Comrades' Association:

...in honoured memory of the Officers, N.C.O.s and men of the 14th Service Battalion, the Welsh Regiment who made the supreme sacrifice at Mametz Wood 10 July 1916.

The newspaper also reprinted some contemporary coverage of the action whilst pointing out that its sister publication, the *Herald of Wales* would, that week, contain a special article on Mametz Wood. One letter writing correspondent ('Veteran') was very grateful for the newspaper coverage stating:

...how grateful I feel to you for the indications that you intend publishing, for the benefit of younger generations, the story of Mametz Wood, the 20th anniversary of which falls on Friday. Voices are vocal today which were in school lessons when Mametz was fought. Their owners can have little idea what that battle meant to every town and hamlet in Wales. The other day I was in one of the most remote districts in Wales in an upland farm miles from anywhere. Here, one felt, the fever of the world was far away. And yet, in a place of honour on the wall of the parlour was a photograph of the only son, who was one of the slain at Mametz. The romance has passed away if, indeed, there ever was any. Mametz showed Wales the cost of war.[28]

On 13 July 1936, T.J. Norris, a surviving member of the Swansea Battalion wrote to the newspaper, paying his erstwhile comrades an eloquent and moving tribute:

Many, many pitched battles were fought in France during the last war, and I personally have taken part in a number, but whether or not Mametz Wood can claim the distinction many of us who took part jealously believe it can, I do not know.

Yet I, and I feel sure many hundreds of the 14th Welsh, recall, on each 10th of July, almost every little incident. This is something not frequently talked about that will go on until that day – let us hope it shall be on the anniversary – when each of us forego the material life, and join those good friends who lay along the banks of the sunken road – Death Valley.

What is there to forget about Mametz? Nothing. What is there to remember? Very much more than I care to record. If human endurance and the suffering of brave men is so small and matter-of-fact a thing, then to those who concur in this way of thought I say 'Forget'; but we who suffered and bled to achieve victory cannot forget the unorthodox gallantry of 'Swansea's Own' in their momentous task on that blistering day.

Can one forget the smiling, cigarette smoking mass of locals who sat on the slope overlooking the sunken road and woods, their faces lit up with the white flashes of exploding shells and myriads of star shells, and showed up undisturbed with the increasing dawn?

Was the alacrity of the well-ordered lines at the word 'Advance' so little to remember? Or the steady but determined march down the grassy slopes to the wood?

Tears of pride collected around my eyes when a blacked and limping soldier informed me: 'The boys are in!'

Did not the slaughter-house on the side of the slope along the sunken road leave any impression on the mind? The picture on the hill along the old German line behind Carnoy is worth a place in the perpetual memory of one who fought that day. I wish I were an artist so that I could paint this picture to be visible for all time. If someone would only tell the whole story from A to Z and omit nothing.

Also at this time the local press, that in 1926 had appeared to harbour some doubts about the level of success of the attack on Mametz Wood and by implication the part that the Swansea Battalion played in it, finally arrived at a clear opinion. Referring to the work of the Welsh Division, which included the Swansea Battalion, its editorial declared:

Never before has so great a body of men drawn from Wales been assembled in our authentic knowledge. Of the 29,380 casualties suffered by the division throughout the war, 4,193 were sustained at Mametz Wood, so that no other day's event has ever so sorely smitten the country.

The tactics may be open to strong criticism. The exact significance of the success – it may have been too belated to yield the rich result that was possible – has still to be disclosed. But there is no question but that for the Welsh Division, for all its severe losses, made a clean job of it. Mametz Wood was taken once and for all. There was no repetition of the ebb and flow that soaked Trones or Delville Woods in blood.[29]

In 1956 'J.R.J.' contributed a piece on the fortieth anniversary of the Mametz Wood attack and noted that even the youngest to participate in the attack was now approaching sixty years of age.[30] In 1966, on 10 July, the fiftieth anniversary of the Mametz Wood engagement, the *South Wales Evening Post* 'Roll of Honour' column displayed a poignant entry:

Swansea Battalion – In honoured memory of the Officers, N.C.O.s and Men who made the supreme sacrifice at Mametz Wood, July 10th 1916. From the few who are left.

The 'few who are left' included Charles Henry Mew, who had come out of Mametz Wood in July 1916 after having his wounds temporarily dressed by Lieutenant Strange and being ordered to retire. After recuperation in England Private Mew had been sent back out to the front though not to the Swansea Battalion. Instead he served with the

9th Battalion of the Royal Welsh Fusiliers and saw further action in the Ypres area.

On one occasion with the 9th Royal Welsh Fusiliers Private Mew and about eight others were sleeping in an underground shelter when a shell dropped on it, burying the men. Mew couldn't breathe at first but, clearing his airways, he spent some time cursing the Kaiser whilst others around him coughed, spluttered or prayed in the darkness. Eventually the men were dug out by their comrades. Private Mew was laid on the ground to recover his senses more fully. He had suffered fractured ribs and a contusion of the back and was sent back to Britain again.

The army had still not finished with Private Mew, however. After convalescing in Knowlesley Park Convalescent Home, he was sent to Limerick in Ireland for a short period. Here he recalled being spat at by local youths on his way to the train station. Joining the 17th Royal Welsh Fusiliers, Mew then returned to France in 1918.

Private Mew was still alive in 1974, when he was living in the Clase area of Swansea. At that time he was interviewed by the then city archivist of Swansea, Dr John Alban, and those taped memories form the basis of the information provided about Private Mew and his eventful life in the army.[31]

Captain John Stanley Strange had been captured by the Germans during the disastrous attack on Aveluy Wood in May 1918, where elements of the Swansea Battalion had the misfortune to be shelled by their own artillery, suffering a number of casualties as a result. Released from captivity in December 1918 Captain Strange was still in Swansea in 1930 when he contributed comments on the attack on Mametz Wood to the Official War historian.

Corporal Colin Charles Thomas of Pontarddulais, near Swansea, had been wounded at Richebourg in February 1916 and again at Mametz Wood in July 1916. After rest and recuperation at a hospital in Lancashire he had returned to the front but this time with the King's Scottish Light Infantry. Demobilized in 1919 he received a War Gratuity of £24-10s, which would be increased by a further £1 provided he returned his military great coat to the proper authorities.[32]

Lieutenant Colonel John Higson Hayes, former Commanding Officer of the battalion, attended several reunions or other ceremonies that involved the old battalion. In 1930 he also contributed comments to the Official History and he was, at that time, living in Market-Drayton, in England.

George Frank Brooke was another former commander of the battalion. He had returned from Cape Town at the outbreak of war and was awarded a DSO in 1917, a Bar in 1917 and a second Bar in 1918. At the end of the war he returned to South Africa where, after a period spent ostrich farming, he became the agent for the White Horse whisky company. In 1920 his father, Frank Theophilus, was murdered in Dublin, allegedly by members of the Michael Collins' gang.

George Brooke retained many of the friendships he had built up on active service, regularly meeting with Thomas Marden, Geoffrey Brewis, 'Puggy' Daniel and 'Birdie' Partridge. His sons both attained high rank within the regiment, Frank eventually becoming Colonel whilst Oliver commanded the 1st Battalion in Italy in the Second World War. George Brooke died in 1966.

Richard Thomas Lyons, the Irish-born Swansea policeman and sometime bayonet instructor to the battalion, attained the rank of Second Lieutenant and eventually

Richard Thomas Lyons in 1918. Kae Warr

resumed his career in the police force. He went onwards and upwards. In 1919 he was promoted to Sergeant at Aberdare and also served in that capacity at Kenfig Hill. The quiet life seemed to totally elude Dick Lyons, however. In 1923 an armed gang raided the offices of the Glantawe Tinworks at Pontardawe and, quickly on the scene, Sergeant Lyons chased two of the culprits.

Despite being shot at during the chase, he apprehended one of the villains after a desperate struggle. A few days later he spotted the other man and, following a motor cycle chase in the Bryncoch area of Neath, caught him as well. I suspect that for a veteran of Mametz Wood and the Ypres salient, a deadly handgun was not too daunting a prospect. The villains were also decidedly lucky that Sergeant Lyons had had to surrender his rifle and bayonet on demobilization!

He was further promoted to Inspector in 1933 and, following the outbreak of the Second World War, he captured an escaped German pilot. From 1944 he was a Superintendent and served at Gowerton and Bridgend before retiring in 1953. At that time he was awarded the Police Medal in the Queen's New Year honours list. He died in 1973, his funeral being afforded full police honours.[33]

Sergeant William Haydn David won the Military Medal for his actions in the raid on the High Command Redoubt in November 1916. On his return to Wales he resumed his employment at the tin plate works in Taibach, Port Talbot. Regrettably, the heat from the furnaces aggravated his war wounds and he was forced to leave the works. A period of unemployment followed during which time Mrs David assisted the family finances by playing a piano accompaniment to silent films in the Port Talbot cinemas.

During the 1930s Haydn was involved in amateur dramatics in the Port Talbot area. In one play he was required to grapple with Leo Lloyd, who played his adversary. Such was the realism that Haydn brought to the scene as he gradually gained the upper hand, that one lady in the audience, who knew Haydn and shared his Taibach roots, suddenly stood up and exclaimed 'Good Old Taibach!' For a moment Haydn and Lloyd peered into the footlights. Then, like actors in the best theatrical tradition, they continued the on-stage struggle.

His daughter, Mrs Connie Evans of Skewen, near Neath, recalls her father standing at a bowl of water, no bathroom being provided in the house at that time, and bathing himself. The wound scars to his left shoulder and the centre of his back were still clearly visible. Indeed, she could place her fist in the wound depression.

During the Second World War Haydn acted as a drill instructor at the local steel works. He was a well-known figure in the area, frequently wearing a large brimmed 'cowboy' style hat around the district. He finally obtained employment as a blast furnace water man at the firm of Guest, Keen and Baldwins, working there until his retirement in 1964. He died in 1968.[34]

Private Edward George Hughes suffered a severe head wound while serving with the battalion and been taken as a prisoner of war to Germany. Returning home after the war he entered the licensed house trade. He ran, at various times, the Maesrhydia Inn at Hirwaun, the Welsh Harp at Trecynon, very appropriately the ex-Servicemen's Club in Aberaman, the Conservative Club in Aberdare and, finally, the Fleur-de-Lys in Kettering, Northants before retiring. He died in 1960.

A sad case is that of Dyson Brock Williams, who had been wounded during his service with the battalion and had also earned a Mention in Dispatches, a Military Cross and a Distinguished Service Order. He came from a well established Swansea family. His father, Morgan Bransby Williams, had been a railway engineer and had worked for a time in Russia. He had used his wealth to build an imposing family home in the Killay area of Swansea. Killay House became a popular venue for the better classes of Swansea, with regular house parties and cricket matches being played on a pitch that was situated within the grounds.

Morgan Bransby Williams died in 1914 and so did not see four of his five sons join the colours. Aubrey served in the Machine Gun Corps whilst Caryl, the youngest, served with Atlantic convoy ships. Dyson and Milbourne were both commissioned into the Swansea Battalion. George was in India at the outbreak of the war and it seems that his work as an engineer in that part of the Empire was judged more important than his being allowed to return home to enlist.

Dyson Brock Williams returned from the war mentally scarred by his experiences and became prone to depression. He lost money in gambling and unsuccessful business ventures and eventually his solicitors' practice in Swansea was closed. Leaving Swansea he went to work for a London based boxing promoter, having himself been a friend of the French boxer Georges Carpentier. The move proved less successful than he had envisaged and he continued to suffer from financial problems. In April 1922 he committed suicide by gassing himself at his London office.[35]

No 'Roll of Honour' entry relating to the Swansea Battalion appears to have been made in 1976, the sixtieth anniversary of the capture of Mametz Wood, though a brief account of the action by Private Ned Bevan, then aged eighty-six years, did appear in the local press on 13 July 1976. This prompted a follow up item by Mrs Connie Evans, the daughter of the late Sergeant Haydn David. It seems likely that after this time any others who remained alive among a dwindling band of Swansea Battalion veterans gradually faded from public view and memory. Time had inevitably reduced their numbers in a manner that the Kaiser's army could never have hoped to equal. With their final passing the memory of the battalion, its men, and its deeds, vanished from the consciousness of most of the people of Swansea.

Whilst during and after the war various Council and other dignitaries had paid tribute to the battalion that they had helped to raise, and had repeatedly promised that its deeds would never be forgotten, little seems to have been done then or since in a practical sense to visibly perpetuate its memory. The cenotaph has stood on the seafront since 1923 as a monument to all who hailed from Swansea and fell in the service of their country. But, as far as 'Swansea's Own' Battalion was concerned, there was to be no prominent, permanent memorial. Perhaps whilst words were easy, actions were somewhat more difficult, especially at times of recurring economic

Part of the large crowd at the dedication. Trevor Tasker

depression in the post-war years. The simple option of naming new streets after significant military actions seems not to have been pursued. Though Swansea has an 'Inkerman Street' and a 'Balaclava Road' and more latterly a 'Normandy Road' there was apparently no local determination to see a 'Mametz Way' or a 'Pilckem Place', let alone a statue or other form of major memorial. The outbreak of the Second World War would have acted as a further factor in relegating the deeds of the battalion to little more than a distant memory in the minds of most of the population of Swansea.

In France, by contrast, the long-held dream of Sergeant Tom Price, a veteran who had served alongside the Swansea Battalion with the 2nd Rhonddas, finally came to fruition in 1987. Tom had long yearned for a permanent memorial to be sited at Mametz Wood in memory of all who fought with the 38th Welsh Division. A fund-raising committee under the able chairmanship of Harold Evans of the South Wales Branch of the Western Front Association raised the large sum required by public subscription and David Peterson of St Clears in Carmarthenshire was commissioned to sculpt the monument.

At an impressive and emotional ceremony in 1987 the result of his toil was revealed in the unveiling of a magnificent Welsh red dragon, set atop a plinth. The dragon glares defiantly at Mametz Wood, one of its claws grasping a piece of German barbed wire found whilst the foundations for the plinth were being excavated. With the wings of a bat, the claws of a lion, the neck, ears and mane of a horse, the head of an alligator, the tongue and tail of a serpent and the horns of a bull, the dragon clearly embodies considerable fighting prowess. This is meant to symbolize the qualities of the Welsh Division, comprising as it did the cream of Welsh manhood.

The nine ton sandstone plinth is carved with the badges of the three infantry regiments of the Welsh Division; the Welsh, the Royal Welsh Fusiliers and the South Wales Borderers. It is inscribed:

> *We revere their endeavours*
> *May we continue to remember*

The dragon atop its plinth. Author

With several veterans attending, a large crowd, a Welsh choir and representatives of the Royal Regiment of Wales and the French Army present, the hymn O Valiant Hearts was sung before Jesu Lover of my Soul, the very hymn that the men of the Welsh Division had sung with great passion as they tensely waited in the trenches before attacking the wood over seventy years earlier.

One who was not there, however, was Sergeant Tom Price, the original driving force behind the plan for a memorial. Tom had sadly passed away in the previous December and it was poignantly left to his grandson to lay a wreath on his behalf. This was judged by many, if not all, to be the most moving part of the ceremony.

In Swansea on 10 July 2003, this being coincidentally the eighty-seventh anniversary of the Swansea Battalion's efforts at Mametz Wood, the Leader of Swansea Council and current Lord Mayor, Councillor Lawrence Bailey, announced that £20,000 would be made available by the Council to complement the fundraising efforts of the local Merchant Navy Association. This would enable a memorial costing about £65,000 to be commissioned from local sculptor Phillip Chatfield in memory of those Swansea men and women who had lost their lives at sea in the service of their country. Councillor Bailey commented that it was a matter of some regret that Swansea did not have such a memorial to those who had provided such service. This is no doubt a very laudable action on the part of the Council and Mr Chatfield is an inspired choice, being a local man who has already produced a striking bust of Swansea's ill-fated Antarctic explorer, Edgar Evans.

However, after a lapse of almost ninety years since the Swansea Battalion was formed at the behest of the then Mayor, is it too late for members of the current Council to visibly honour the pledges that its predecessors so freely gave to the men who enlisted, that they would never be forgotten? It need not cost anything like £20,000; a street or mall name on one of Swansea's new developments would provide a long overdue link and reminder to a heroic chapter in Swansea's long history whilst even a modest plaque at the Dylan Thomas Centre would be better than nothing. It was in this building after all, at that time the town's Guildhall, that early recruits for the battalion signed up. Perhaps this book will act as a small reminder to those currently in public office, who understandably have little or no personal knowledge of the situation, of a debt that has not been fully settled and is now long overdue.

Notes

1. PRO/WO/95/2540.
2. PRO/WO/95/2559.
3. SWDP, 19 February 1919.
4. PRO/WO/95/2559.
5. SWDP, 27 February 1919.
6. SWDP, 16 April 1919.
7. SWDP, 26 May 1919.
8. SWDP, 3 June 1919.
9. SWDP, 25 October 1918.
10. SWDP, 19 September 1919.
11. SWDP, 7 April 1916.
12. SWDP, 27 December 1916.
13. SWDP, 13 March 1917.
14. SWDP, 3 April 1917.
15. SWDP, 14 August 1919.
16. SWDP, 14 July 1919.
17. SWDP, 9 November 1920.
18. SWDP, 26 July 1922.

19. SWDP, 23 July 1923.
20. SWDP, 1 August 1923.
21. SWDP, 11 July 1930.
22. SWDP, 15 July 1930.
23. *Herald of Wales*, 7 February 1931.
24. Information provided by Mrs Shirley Ferguson.
25. *South Wales Evening Post*, 2 February 1934.
26. SWEP, 10 February 1934
27. SWEP, 11 February 1935.
28. SWEP, 9 July 1936.
29. SWEP, 10 July 1936.
30. SWEP, 10 July 1956.
31. WGAS/Mew.
32. Thomas.
33. Warr.
34. Evans.
35. SWEP, 30 June 2003 article by Jill Forwood.

CHAPTER TWELVE

The Price of Victory

In the years immediately following the end of the Great War both the men who had fought, and their commanders, were much revered. When the Earl Haig visited Swansea in 1922 not only did he unveil the foundation stone of the cenotaph but he was also granted the freedom of the County Borough of Swansea by a thankful citizenship. He was greeted with great acclaim by a large gathering of ex-soldiers.

How can we reconcile this contemporary image of Haig as the conquering hero with the more modern day version, in some quarters at least, of 'Butcher Haig' and his bungling, callous generals? Were the men indeed 'Lions led by Donkeys', a remark that apparently has its real origins in the Franco-Prussian War, but is now regularly applied to the British Army in the Great War?

There can be no doubt that, at the outbreak of war, the technological advances that had spawned the rapid firing machine gun and a vastly improved artillery arm had tipped the scales of battle firmly against the infantry, the bedrock of all armies up to the middle of the twentieth century. Faced with these weapons and, for much of the Great War at least, the absence of effective armoured forces and air power, the infantry attack was almost always doomed to run the risk of heavy casualties when assaulting prepared defences.

It is a little known fact that most casualties of the Great War were the result of artillery fire. This could reach the soldier whether he be in no man's land in the act of attacking, in the front line trenches, in the support trenches or, indeed, even as far back as the reserve trenches. Machine-gun or rifle fire, by contrast, was of a much shorter range and the men were only exposed to it for relatively short (though admittedly deadly) periods, such as when making an attack or working in no man's land.

Field Marshal Sir Douglas Haig. Taylor Library

Given these facts, would it have been better to merely remain in one's trenches and not to attack at all? Personally, I do not think that this was a viable option at the time. Germany had violated Belgian neutrality and invaded France. Britain was linked to Belgium by a treaty and to France by a largely unspoken attachment, based on a mutual desire to restrain the growing strength of the German Empire. Assuming that the cause is just, it is usually good, I think, to stand by your allies in circumstances such as these.

Most of Belgium and a large part of northern France lay under the heel of an oppressor who, left unchecked, might in time expand his territorial ambitions towards mainland Britain. The Belgians and the French had little option other than to defend, and try to recover, their homelands. Can we imagine Winston Churchill in the Second

World War accepting a lasting German presence on British soil on the basis that it would be very costly in human terms to evict them by force?

A book of this nature is not the place to debate at length whether the commanding officers were indeed butchers or bunglers or whether they were rather men, thrust into unfamiliar positions of responsibility for which some of them were hopelessly unsuited. A few brief comments are, however, in order on this issue.

Modern historians seem to be moving towards the analysis that as the war progressed the British Army did indeed learn from its experiences as well as its mistakes, though views, almost ninety years afterwards, are still very divided on this.

There can be no doubt that the British Army, that at the outbreak of war could muster only six divisions, suffered from the rapid and necessary promotion of men to meet the needs of an army that expanded to fifty-six divisions on the Western Front alone by July 1916. A total of only eighteen brigadiers were required for the six pre-war divisions, whilst the 1916 requirement was 168. Many of those promoted to these posts simply lacked the battle skills and experience necessary to effectively lead those for whom they were responsible. If some of them were indeed bunglers, it should not be found too surprising and some sympathy is due to them. They were frequently propelled into positions far in excess of their capabilities by desperate circumstances that were totally beyond their control.

Terrible though it may seem, we should also recognize that at the turn of the century the real value of human life was not as well respected as it is today. The heavy industries of the day were dangerous places to work and regularly killed members of the workforce by way of industrial accidents. These were, to a degree, seen as being almost necessary if 'progress' was to be continued. Health and safety legislation was, at first, resisted and was, in any event, a long time in coming. Thus the deaths of a few

The Cenotaph in Whitehall and the focus of the nation's mourning for its lost children.
Taylor Library

workers did not matter that much, provided that production was not unduly affected. A similar attitude could be displayed by some (but not all) army commanders towards the lives of their soldiers, placed in mortal danger in the cause of their country. Thus, given the mores of the time, it is likely that casualties would often be more readily accepted than would be the case today, provided that the objective was achieved.

The Swansea Battalion was not in any way a 'special' battalion. Like many others it was formed in a wave of patriotic fervour although, at the time, the local recruiting authorities apparently found the enthusiasm to enlist not quite as evident in all quarters as they would have wished. The battalion was duly formed, however, and during its service took part in many significant actions, the most important being that of the capture of Mametz Wood in 1916.

Overall the battalion was better than some, as good as others, and inferior to the very best. I think it true to say that it learned how best to fight the war from bitter and painful experience, a trait it no doubt shared with countless other units. In time, with mounting losses due to death and injury, the makeup of the battalion changed and the local element became, inevitably, much reduced. This was true of all formations.

At the end of almost three years' fighting in France and Flanders, the battalion, which had started out for the front with less than 1,300 men, had lost over 600 killed and probably at least twice that number wounded. Indeed, some of the wounded had later returned to the front to be wounded again or killed.

Many of the dead did not even have the dignity of a marked grave, their bodies being lost in the fighting or found to be unidentifiable on recovery.

We must be mindful of the effect of revisionist histories of the war who have, in many instances, overturned what was once the long accepted understanding of events. This is natural and sound, provided that it is based on a full and proper analysis of the evidence. Some historians came to see the men who fought these battles as mere pawns in a higher, more deadly game, and terms such as 'the lost generation', 'lambs to the slaughter' and 'cannon fodder' are routinely applied today to those who fought in the Great War.

However, is this how the men who fought really saw it at the time? During my research it has become apparent to me that either very few men left a written record of their thoughts and experiences or, if they did, they have apparently been sadly mislaid or destroyed. I certainly struggled to come across any surviving firsthand accounts. The ones I did find (often in the newspapers of the day) naturally tended to focus on the actions they took part in with very little, if indeed any, comment on their general feelings towards the war or its conduct.

The author Malcolm Brown has written extensively on the Somme and the Western Front in general. In the contemporary writings of both officers and other ranks he found surprisingly little that challenged the general conduct of the war or indicated that the men at the front saw themselves in any way as victims. Naturally, many of these men were fated to be killed or injured, and some military objectives were only to be taken, if taken at all, at great cost. But this was usually seen at the time as being the price that had to be paid, if the invader was to be ejected from friendly soil. They would have undoubtedly complained about some of the plans that they were forced to follow but it is likely that most felt that they were fighting in a just cause.

At a memorial service held in Swansea for Sergeant Stanley O. John, who was not a member of the Swansea Battalion, the congregation heard tributes from his Commanding Officer, two comrades, friends and his former employer. At the end of the service the congregation:

...asked the Lord to raise up men of like spirit in their churches, and all churches in the town and country so that God's Kingdom might come with all its power and glory... .[1]

This occurred in October 1917, long after the sacrifices on the Somme and with the losses of the Passchendaele offensive presumably still fresh in the minds of those present, and the end of the war apparently no nearer in sight. Nevertheless, the tone of the proceedings does not appear to reveal any feeling of futile sacrifice as regards the progress of the war and the need for more men.

A similar tale appeared the following month when it was reported that the mother of the late Private S. Gordon of Sketty, Swansea, (again, not of the Swansea Battalion) felt:

...honoured by such a goodly company of heroes, and posterity will feel proud that a small suburban district bore so much of the brunt in shaping the destiny of the Empire and punishing the Huns...[2]

Private Gordon was reported as being the 39th Sketty lad to fall in the conflict.

I think it a great pity that men who, over the years, saw their wartime service become almost the subject of pity should perhaps come to regard themselves in some way as victims. They did not do this out of a sense of self-pity, but probably over time came to merely unconsciously reflect what seemed to be the modern consensus on the conduct of the war and their role in it. This distorted perspective overlooks the great courage displayed by these gallant men, many of whom had responded voluntarily to their country's call at a time of crisis. Their bravery, determination and stoicism in the face of a terrible and prolonged trial are far more deserving of our gratitude and admiration than of our pity.

The early volunteers enlisted in answer to their country's call. They went to help 'Little Belgium' and France fight a powerful oppressor, as well as to uphold the obligations of their country to their allies in a time of extreme crisis. The cost of meeting and defeating this threat was enormous, both in terms of lives lost, human suffering and property destroyed.

But they did indeed prevail, and finally ejected the invader, just as they had set out to do in those heady days of patriotic fervour in 1914. The people of France and Belgium had themselves suffered terribly and, whilst appreciating the sacrifices made by others on their behalf, they could not help but rejoice at their newly restored freedom. I doubt if they thought of the sacrifices as being 'futile', terrible though they were. It was certainly not the fault of the 'Pals' battalions that an altogether more dangerous threat to peace would arise from an impoverished Germany within the short space of fifteen years. That threat, too, would eventually be squared up to by the British and their allies and seen off in the cause of liberty and freedom, again at a very heavy cost.

I will leave the final word not to a general, or a captain, or a sergeant; not to a corporal, or an other-ranker or a politician. I will, instead, quote the words placed in the South Wales Daily Post 'In Memoriam' column on 10 July 1917, by the widow of Corporal William Henry T. Phelps, of Montana Place, Swansea and late of the Swansea Battalion. Corporal Phelps had enlisted in 1914 in answer to the Mayor of Swansea's appeal. He had been killed in the attack on Mametz Wood. The general sentiment expressed is, in my view, appropriate to both those battalion members who died, as well as those who served, suffered, but luckily survived. The notice concluded:

   In Manhood's prime he nobly died
   That wrong should not the right o'er ride... .
Could anyone be unhappy to have such an epitaph applied to them?

Notes

1. SWDP, 29 October 1917.
2. SWDP, 19 November 1917.

1914 1918
TO THE IMMORTAL MEMORY OF THE MEMBERS OF THE SWANSEA CRICKET & FOOTBALL CLUB WHO GAVE THEIR LIVES FOR THEIR COUNTRY IN THE GREAT WAR

B. BOYS	G. T. GREGOR	E. JONES
G. T. BENSON	D. HOWELLS	B. R. LEWIS
C. B. DAVIES	J. H. HOWELLS	J. MORRIS
W. A. S. DAVIES	G. HOWELLS	J. S. REID
W. A. EDWARDS	E. R. JEFFORD	D. ROBOTHAN
D. E. CHILES EVANS	D. R. JENKINS	A. ROSSER
L. P. GODFREY	L. JENKINS	D. A. SANDBROOK
W. S. GOFF	O. JENKINS	B. WILLIAMS

The Swansea Cricket and Football Club memorial. It includes the names of Swansea Battalion members W.A.S. Davies, L.P. Godfrey, G. Howells, A. Rosser and D.A. Sandbrook. Patriotism came with a very high price. A. Thomas

Select Bibliography

Manuscript Sources
War Office Records, National Archives, London
Town Clerk's Records, (Battalion Formation Committee), West Glamorgan Archive
    Service, Swansea

Periodicals
Herald of Wales
Rhyl Guardian
South Wales Daily Post
South Wales Evening Post

Secondary Sources
Alban, J.R., *The Formation of the Swansea Battalion 1914-1915*, Gower volume 25,
    1974
Balchin, W.G.V., (Ed.) *Swansea and its Region*, Swansea, 1971
Brown, M., *The Imperial War Museum Book of the Somme*, Pan Books, 1997
    The Imperial War Museum Book of 1918 – Year of Victory, Pan Books, 1999
    The Imperial War Museum Book of the Western Front, Pan Books 2001
Gilbert, M., *First World War*, Harper Collins, 1995
Graves, R., *Goodbye to All That*, Penguin, 1960
Griffith, W., *Up to Mametz*, Gliddon Books, 1988
Hughes, C., *Mametz: Lloyd George's 'Welsh Army' at the Battle of the Somme*,
    Orion Press, 1982
Jones, D., *In Parenthesis*, Faber and Faber, 1963
Marden, T.O., *The History of the Welch Regiment, Part II, 1914-1918*, Cardiff,
    1932
Munby, J.E., (Ed.) *A History of the 38th (Welsh) Division*, Hugh Rees, 1920
Renshaw, M., *Mametz Wood*, Leo Cooper, 1999
Richards, F., *Old Soldiers Never Die*. Publisher/date not stated
Sassoon, S., *Memoirs of an Infantry Officer*, Faber and Faber, 1997
Steel, N., and Hart, P., *Passchendaele – the Sacrificial Ground*, Cassell, 2003
Westlake, R., *British Battalions on the Somme*, Leo Cooper, 1998

14th (Service) Battalion The Welsh Regiment
Next of kin of men proceeding overseas
December 1915

West Glamorgan Archive Service TC/26/40

1.

	Rank and Name	Relationship	Next of Kin	2/12/15.
19	R.S.M. Alexander C.	Wife	Mrs Jane Alexander,21,Old Road, Huntley,Aberdeenshire.	
19	C.S.M. Thomas.W.C.	Wife	Mrs Thomas,23,Barsbury Terrace Hafod,Swansea.	
15	C.Q.M.S. Norman.E.	Mother	Mrs Selina Norman, 6 Pleasant Street,Swansea.	
3	Sergt. Batchelor.F.A.	Wife	Mrs Eva Batchelor,4,Hall Bank Terrace,Mumbles,Glamorgan.	
9	" Bidder.W.	Mother	Mrs Emma Bidder,61,Terrace Road Swansea.	
8	" Carter.G.A.	Wife	Mrs Jane Carter,43,Vera Road, Clydach, Near Swansea.	
3	" Hopkins.D.A.	Mother	Annie Hopkins,6,Alberta Place, Penarth.	
0	" John.A.L.	Wife	Mrs Isabell John,10 Margaret Terrace,Swansea.	
8	" Lilley.D.	Wife	Mrs Alice Lilley, 3 Bryngolew Terrace,Sketty,Swansea.	
2	" Morley.H.	Mother	Mrs Elizabeth Morley,Coedbach, Pontardulais.	
9	" Stansbury.T.	Wife	Mrs Eliza Jane Stansbury, 52 Shelly Crescent,Swansea.	
4	" Thomas.J.H.	Wife	Mrs Mary Thomas,149 Eaton Road, Brynhyfyyd, Swansea.	
0	" Williams.S.J.C.	Mother	Mrs Edith Williams,11,Bridge Street,Swansea.	
3	Corporal Clements.C.J.	Wife	Mrs Ruth Clements,2,Pottery St. Swansea.	
2	" Evans.D.E.	Wife	Mrs Florrie Evans,48,Orchard St. Swansea.	
2	" Morgan.J.	Wife	Mrs Kate Morgan,15,Northampton Place,Swansea.	
9	" Thomas.H.M.	Wife	Mrs Mary Ellen Thomas,19,Brynsifi Terrace,Swansea.	
9	" Melmoth.A.	Friend	Miss Laura Williams,Cefndy Farm Rhyl.	
3	" Williams.J.G.	Mother	Mrs Edith Williams,11,Bridge Street,Swansea.	
6	" Walker Harry	Mother	Mrs Martha Walker,11 Siloh Rd. Swansea.	
8	Private Absolom.J.H.	Mother	Mrs Elizabeth Absolom,Causeway, Cambros,Pembroke.	
1	" Allen.J.	Wife	Mrs Laura Allen,425 Pentregethin Road,Swansea.	
5	" Allen.E.G.	Wife	Mrs Eleanor Allen,26 Mabel Street Port Talbot.	
1	" Arnett F.R.	Wife	Mrs Daisy Arnett,The Manse, Reynoldstone,Swansea.	
8	" Arnold.D.	Wife	Mrs Elizabeth Arnold,15 Bethesda Terrace,Swansea.	
5	" Border C.	Wife	Mrs Catherine Border,26 Waterloo Place,Brynmill,Swansea.	
5	" Bennett T.	Wife	Mrs Margaret Bennett,51 Sand- -field Road,Aberavon.	
4	" Brain S.H.	Wife	Mrs Sarah Brain,Cefn Stylla, Gowerton,Glamorganshire.	
0	" Brown S.H.	Mother	Mrs Mary Ann Brown,7 Marlborough Road,Swansea.	
5	" Brice H.W.	Wife	Mrs Rose,32 Arthur Street, Aberavon.	
5	" Berry R.E.	Wife	Mrs Jennie Berry,13 St.Davids Place,Swansea.	

Regtl. No.	Rank and Name	Relationship	Next of Kin.
17116	L.Cpl. Berry W.L.	Wife	Mrs Evelyn Berry,10 St.Davids Place,Swansea.
17189	Private Beresford.D.G.	Mother	Mrs Emily Beresford,4 North Prospect Place,Swansea.
17190	" Bevan E.J.	Wife	Mrs Bevan,280 Carmarthen Road, Swansea.
17038	" Bishop.G.W.	Wife	Mrs Minnie Bishop,53 Baptist Well Street,Swansea.
17313	" Blain.E.	Mother	Mrs Mary Blain,97 Cecil Street Manselton,Swansea.
17040	" Bolch.W.	Wife	Mrs Bridget Bolch,24 Byron Crescent,Swansea.
17170	" Border.F.W.	Wife	Mrs Beatrice Border,22 Bay St. Swansea.
17314	Corporal Browning.G.A.	Sister	Mrs Annie Browning,3 White St. Swansea.
17041	Private Brown R.	Mother	Celia Brown,85 Rhondda Street, Swansea.
17019	L.Cpl. Bushell S.	Wife	Mrs Mary Bushell,2 Hall Terrace Geitre Road,Dunvant.
17112	Private Bancroft F.G.	Mother	Mrs Florence Bancroft,96 King Edwards Road,Swansea.
29187	" Crossland A.	Mother	Mrs Rachel Crossland,6 Nelson Terrace,Sherburn Colliery,Near Durham.
29174	" Collins C.E.	Mother	Mrs Emma Collins,6 Horton Street Swansea.
29232	" Crabbe J.	Wife	Mrs Mary Crabbe, 4 Charles Row Gendros, Swansea.
29200	" Cook P.	Wife	Mrs Emily Cook,75 Sommon Street Waunwen,Swansea.
17935	" Cole W.	Wife	Mrs Esther Cole,22 Pegler Street Brynhyfryd, Swansea.
17498	" Carroll M.	Mother	Mrs Mary Carroll,19 Skinner St.
17020	" Chaplain J.	Brother	Mr Thomas Chaplain,75 Alscot Rd. Bermondsey,London.
17172	" Charles O.B.	Mother	Mrs Sofia Charles,18 Milton Terr. Swansea.
17499	" Clancy J.	Mother	Mrs Catherine Clancy, 24 The Common,Plasmarl,Swansea.
17119	" Cole R.	Wife	Mrs Amy Cole,16 David Street Swansea.
17226	" Connors H.	Mother	Mrs Margaret Connors,23 Croft Street,Swansea.
17500	" Cole W.	Mother	Mrs Hannah Cole,13 AberClydach Place,Clydach.
17501	" Cutcliffe E.J.	Mother	Mrs Martha Cutcliffe,Hynberg, Church Park,Tenby.
29065	" Davies W.G. 21st Batt.did not go overseas.	Wife	Mrs Harriet Davies,23 Brynsifi Terrace,Swansea.
29128	" Davies W.E.	Mother	Mrs Margaret Davies,29 Powell Terrace,Swansea.
17044	" Danielson O.	Mother	Mrs Eliza Danielson,56 Rodney Street,Swansea.
17435	" Davies D.	Wife	Mrs Ann Davies,Brynamlwg,Dunvant.
29153	" Davies O.	Mother	Mrs Mary Davies,3 North Hill Road,Swansea.
29015	" Dew W.H.	Wife	Mrs Dew,1 Park Street,Swansea.
29028	" Davies W.J.	Wife	Mrs Catherine Davies,121,Malta Street,Aberavon.
29029	" Davies D. (21st Batt. did not go Overseas).	Wife	Mrs Lily Davies,Cilmaengwyn Rd. Ynysmeudew.
29030	" Doran J.	Wife	Mrs Margaret Doran,Lamb Cottage Godregraig.
17995	" Davies L.	Wife	Mrs Eliz.Davies,35 Greenpark St. Aberavon.

Regtl. No.	Rank and Name	Relationship	Next of kin
17996	Private Dowse J.	Sister	Catherine Dowse, 20 Pendarvis Terr Port Talbot.
17229	" Davies F.	Brother	Mr William Davies 135 Rhondda Street Swansea.
17296	" Davies A.J.	Wife	Mrs Mary Davies 8 Grove Street Swansea.
17315	" Davies Z.	Wife	Mrs Davies, Wern, Gowerton, near Swansea.
17348	" Davies E.J.	Wife	Mrs Kate Davies, 6 Plasmarl Terr. Swansea.
17370	" Davies W.J.	Mother	Mrs Mary Davies 19 Portia Terr. Swansea.
17503	" Davies D.	Wife	Mrs Mary Davies, 14 Llangyfelach Street, Swansea.
17209	" Dann E.S.	Mother	Mrs Martha Dann, 162 St. Helens Road, Swansea.
17355	" Dupree H.A.	Mother	Mrs Annie Dupree 10 Short Street Swansea.
29008	" Evans E.	Wife	Mrs Alice Evans, 34 Verig Street, Manselton, Swansea.
29116	" Evans L.	Sister	Mrs Elizabeth Evans, 6 Crumlin Street, Swansea.
18043	" Evans T.W.A.	Wife	Mrs Evans, 5 Marine St. Llanelly.
17926	" Evans A.B.	Wife	Mrs Maud Evans, 41 Byron Crescent Swansea.
17927	" Evans W.T.	Mother	Mrs Gwen Evans, 2 Welcome Lane, Swansea.
17004	" Endres J.F.	Father	Mr Fred Endres, Normanhurst, Kilcot, Newent, Gloucester.
17175	Corporal Evans S.C.	Mother	Mrs Evans, 6 Bishopston Road, Gloucester.
17356	Private Evans A.E.S.	Mother	Mrs Edith Evans, 2 Cory St, Sketty Swansea.
17431	" Evans S.J.	Wife	Mrs Beatrice Evans, 52 Odo Street Swansea.
17471	" Evans C.	Mother	Mrs Mary Evans Victoria House Llanstephan Carmarthen.
29141	L.Cpl. Finch P.K.	Wife.	Mrs Amy Finch, Sunnybank, Cambros. Pembrokeshire.
29003	Private Folland R.J.	Wife	Mrs Maggie Folland, 25 Mynydd Terr Landore, Swansea.
17931	" Fisher T.	Father	Mr Thomas Fisher, 15 Greenpark Street, Aberavon.
17054	" Flowers W.O.	Wife	Mrs Ruth Flowers, 69 Manor Road Swansea.
17055	" Fox D.	Mother	Mrs Mary Fox, 10 Clarence Court Swansea.
29105	" Griffiths W.E.	Mother	Mrs Mary Griffiths, 39 Freeman Street, Brynhyfryd, Swansea.
29149	" Gammon S.	Wife	Mrs Gladys Gammon, Georgebank, Southend, Mumbles, Swansea.
18075	" Geary E.T.	Mother	Mrs Mary Geary, Williams Place, Colombus St. St Helens, Jersey, C.I.
17928	" Griffiths F.	Mother	Mrs Mary Griffiths, Ynysmeudew, Pontardawe.
17124	" Gard C.	Father	Mr John Thos. Gard, 28 Terrace Road, Swansea.
17056	" Gent G.M.	Mother	Mrs Elizabeth Gent, 36 Pentre-guinea Road, St. Thomas, Swansea
17057	" Gifford G.R.	Mother	Mrs Mary Gifford, Brig-y-don, Carnglas, Sketty, Swansea.
17261	" Gorman H.J.	Mother	Mrs Edith Gorman, 28 Villiers St. Hafod Swansea.
17214	" Griffin J.	Wife	Mrs Margaret Griffin, 8 Compass Street, Swansea.
17810	" Husband F.	Mother	Mrs Elizabeth Husband, Kingston, Hereford.
29033	Private Hassell H.	Mother	Mrs Hassell, Brynmair, Bryntawe, Terrace, Ystradgynlais.
29196	" Hurford W.H.	Mother	Mrs Florrie Hurford, 5 Clifton Row, Swansea.
29138	" Hoggs F.	Sister in Law	Mrs Jane Hogg, Penybryn, Dunvant, Swansea.
29139	" Howells B.	Wife	Mrs Winifred Howell, 16 Landeg St, Swansea.
29179	" Harris J. 21st Batt. did not go overseas.	Wife	Mrs Mary Harris, 4 Phillips Place, Swansea
29155	" Harris T.	Wife	Mrs Gwenllian Harries, 3 Danybryn Gorseinon.
17065	" Hughes J.G.	Mother	Mrs Mary Hughes, Rhianfa, Llangennech, Carmarthen.
17929	" Hughes D.	Mother	Mrs Elizabeth Hughes, 22 Pegler Street, Brynhyfryd, Swansea.
17513	L.Cpl. Hawes H.F.	Mother	Mrs Annie Hawes, 112 Plough Road, Clapham Junction, London.
17062	Private Hayward J.	Mother	Mrs Jane Hayward, Eclipse Buildings, Llanelly.
17059	" Hall J.	Wife	Mrs Amy Hall, 77 Lone Road, Clydach, Swansea.
17060	" Haskins H.H.	Mother	Mrs Mary Haskins, 16 Pavillion Terrace, Wood Lane, London.
17128	" Hare E.S.	Brother	Mr Thomas Hare, 5 St Illtyd Crescent, Danygraig, Swansea.
17130	" Harris W.T.	Mother	Mrs Lucina Harris, 28 Mariner Street, Swansea.
17215	L.Cpl. Harcourt C.F.	Mother	Mrs Polly Harcourt, 7 Willow Place, Swansea
17253	Private Hardy H.J.	Mother	Mrs Laura Hardy, 10 Scyborfach Street, Swansea.
17177	" Hodgins W.E.	Wife	Mrs Mary Hodgins, Lofthouse, Burridge Rd, Chelston, Torquay.
17268	" Hopkins, J.	Wife	Mrs Mary Jane Hopkins, 11 Kilvey Terrace, Swansea.
29235	" Jones P.P.	Mother	Mrs Margaret Jones, Childwall House, Wellington Road, Rhyl.
29256	" Jones J.	Child	Miss Sarah, 13 Dalrymple Street, Aberavon
29234	" Jackson A.	Father	Mr Thomas Jackson, Ship Inn, Foxhole, Swansea.
29183	" John R.D.	Mother	Mrs Emma John, 11 Gorse Road, Cwmbwrla, Swansea.
17138	" Jones F.	Wife	Mrs Alice Jones, 130 Oxford St, Swansea.
29215	" Jones J.L.	Mother	Mrs Margaret Jones, Tanybryn, Heolgwaith, Ystradgynlais.
29027	" John W.	Wife	Mrs Edith John, 41 Greenpark, Aberavon.
29034	" Jones A.	Mother	Mrs Fanny Jones, Kington Road, Weobley, Hereford.
17998	" John J.J.	Wife	Mrs Annie John, 41 Greenpark Street, Aberavon.
17930	" Johnson C.H.	Wife	Mrs Florence Johnson, 16 Villiers Street, Hafod Swansea.
17518	" Jerram W.C.	Mother	Mrs Mary Jerram, 12 Wellington Street, Swansea.
17069	" Jenkins J.J.	Father	Mr Thomas Jenkins, 9 Smyrma Street, Plasmarl, Swansea.
17071	L.Cpl. John S.O.	Mother	Mrs Margaret John, The Woods, Sketty, Swansea.
17605	Private John J.G.	Wife	Mrs Catherine John, 2 Bryngolew Terrace Sketty, Swansea.
29125	" Johnson B.	Mother	Mrs Mary Johnson, 1364 Neath Road, Swansea.
17072	" Jones D.T.	Mother	Mrs Eliza Jones, 57 Vincent St, Swansea.
17075	L.Cpl Jones J.H.	Mother	Mrs Rose Jones, 33 Green Hill, Swansea.
17136	Private Jones C.	Mother	Mrs Carrie Jones, 74 Norfolk St, Swansea
17139	" Jones J.H.	Father	Mr David Jones, 4 Brynsifi Tce, Swansea

No.	Rank and Name	Relationship	Next of Kin.
17319	Pte. Jones W.H.	Mother	Mrs Mary Jones, 117 Robert St. Swansea.
18047	" Keyes W.J.	Wife	Mrs Flossie Keyes, 41 Rodney St. Swansea.
17273	L.Cpl. Keen J.W.	Wife	Mrs Selina Keen, Ynysydaren Rd. Ystalyfer
17180	Pte. Kneath A.	Mother	Mrs Annie Kneath, 5 Milton Terr. Swansea
29016	" Lake A.E.	Mother	Mrs Mary Lake, 10 Tycoch Road, Swansea.
29023	" Lewis W.	Mother	Mrs Janet Lewis, 10 Curtis Row, Ynysmedew
29024	" Logan J.A.	Wife	Mrs Florence Logan, 2 Bethesda St. Swanse
18037	" Lloyd J.	Mother	Mrs Elizabeth Lloyd, 23 Coalport Rd, Made Shropshire.
17924	" Lawrey T.H.	Wife	Mrs Sarah Lawrey, 69 Strand, Swansea.
17933	" Lean J.H.	Wife	Mrs Eliz. Lean, 8 Michna Street, Aberavon.
17940	" Lewis D.	Wife	Mrs Maud Lewis, 17 Grey Street, Swansea.
17078	" Landers M.	Wife	Mrs Bridget Landers, Charles St. Swansea.
17196	" Lovering F.	Father	Mr John Lovering, 21 Vardre Rd. Clydach, n Swansea.
17197	" Lovering J.O.	"	Mr John Lovering, do.
17421	" Morse T.	Wife	Mrs Beatrice Morse, 4 Hall Bank Tce, Mumb Swansea.
29225	" Melling J.	Wife	Mrs Catherine Melling, 54 Windmill Tce, S
29194	" Marles W.E.	Mother	Mrs Lucy Marles, Clapperbrook, Alpington, Exeter.
18044	" Morgan A.E.	Sister	Mrs S.A. Rickard, 33 Lyon St. Swansea.
17358	" McCarthy T.	Wife	Mrs Mary McCarthy, 152 Eaton Rd. Swansea.
17144	" Milne G.A.	Mother	Mrs Annie Milne, 357 Neath Road, Swansea.
17084	" Moss A.	Mother	Mrs Moss, 15 Battaera (Bethania ?) Road, Clydach, Swansea.
17218	" Morgan C.H.	Mother	Mrs Catherine Morgan, 46 Odo Str. Swanse
17321	" Moreton E.T.	Mother	Mrs Mary Moreton, 13 Benthall Place, Swar
17459	" Morgan J.	Mother	Mrs Mary Morgan, 5 Market St. Morriston, S
17148	" Nash F.J.	Wife	Mrs Nellie Nash, 6 Crole Street, Swansea.
29208	" Owen J.G.	Grantmother	Mrs Hellen Owen, 127 Shiperton Road, London, S.E.
17088	" Owen W.G.	Wife	Mrs Margaret Owen, 37 Vincent St. Swanse
29175	" Peters A.J.	Wife	Mrs Hannah Peters, 3 Slip Rd. Swansea.
18002	" Phillips J.	Wife	Mrs Margaret Phillips, 15 Bouough St, S'
29017	" Phillips W.G.	Wife	Mrs Catherine Phillips, 2 Boarspit Lane, Norton, Swansea.
29037	" Plimmer F.	Mother	Mrs Eliz. Plimmer, 21 Bridge St. Swanse
17322	" Parkin G.H.	Wife	Mrs Maria Parkin, 3 Pleasant Str. Swanse
17279	" Pentland C.	Mother	Mrs Amelia Pentland, 15 Frederick St, S'
17089	" Phillips C.J.	Mother	Mrs Eliz. Phillips, 76 Gethin Tce, Mansel Swansea.
29131	" Price F.W.	Mother	Mrs Annie Price, 422 Pentregethin Rd, S'
17280	" Preece R.	Wife	Mrs Rose Preece, Trevellian Cottage, Tre
17151	" Pugsley T.	Mother	Mrs Sarah Pugsley, 9 Duke Str. Swansea.
18005	" Roberts J.R.	Wife	Mrs Cath. Roberts, 3 Albion Cottage, Waun-llwyd, Swansea.
29154	" Rees E.	Father	Mr Evan Rees, Penfordd, Llanybyther, Card
29173	" Richards W.	Wife	Mrs Amy Richards, 8 Gelli Str, St, Thomas
18006	" Robins S.H.	Wife	Mrs Annie Robins, 16 Byron Cresc. Swanse
18046	" Richards T.H.	Mother	Mrs Lucy Richards, 5 Aberdyberthi St. S'
17091	" Rapsey W.J.	Mother	Mrs Sarah Rapsey, 108 Pentre Road, Swans
17152	" Rees A.B.	Mother	Mrs Sarah Rees, 26 Plymouth Str. Swanse
17221	" Rees D.J.	Mother	Mrs Eliz. Rees, 8 Mariner Street, Swansea
17364	" Rees W.H.	Mother	Mrs Margaret Rees, 4 Llewellyn St, Skett Swansea.
17095	" Richards G.	Mother	Mrs Ann Richards, 6 Croft Street, Swanse
17488	" Rowlands I.	Mother	Mrs Mary Rowlands? Braemar Cottage, Sket Swansea.
17487	" Robertson R.	Wife	Mrs Emily Robertson, 66 Martin Street, Morriston, Swansea.
29007	" Rosser F.G.	Wife	Mrs Emily Rosser, 1 Park St. Mumbles. S's
29198	" Smith C.	Wife	Mrs Eliz. Smith, 12 Laburnham Tce. Dunvar Swansea.
29151	" Swann J.	Mother	Mrs Eliz. Swann, 201 Newmarket Rd. Cambri
29136	" Sewell C.	Wife	Mrs Jane Sewell, 115 Graig Rd, Morriston
29185	" Stephens E.	Wife	Mrs Ethel Stephens, 28 B Jones Rd. Bush Wolverhampton.
17942	" Shingles F.	Friend	Rachel Fright, 3 Upperdumpton Park Road Ramsgate, Kent.
17155	Pte Seeley W.A.	Wife	Mrs Annie Seeley, St. Helens Ave. Swansea
17156	L.Cpl. Simpson C.H.	Mother	Mrs Helen Simpson, 156 Odo Street, Swansea.
17201	Pte. Snowden R.	Mother	Mrs Eliz. Snowden, 14 Fairfield Tce. Swanse
17185	" Stonehouse R.	"	Mrs Rhoda Stonehouse, 53 Cambridge St. Swa
17100	Cpl. Stephens W.	Wife	Mrs Minnie Stephens, 3 Langdon Place, Swan
17286	Pte Sullivan J.	Brother	Mr John Sullivan, 6 Well Street, Swansea.
29018	" Stephens W.A.	Mother	Mrs Ann Stephens, 113 Pentre Tce. Swansea
29026	" Smith E.	Mother	Mrs Lydia Smith, 106 Cowbridge Road, Cardi
29204	" Thomas W.G.	Mother	Mrs Hannah Thomas, Crumlin Villa, Llansaml Swansea.
29205	" Thomas. W.G.	Mother	Mrs Hannah Thomas, 76 High St. Llandovery
18045	" Thomas R.E.	Wife	Mrs Rachel Thomas, 4 Pontardulais Rd, Gors
17534	" Taylor B.	Wife	Mrs Annie Taylor, 76 Norfolk Street, Swans
17014	" Thomas D.	Mother	Mrs Mary Thomas, 7 Baptist Well St. Swans
17015	" Thomas H.	Mother	Mrs Mary Thomas 3 Lyon Street, Swansea.
17205	" Thomas W.	Wife	Mrs Eliz. Thomas, 76 High St. Clydach.
17290	L.Cpl. Thomas. S.L.	Mother	Mrs Agnes Thomas, 32 Marlborough Rd. Swans
17538	" Thomas. G.B.	Brother	Mr Wm. Thomas, 3 Bay View Terrace, Swansea.
17410	Pte. Tyrell J.	Wife	Mrs Violet Tyrell, 31 River St. Rhyl.
29025	" Thomas F.	Wife	Mrs Margt. Thomas, 10 Owens Row, St. Thomas,
29197	" Williams. T.H.	"	Mrs Bertha Williams, Temperance House, Kin Street, Laugharne, Carmarthen.
29206	" Williams R.T.	Mother	Mrs Catherine Williams, 5 Beaconsfield St Cadoxton, Neath.
29113	" Williams. D.	Mother	Mrs Annice Williams, Graig Road, Trebanos,
17162	L.Cpl. Walsh F.	Wife	Mrs Margt. Walsh, 56 Fern St. Cwmbwrla, S'se
17163	Pte. Watkins. D.E.	Mother	Mrs Eliz. Watkins, 23 Portia Tce. Swansea.
17291	" Walker J.	Wife	Mrs Catherine Walker, 30 Charles St, Swans
17207	L/C. West A.	Wife	Mrs Ellen West, 53 Vera Rd. Clydach. Swanse
17541	Pte Welsh G.E.	Wife	Mrs Rose Ellen Welch, Garden City, Clydach
17033	" Williams R.	Sister	Mrs Mary Williams, Iscoed, St. Helens Rd, Sw
17108	L/C. Williams. I.	Mother	Mrs Jane Williams, 10 Forest Tce, Hendy, Pon-dulais.
17223	Pte Williams D.H.	Father	Mr Dd. Williams, Rose Cottage, Phillys St Cwmdu, Swansea.
17246	" Williams D.V.	Wife	Mrs Alice Williams, 17 Barbers Court, High Swansea.
17294	" Winter W. 21st Batt. did not go.	Mother	Mrs Emma Winter, 9 Wernfawr Rd, Swansea.
17326	" Winch B.G.	Wife	Euronwy Winch, Eversley Road, Swansea.
29012	" Williams. T.F.	Wife	Mrs Cath. Williams. 19 Tudor St. Port Talbo
17300	" Evans. W.J.	Wife	Mrs Nellie Evans, 9 Dyfatty Street, Swanse
17458	C.S.M. Leach J.	Wife	Mrs E. Leach, 74a Dagnan Rd. Balham. S.W.
17613	C.Q.M.S. Bourne. A.	Mother	Mrs W. Bourne, Wilden, near Stourport, Worce
17316	Sgt. Greenland T.H.	Wife	Mrs E.A. Greenland, 59 Oxford St. Swansea.
17006	" Harding. A.G.	Father	Mr A.C. Harding, 64 St. Lukes Rd. Totterdown Bristol.
17042	" Carey T.H.	Wife	Mrs N.J. Carey, 4 Greyhound St, Swansea.
17430	" Earle J.A.	Wife	Mrs A.G. Earle, 8 Paxton Street, Swansea.
17361	" Prangle W.H.	"	Mrs N.J. Prangle, 22 Spring Terrace, Swanse
17013	" Strawford. H.F.	Father.	Mr T. Strawford, 73 Manselton Rd. Swanse
17167	" Absolom A.H.	Wife	Mrs E. Absolom, 3 Penmaen Terrace, Swansea.
17103	" Thomas H.	Mother	Mrs P. Thomas, 5 Edgeware Road, Swansea.
17032	" Williamson G.E.	Wife.	Mrs Williamson, 7 Pleasant Row, Swansea.
17037	L/S Bevan E.L.	Wife	Mrs E.L. Bevan, 9 Dyfatty Street, Swansea.
17114	Cpl. Begley I.	Wife	Mrs R. Begley, 41 Phillips Street, Swansea.
17257	" Edwards O.	Father	Mr J. Edwards, 8 Bryn Terrace, Swansea.
17132	" Harvey R.	Wife	Mrs R. Harvey, 27 Scyborfach Street, Swanse
17438	" Glover. W.J.	Wife	Mrs M. Glover, 116 Wellington Road, Rhyl.
17077	" King C.F.	Wife	Mrs E.J. King, 21 Dyfatty Street, Swansea.
17219	" Phelps W.	Wife	Mrs S.A. Phelps, 2 Montana Place, Plough R Swansea.
17146	" Morris J.	Aunt	Miss Miller, 20 Plymouth Street, Swansea.
17457	" Howell F.D.J.	Wife	Mrs F. Howell, 11 Port Tennant Rd. Swansea
17519	" Jupp C.R.W.	Wife	Mrs H. Jupp, 1 Bryn Terrace, Swansea Road, Trebanos Pontardawe.
29303	" Lewis M.	Son	Richd. Thos. Lewis c/o Mrs Arnott, 80 Caer Road, Caerau.

Regtl. No.	Rank and Name	Relationship	Next of Kin.
17367	L/Cpl.Berry R.	Mother	Mrs S.Berry c/o Mrs Trickett,Mayfield,Villa Ormskill,Lancs.
17859	" Evans D.H.	Father	Mr W.Evans,1 Armine Rd.Fforestfach,NrS'sea
18062	" Mew C.H.	Wife	Mrs M.Mew,Ty-drow,Bonymaen,Nr,Swansea.
29094	" Williams R.	Son	Mr R.Williams,1a Argo Terr,Landore,Swansea
29097	" Williams L.	Mother	Mrs A.Williams,54 Walters Rd.Swansea.
17568	" Williams T.I.	Mother	Mrs M.Williams,50 Tymawr St.Cwmavon.
17976	" Williams J.P.	Mother	Mrs A.Williams,18 Sebastopol St,St Thomas,"
17597	" Richards G.	Mother	Mrs S.Richards,14 Queens Road,Mumbles,Ssea.
17564	" Rogers H.	Mother	Mrs J.Rogers,Rock House,Court Sart,Briton Ferry,Glamorgan.
17573	Pte Cook R.H.	Mother	Mrs M.Cook,144 Robert St. Swansea.
17415	L/cp. Davies M.	Mother	Mrs R.Davies,11 Cwm Rd.Swansea.
17959	Pte Allen E.	Wife	Mrs C.Allen,26 Vivian St.Swansea.
17570	" Austin D.	Wife	Mrs M.Austin,2 Tudor St.Garden City, Ystradgynlais,Swansea Valley,Glam.
17581	" Austin T.R.	Wife	Mrs C.Austin,61 Rodney St. Swansea.
17879	" Ace H.G.	Father	Mr W.Ace,Tyle House,Reynoldstone,Gower,Glam
29144	" Argent I.G.	Mother	Mrs M.Argent,52 Garden St.Swansea.
17880	" Beard A.	Wife	Mrs L.A.Beard,Wern-Goch Farm,Skewen,Glam.
17368	" Booth J.	Friend	Miss L.Williams,59 Penhyrn Ave.Liverpool.
17858	" Black P.	Mother	Mrs M.Black,Cwmbach Rd.Cockett,Swansea.
17860	" Beynon S.	Father	Mr G.Beynon,Rhossilly,Gower,Nr.Swansea.
17544	" Brown H.	Father	Mr H.Brown,4 Town Hill,Swansea.
17598	" Brown H.J.	Wife	Mrs P.Brown,19 Lamberts Cottages,Port Tennant,Swansea.
17599	" Bryant F.	Sister	Miss K.Maggs,42 Twinnel St.Easton Rd. Bristol.
29095	" Bellew E.	Mother	Mrs A.Bellew,57 Rodney St.Swansea.
29101	" Beynon E.	Father	Mr W.H.Beynon,19 Princess St.Swansea.
29106	" Britton A.G.	Father	Mr W.Britton,13 Victoria Avenue,Swansea.
17434	" Beresford J.H.	Mother	Mrs E.Beresford,4 North Prospect Place,Ssea
17254	" Chappell J.	Wife	Mrs R.Chappell,44 Ebenezer St.Swansea.
17329	" Christensen J.	Wife	Mrs M.J.Christensen,121 Oxford St.Swansea.
17912	" Clark G.	Father	Mr.F.Clark,Level Crossing,Barbes Green, Nr.Hostham,Sussex.
17600	" Clement J.	Wife	Mrs M.Clement,54 Catherine St.Swansea.
18013	" Collins W.	Wife	Mrs O.Collins,2 Julian Terr.Aberavon.
17917	" Cullis D.E.	Mother	Mrs S.Cullis,32 Pelby St.Swansea.
17882	" Curtis W.T.	Wife	Mrs J.Curtis,2 Gorse Rd.Cwmbwrla,Swansea.
29098	" Carr A.	Wife	Mrs S.Carr,20 Michna St.Aberavon.
29228	" Chadford J.T.	Mother	Mrs E.D.Chadford,1 Oddfellow St.Ystradgyn--lais.
17504	" Davies J.	Mother	Mrs E.Davies,100 Cyfing Rd.Ystalyfera.
17547	" Davies D.J.	Mother	Mrs R.Davies,13 Hill Street,Swansea.
17550	" Davies W.J.	Wife	Mrs F.Davies,2 Brynmelin St.Swansea.
17696	" David H.	Mother	Mrs M.David,Scutare Rd.Taibach,Pt.Talbot.
17594	" Dobbs W.J.	Mother	Mrs A.Dobbs,1 Pinkney St.St Thomas,Swansea
18070	" Davies J.C.	Mother	Mrs J.Davies,11 Mabel St.Sandfields, Aberavon.
29110	" Durk W.O.	Mother	Mrs M.E.Durk,6 Earl St.Hafod,Swansea.
29171	" Davies J.	Mother	Mrs G.Davies,4 Monterey St.Manselton,S'sea
17883	" Edwards A.G.	Mother	Mrs F.Edwards,14 Graig Terrace,Swansea.
17372	" Evans W.J.	Sister	Mrs M.J.Evans,1 Hill St.Swansea.
17508	" Evans G.	Mother	Mrs A.Evans,5 Springfield Terr,Morriston,"
17551	" Evans D.	Aunt	Mrs Mar Evans,62 Castle Graig,Landore,S'sea
18015	" Evans J.	Mother	Mrs E.E.Evans,3 Corporation Rd.Aberavon.
17872	" Evans T.J.	Mother	Mrs B.Evans,1 Corporation Rd.Aberavon.
29142	" Evans D.	Wife	Mrs A.Evans,Ddol Cottage,Dunvant,Swansea.
29213	" Evans T.R.	Father	Mr W.Evans,22 Pelican St.Ystradgynlais.
17584	" Finch C.B.	Mother	Mrs L.Finch,31 Hawthorne Ave,Swansea.
17373	" Floyd D.J.	Mother	Mrs E.Floyd,10 Washington Terrace,Swansea.
17375	" Franks P.	Wife	Mrs M.Franks,5 Belle-vue Street,Swansea.
18071	" Fisher D.	Mother	Mrs M.Fisher,15 Greenpark St.Aberavon.
17969	" Godfrey R.	Mother	Mrs L.Godfrey,Gower Rd,Killay,Nr.Swansea.
17473	" Grey G.	Mother	Mrs M.A.Grey,45 Penvillia Road,Swansea.
17863	" Griffiths J.J.	Father	Mr D.Griffiths,29 Langdon Place,Swansea.
17865	" Guy G.	Father	Mr R.Guy,84 Rhyddings Terrace,Swansea
29102	L/C Griffiths D.	Wife	Mrs M.Griffiths,28 Millbrook St,Plasmarl,"
29233	Pte Griffiths D.J.	Wife	Mrs D.Griffiths,Duffryn Rd,Alltwen, Pontardawe.
17318	" Harris W.J.	Wife	Mrs E.Harris,62 Byron Crescent,Swansea.
17377	" Hawkins J.A.	Wife	Mrs E.J.Hawkins,139 Rodney St.Swansea.
17455	" Heddon W.F.	Aunt	Mrs E.Jenkins,The Bank,Oxwich,Nr.Swansea.
17553	" Hellyer W.R.	Wife	Mrs J.Hellyer,4 Port Tennant Place, St Thomas,Swansea.
17516	" Howard M.	Wife	Mrs T.Howard,62 Strand,Swansea.
18074	" Hodgkinson H.	Brother	Mr S.Hodgkinson,Richmond Villas,May Hill, Swansea.
29099	" Hughes B.	Father	Mr I.Hughes,Belgrave Rd,Loughor,Nr.Swansea
29103	" Hopkins S.J.	Wife	Mrs E.Hopkins,18 Lyon St.Swansea.
29111	" Henry G.	Mother	Mrs J.Henry,10 Waterloo St.Swansea.
29245	" Hutchins W.	Stepmother	Mrs L.Williams,7 Edward Street,Swansea.
17913	" Incledon W.H.	Father	Mr G.Incledon,8 Margaret St.St Thomas,Ssea
29260	" Ibbitson S.	Wife	Mrs L.Ibbitson,Sterry Rd.Gowerton,Swansea.
29137	" Hooper W.	Wife	Mrs M.J.Hooper,115 Graig Rd,Morriston,Glam.
17333	" James E.G.	Wife	Mrs V.E.James,32 Heol-fach,Treboeth,Swansea
17602	" James W.D.	Mother	Mrs E.James,10 Short Street,Swansea.
17902	" James L.R.	Mother	Mrs K.James,19 Tudor Street,Port Talbot.
17475	" Jenkins S.	Mother	Mrs M.H.Jenkins,183 Foxhole Rd.Swansea.
17864	" Jenkin J.	Father	Mr D.Jenkin,Gendroe,Fforestfach,Swansea.
17586	" Jensen C.N.	Mother	Mrs.J.Jensen,28 Danygraig Rd,Swansea.
17587	" Jensen M.	Mother	Mrs J.Jensen,28 Danygraig Rd.Swansea.
18019	" John S.	Mother	Mrs H.John,6 Western St.Swansea.
17137	" Jones D.T.	Mother	Mrs A.Williams,24 Pelly St.Cwmavon.
17272	" Jones G.	Wife	Mrs D.Jones,136 Eaton Rd.Swansea.
17334	" Jones D.	Mother	Mrs E.Jones,Ystrad Rd,Fforestfach,Swansea.
17380	" Jones J.	Mother	Mrs M.A.Jones,1 Pentremawr Rd.Swansea.
17478	" Jones R.H.	Mother	Mrs K.F.Jones,5 Forge & Hammer Place, Plasmarl,Swansea.
17576	" Jones D.	Wife	Mrs H.Jones,Cross Street,Glantawe,Ystrad--gynlais,Swansea Valley,Glam.
17875	" Jones I.	Mother	Mrs A.Jones,5 Glenview Tce.Port Talbot.
17914	" Jones S.	Wife	Mrs M.Jones,BrynGailia,Caersalem,Landore, Swansea.
17915	" Jones W.	Mother	Mrs E.Jones,42 Dynevor Rd,Skewen,Glam.
29100	" Jones I.D.	Mother	Mrs C.Jones,Belgrave Rd.Loughor,Swansea.
29158	" Jones D.J.	Aunt	Mrs M.A.Aplin,41 Monterey St.Swansea.
29219	" Jones S.	Father	Mr.E.Jones,Brook Tce.Gwaun-Cae-Gurwen,Near Swansea.
18073	" Jones J.	Mother	Mrs M.A.Jones,6 Mabel St.Aberavon.
18020	" Kevan E.H.	Mother	Mrs A.Kevan,4 Torridge Place,East-the--Water?Bideford,N.Devon.
17559	" King G.L.	Father	Mr.J.King,32 Catherine Street,Swansea.
17561	" Lewis J.O.	Mother	Mrs J.Lewis,Harry Street,Morriston,Glam.
17595	" Locker F.	Wife	Mrs B.Locker,27 Wellington St.Swansea.
17588	" Lynn V.	Sister	Miss L.Lynn,16 Quarry Street,Swansea.
17713	" Lewis L.	Mother	Mrs M.Lewis,Llanmadock,Reynoldstone,Gower, Nr.Swansea
29239	" Long F.	Wife	Mrs E.Long,1 New Cottages,Blackpill,Swansea
29217	" Lucas W.	Mother	Mrs A.Lucas,Burry Head,Reynoldstone,Gower."
29190	" Luckwill T.	Wife	Mrs S.Luckwell,10 Bethesda St.Swansea.
29236	" Lynch E.	Mother	Mrs J.Lynch,4 Brook Street,Swansea.
17562	" Manship H.	Mother	Mrs M.Manship,353 Trewyddfa Rd.Landore,"
17897	" Millard A.C.	Wife	Mrs K.Millard,11 Carmarthen Row,Port Talbot
17874	" Mills I.	Mother	Mrs A.Mills,10 Angel St.Aberavon.
17898	" Minchin A.	Mother	Mrs A.Minchin,27 Maesycoed Tce.Port Talbot
17351	" Morgan H.J.	Wife	Mrs M.Morgan,Gelly Gron Rd.Pontardawe,Glam
17596	" Morgan E.	Mother	Mrs E.Morgan,6 Cornwall Tce.Mumbles,Swansea
17630	" Morgan W.J.	Wife	Mrs E.Morgan,2 Glun St.Hafod,Swansea.
17878	" Morgan T.	Brother	Mr W.Morgan,13 Pentrepoeth Rd.Morriston,"
17888	" Morris J.H.	Wife	Mrs E.M.Morris,88 Colbourne Terr.Swansea.
17147	" Mort R.	Wife	Mrs M.A.Mort,210 Cwm Rd.Pentre,Swansea.
17887	" Morgan R.	Sister	Miss G.Morgan,Miners Arms,Ystradgynlais,Gla
17336	" Murphy F.	Wife	Mrs A.Murphy,1 Woodfield St.Morriston,Glam.
29134	" Mellor W.H.	Aunt	Mrs E.Jones,1 Clifton Villas,Manninghan Lane,Bradford.
29253	" Murphy W.	Wife	Mrs M.Murphy,3 Ann Street,Swansea.

Regtl. No.	Rank and Name	Relationship	Next of Kin.
18039	Pte Nicholls H.W.J	Mother	Mrs E.M.Nicholls,Brownwood Ave.Barnes, London.W.
17608	L/C Norvell W.	Wife	Mrs J.Norvell,32 Fitzarthur St.Leeds.
29104	Pte Nicholson C.T.	Wife	Mrs A.Nicholson,103 Camden St.Birmingh
17972	" O'Brien P.	Cousin	R.Q.M.S.Hughes J.9 Millmount Place,Dur--condia,Dublin,Ireland.
17867	" Lynch T.	Wife	Mrs S.Lynch,156 Llangyfelach Rd.Swanse
17868	" Owen W.J.	Wife	Mrs A.Owen,6 Shepherds Rd.Graig,Plasma Swansea.
17359	" Palmer S.J.	Wife	Mrs E.Palmer,8 Washington Terr,Landore
18022	" Paton J.	Mother	Mrs S.Paton,4 Thomas Street,Swansea.
17916	" Parry H.E.	Father	Mr W.Parry,Moorhampton,Hereford.
17362	" Pearson W.R.	Wife	Mrs E.Pearson,17 Kynaston Place,Swanse
17889	" Phillips D.A.	Father	Mr J.Phillips,Gwendraeth House,Brecon Ystradgynlais,Glam.
17220	" Phillips R.I.	Father	Mr W.Phillips,20 Arthur St.Pembroke Do
29237	" Parkin G.H.	Sister	Mrs F.Dyer,87 Mermaid Row,Port Tennant Swansea.
29242	" Pilkington J.	Mother	Mrs M.Pilkington,14 Strand,Swansea.
29243	" Phillips S.P.	Mother	Mrs K.Phillips,49 North Hill Rd.Swanse
17384	" Quick W.J.	Grand-Mother.	Mrs A.Quick,1 Ivy Bush Rd,Swansea
17363	" Rafferty P.	Mother	Mrs R.Rafferty,12 Percy St.Cwmbwrla,S'
17423	" Rees C.G.	Mother	Mrs M.Rees,16 Brynmelin St.Swansea.
17528	" Richards S.G.	Wife	Mrs A.Richards,The Gardens,Dinder,Nr.W Somerset.
17899	" Richards A.	Father	Mr H.Richards,4 James St.Port Talbot.
18023	" Richards P.	Father	Mr C.Richards,Pitton,Gower,Nr Swansea.
17890	" Ridd R.E.	Mother	Mrs M.Ridd,90 Rodney St,Swansea.
17869	" Rowlands F.	Wife	Mrs D.Rowlands,32 Chapel St.Mount Plea Liverpool.
17973	" Rowlands B.J.	Mother	Mrs B.Rowlands,20 Little Wind St. Swan
18064	" Randall W.	Mother	Mrs E.Randall,6 Dany-coed Rd.Cwmavon,G
29221	" Rees W.	Step-Mother	Mrs M.Jones,46 Cae-bricks Rd.Cwmbwrla,
29117	" Richards J.H.	Mother	Mrs M.Richards,509 Neath Rd.Morriston,
29176	" Richards J.H.	Mother	Mrs M.Richards,15 Mabel St.Aberavon,G
17385	" Screech L.J.	Wife	Mrs D.Screech,21 Delhi St,St Thomas,S'
17531	" Shepherd S.J.	Mother	Mrs E.Shepherd,Rose Cottage,Park Mill, Swansea.
17974	" Short W.J.	Wife	Mrs E.Short,2 Hendrefoilan Rd,Sketty,S
17900	" Slade R.T.	Mother	Mrs E.Slade,3 Pleasant Terr,Walter Rd, Llansamlet,Nr.Swansea.
17386	" Smith W.H.	Wife	Mrs M.Smith,37 Shelly Crescent,Swansea
17578	" Smith T.F.	Wife	Mrs A.Smith,12 Polson Place,Winchester
17909	" Stoker A.J.	Son	Mr T.H.Stoker,22 Lion St.Easton Rd.Br
17975	" Summerfield W.	Wife	Mrs M.Summerfield,7 Marsden Street,Swa
17287	" Swain E.	Wife	Mrs C.Swain,5 Charles Place,Swansea.
29191	" Sandywell W.J.	Wife	Mrs F.E.Sandywell,13 Vincent Street,S'
29108	" Short W.	Mother	Mrs C.H.Hext,27 Edgeware Rd,Uplands,S'
29170	" Short E.S.	Wife	Mrs M.A.Short,1 Richard St.Swansea.
29227	" Short W.	Wife	Mrs G.Short,15 Stanley Terr.Swansea.
29143	" Smith W.	Mother	Mrs E.Smith,Plasycoed,Dunvant,Nr Swan
29254	" Swaffield S.	Wife	Mrs M.Swaffield,2 Cae Rowland,Cwmbwrl
17891	" Thomas D.	Wife	Mrs M.Thomas,Sterny Road,Gowerton,Gla
18066	" Thomas C.	Wife	Mrs J.Thomas,1a Bevan St.Aberavon.
29096	" Thomas J.F.	Father	Mr D.Thomas,11 Aberclydach,Clydach,Gl
29004	" Tebby W.J.	Father	Mr T.Tebby,Rye Corner,Broadway,Winche (Worcester)
17724	" Thomas D.	Father	Mr W.Thomas,Cheriton,Gower,Nr,Swansea
29176	" Thomas J.	Brother	Mr.D.Thomas,64 Piscah St.Kenfig Hill,
17612	" Wallace F.	Mother	Mrs E.Wallace,6 Tintern Terr,Sketty,S
17387	" Walters G.H.	Mother	Mrs M.J.Walters,42 Love Lane,Romsey.
17492	" Webber R.E.	Mother	Mrs E.Webber,1 Station Rd.Llansamlet,
17466	" Wheale J.	Mother	Mrs A.Wheale,Perris Wood,Penmaen,Gowe
17895	" Wheaton J.	Mother	Mrs A.Wheaton,26 Holland St.Barnstapl
17911	" Whyeth W.S.	Mother	Mrs E.S.Whyeth,72 Argyle Street,Swans
17427	" Williams J.	Mother	Mrs A.Williams,93 Milton Terr.Swansea
17569	" Williams W.	Mother	Mrs C.Williams,41 Lan Street,Morristo
17593	" Williams B.G.	Mother	Mrs E.Williams,16 Catherine St.Swanse
17580	" Williams E.	Mother	Mrs S.Williams,1 Williams Cottage,Ffo -fach,Glam.
17644	Pte Williams D.G.	Mother	Mrs E.Williams,9 Watkin St.Swansea.
17871	" Williams A.	Mother	Mrs M.Williams,BrynHeulog House,Mile
17325	" Williams W.H.	Wife	Mrs E.Williams,12 Gordon Tce.Swansea.
17295	" Woollard H.	Wife	Mrs J.Woollard,12 Llangyfelach St.Swan
18061	" Watkins J.J.	Wife	Mrs R.Watkins,16 Edward St.Swansea.
29118	" Wilkes N.	Wife	Mrs L.M.Wilkes,10 Midland Tce.Morrist
29249	" Watkins A.F.	Wife	Mrs M.J.Watkins,9 Campbell St.Swansea
17206	" Wallace W.	Mother	Mrs J.Wallace,93 Caledonian Rd.Leeds.
29181	" Heddon A.H.	Wife	Mrs A.R.Heddon,238 Neath Rd.Landore,S
18024	" Thomas T.J.	Wife	Mrs A.M.Thomas,12 Thomas St.Swansea.
29246	" Thomas W.D.	Father	Mr S.Thomas,53 Garden St.Swansea.
18063	" Thomas J.	Sister	Miss E.Thomas,18 Wem Square,Aberavon.
17343	" Vernon F.	Mother	Mrs A.M.Vernon,46 Cromwell Tce,Swanse
17567	" Williams T.A.	Brother	Mr W.H.Williams,97 Port Tennant Rd,Sw
17164	" Williams D.	Wife	Mrs C.Williams,12 Cwm Terrace,Swansea
18084	" Williams W.	Mother	Mrs M.Williams,86 Eaton Rd.Swansea.
29152	" Walker I.	Wife	Mrs C.Walker?Tansley Villa,Cynonville Port Talbot.
29230	" Williams B.A.	Wife	Mrs S.Williams,116 Glyndu St.Morristo
29251	" Walker W.H.	Stepmother	Mrs E.Walker,7 Watkin St.Swansea.
17977	" Young W.T.	Mother	Mrs M.Young,2 Gore Terrace,Swansea.
17225	" Ahearne P.	Wife	Mrs C.Ahearne,5 Brook St.Swansea.
17923	" Owens W.H.	Wife	Mrs A.Owens,6 Colebrook Rd.Grovesend, Swansea.
17932	" Jones G.W.T.	Wife	Mrs L.Jones,7 Michna St.Aberavon.
17011	" Norris D.J.	Wife	Mrs E.M.Norris,40 James St.Swansea.
17125	" George T.H.	Brother	Mr George,87 Baptist Well St.Swans
17705	" Carter G.L.	Mother	Mrs S.Carter,Gorfield,High Rd.Wisbech Cambridge.
17574	" Davies J.	Mother	Mrs A.Davies,Parkmill,Near Swansea.
29280	" Hurford W.W,	Wife	Mrs E.Hurford,44 Corporation Houses, Morriston.
18035	C.S.M.Mallin F.	Mother	Mrs S.Mallin,Cow & Hare,Easton St.Hig Wycombe.
17654	C.Q.M.S. Sewell R.	Wife	Mrs M.A.Sewell,71 Stephey Green,Londo
17074	Sgt Jones J.	Wife	Mrs Jones,28 St.Helens Rd.Swansea.
17641	" Silk R.	Wife	Mrs Silk,3 South View,Gorseinon,Nr S'
17663	" Goad A.	Mother	Mrs S.Goad,4 Fabian St. St Thomas,Swa
17946	" Hamens A.	Mother	Mrs A.Hamens,28 Commercial St.Kenfig Bridge.
17634	" Buse G.	Father	Mr Buse,116 King Edwards Rd.Swansea.
17941	" Roberts T.	Wife	Mrs M.Roberts,Fairview,Newton,Mumbles
17939	" Lyons R.T.	Mother	Mrs M.A.Lyons,10 St Alphonso's Rd.Wat -ford, Ireland.
17945	L/Sgt.Griffiths J.	Mother	Mrs G.Richards,5 Fleet St.Pennar,Pemb Dock.
17698	C.Q.M.S. Mitchell G.	Wife	Mrs E.E.Mitchell,48 Norfolk St,Swanse
17943	Cpl Flaherty S.	Mother	Mrs A.Flaherty,94 Marighan St.Penarth
17749	" White F.W.	Wife	Mrs E.White,Rhydefaid,Killay,R.S.O.Gl
17787	" Rawlins A.	Wife	Mrs M.Rawlins,1347 Neath Rd,Hafod,Swa
17700	" Puxley H.	Wife	Mrs M.Puxley,54 Fern St.Cwmbwrla,Swan
17658	L/C Margetts A.L.	Wife	Mrs E.B.Margetts,2 Harbour View Swan
17674	" Cloke W.G.	Wife	Mrs Cloke,55 Colbourne Tce.Swansea.
17640	Cpl Russell V.J.	Mother	Mrs Russell,77 Wyldes Lane,Worcester.
17847	L/C Pascoe T.	Father	Mr T.Pascoe,67 Velindre St. Aberavon.
17746	" Whitty P.	Wife	Mrs J.Whitty,9 Grove St,Greenhill,S'a
17689	" Whittaker W.	Sister in law	Mrs C.Cameron.119 Harrow Side, S.Sho Blackpool.
17489	Cpl Seddon S.	Father	Mr W.Seddon,25 Laba St.Manchester.
17635	L/C Phillips G.	Wife	Mrs E.Phillips,3 Rutland Place,Swanse
17826	" Arnold J.W	Mother	Mrs E.Arnold,170 Port Tennant,Swansea
17833	" Wiltshire W.	Cousin	Miss Maria Wiltshire,The Chantry,Wimb Dorset.
29115	" Nunn B.A.	Wife	Mrs M.Nunn,20 Ingateshore Rd.S Norwoo London.
29292	Pte Armor F.	Wife	Mrs E.F.Armor,3 Paxton St,Swansea.
17571	" Bean G.E.	Mother	Mrs A.Bean,36 Bonymaen Rd.Swansea.
17744	" Beale E.	Father	Mr W.Beale,17 Gerald St.Hafod,Swansea

Regtl. No.	Rank and Name	Relationship	Next of Kin.
17805	Pte Beck C.H.	Mother	Mrs R.Beck,46 Madoc St.Swansea
17704	" Bull G.	Mother	Mrs J.Bull,7 Rectory St.Woodsley,Stour--bridge.
17614	" Bevan W.J.	Mother	Mrs M.Bevan,Cwmbach Rd.Cockett,Nr,Swansea.
29267	" Bevan W.	Wife	Mrs K.Bevan,2 Rutland Place,Swansea.
17693	" Bowen J.	Mother	Mrs C.Bowen,25 Lambert Cottages,Swansea.
17733	" Bradshaw W.	Wife	Mrs K.Bradshaw,47 Rodney St.Swansea.
17672	" Brereton A.J.	Mother	Mrs E.Brereton,3 Windsor Place,Mumbles,Glam
17828	" Britton J.	Mother	Mrs A.Britton,95 Foxhole Rd,St.Thomas,Ssea
17770	" Buckmaster R.	Mother	Mrs E.Buckmaster,West Cross,Swansea.
17680	" Burge F.G.	Mother	Mrs Burge,112 Oxford St.Swansea.
17836	" Chapple P.W.	Mother	Mrs F.Chapple,56 Ysgol St.Swansea.
17829	" Charles D.J.	Wife	Mrs Charles,7 Armine Rd.Fforestfach,S'sea
29278	" Charles G.	Mother	Mrs C.Charles,28 Twynybedw Rd.Clydach,Ssea
17681	L/C Conway E.	Wife	Mrs F.Conway,51 Colbourne Tce.Swansea
29001	Pte Cook T.	Wife	Mrs E.L.Cook,8 Ford ~~Street~~,Aberavon.
17881	" Corris J.	Uncle	Mr F.Corris,Shore Rd.Port St.Mary.I.O.M.
17706	" Cossins W.	Father	Mr J.Cossins,8 Elias St,Neath,Glam.
18029	" Coupland W.H.	Wife	Mrs W.H.Coupland,10 Heolycae,Clydach,Ssea.
7617	" Cowley H.	Brother	Mr H.Cowley,34 Eaton Rd.Swansea.
7616	" Critchley S.	Father	Mr H.Critchley,41 Coedsaeson Cres,Sketty.
7844	" Crowley D.	Mother	Mrs B.Crowley,159c Water St.Aberavon.
8034	" Cuell W.H.	Mother	Mrs M.Cuell,60 Baptist Well St,Swansea.
7618	" Cundy C.H.	Father	Mr R.Cundy,27 Wellington St.Swansea.
7675	" Davies J.A.		Miss Mary Thomas?Buarth Newydd,Dinorwu, Cwmydo,Carnarvon.
7646	" Davies R.E.	Father	Mr G.H.Davies,Bridge House,Blackpill,Glam
9212	" Davies S.G.	Mother	Mrs M.H.Davies,19 Woodlands Tce.Swansea.
7745	" Dorkins W.	Father	Mr W.Dorkins,Back of Brickworks,Morriston.
7773	" Day F.H.	Mother	Mrs C.M.Day,39 Ysgol St.Swansea.
7772	" Dennis R.	Mother	Mrs E.Dennis,3 Gorse Road,Swansea.
088	" Dew J.	Sister	Mrs E.Dew,669 Oxford Road,Reading.
114	" Duckmanton G.H.	Mother	Mrs M.Duckmanton,New Westwood,Jocksdale. Nr Liston,Notts.
735	" Dyer T.J.	Mother	Mrs M.Davies,48 Compass St.Swansea.
507	" Edwards E.	Father	Mr G.Edwards,Grayfawr,Pontardulais.
086	" Edwards E.R.	Father	Mr J.Williams,Cinema,Ystalyfera.
620	" Edwards F.	Mother	Mrs E.Edwards,80 Carmarthen Road,Swansea
132	" Edwards W.H.	Wife	Mrs E.Edwards,3 West End,New Street,Aberavo:
273	" Egan M.	Mother	Mrs M.A.Calnan,6 Michna St.Port Talbot
774	" Essenhigh W.G.	Father	Mr W.Essenhigh,21 Mathew St.Swansea.
648	" Evans F.C.	Mother	Mrs Evans,41 Vivian Rd,Sketty,Swansea.
279	" Evans J.S.	Wife	Mrs B.Evans,14 Maliphant St.Swansea.
708	" Evans L.G.	Wife	Mrs M.J.Evans,3 Jones's Row,Ystrad,Glam.
647	" Evans T.	Wife	Mrs A.J.Evans,141 High St.Swansea.
261	" Evans T.H.	Wife	Mrs S.Evans,29 Midland Terrace,Swansea.
737	L/C Fewings E.	Wife	Mrs G.Fewings,27 Landeg St.Landore,S'sea.
838	Pte Fleming W.	Sister	Miss P.Fleming.
664	" Flynn W.G.	Mother	Mrs A.Flynn,5 Albert Place,Swansea.
349	" Francis W.	Mother	Mrs P.Francis,Salem Place,Rhydyfro,Pontar--dawe.
775	" Furness H.P.	Mother	Mrs M.J.Furness,Mount Pleasant,Swansea
752	" Gammon A.J.	Wife	Mrs L.Gammon,6 Kinbel St.Swansea.
855	" George H.	Mother	Mrs M.George,Sunny Bank,Griffithstown.
753	" Gilchrist L.	Wife	Mrs R. Gilchrist,33 Tirpenry St.Morriston
259	" Gilchrist T.J.	Wife	Mrs M.Gilchrist,Chemical Rd,Morriston,Ssea
845	" Godbear W.	Father	Mr H.Godbear,8 Croft St.Swansea.
840	" Grinter F.W.	Wife	Mrs L.Grinter,Arosfa House,Bryn Rd.Loughor
656	" Griffiths D.	Mother	Mrs E.Griffiths,39 Jersey St.Swansea.
808	" Hacche P.F.	Father	Mr F.Hacche,57 Bond St.Swansea.
623	" Harris S.	Wife	Mrs L.Harris,Rhydyr-Afon House,Sketty,Ssea
809	" Holt L.	Mother	Mrs Holt?Oakfield House,Cwmphil,Nr,S'sea
776	" Hopkins W.	Mother	Mrs E.Hopkins,42 Argyle St.Swansea.
276	" Hoskins E.	Mother	Mrs M.Hoskin,101 Fleet St.Swansea.
214	" Hoskin R.	Wife	Mrs B.Hoskin,20 Aberdyberthi St.Swansea,
695	" Hughes T.J.	Mother	Mrs C.Jones,43 Comman,Landore,Swansea.
189	" Hughes W.S.	Father	Mr J.Hughes,64 Lamb St.Swansea,
980	" Ingham J.	Wife	Mrs Ingham,26 Belthania Rd,Clydach,Swansea
1852	Pte James O.	Wife	Mrs M.A.James,Blackwood,Monmouth.
17202	" Jenkins B.	Mother	Mrs E.Jenkins,27 Pant St.St Thomas,Swansea.
17777	" Jenkins	Mother	Mrs J.Jenkins,Tanygroes St.Port Talbot.
17626	" Jenkins R.E.	Mother	Mrs E.Jenkins,3 Winstone St.Swansea.
17710	" Jenkins R.T.	Wife	Mrs T.Jenkins,6 Tip Row,Hafod,Swansea.
17739	" John W.M.	Wife	Mrs A.John,37 Lambert Cottages,Swansea.
17981	" John J.	Wife	Mrs J.John,24 Quarr Rd,Clydach-on-Tawe.
17841	" Johns W.R.	Mother	Mrs E.Johns,23 Westbourne St.Swansea.
17671	" Jones C.L.	Wife	Mrs Jones,47 Garden St.Swansea.
17696	" Jones D.	Wife	Mrs A.Jones,13 David St.Cwmbwrla,Swansea.
17477	" Jones D.	Mother	Mrs E.Jones,22 Neath Rd.Hafod,Swansea.
17811	" Jones D.	Wife	Mrs E.Jones,29 Woodville Rd.Mumbles,Swansea.
17381	L/C Jones J.	Wife	Mrs Jones,23 Rose Hill Tce,Swansea.
18026	Pte King G.	Wife	Mrs King,4 Galpine Ter.Brown Hill,Dartmouth Devon.
17778	" Landeg W.	Father	Mr D.Landeg,1 Tudor St.Port Talbot.
17697	" Leary A.	Guardian	Mrs Taglom,37 Singleton Terrace,Swansea.
7842	" Lewis J.	Sister	Mrs L.Lewis,Bwllfa,Clydach-on-Tawe.
9271	" Lewis L.	Mother	Mrs E.Lewis,1 Ynysforgan,Morriston,Swansea
7812	" Llewellyn J.G.	Father	Mr B.Llewellyn,3 Bryn St.Cwmphil,Lower Cwmtwrch,Swansea.
8095	" Lowe G.H.	Wife	Mrs E.A.Lowe,Swansea.
7756	" Lumsdaine J.	Wife	Mrs L.A.Lumsdaine,84 Port Tennant Rd,S'sea.
7846	" Mathias W.	Mother	Mrs L.Mathias,9 Church Square,Cwmavon.
7781	" Mapstone A.	Wife	Mrs M.Mapstone,15 Jordon Cottages,Aberavon.
7985	" Mayne R.	Father	Mr Mayne,2 Carmel Tce.Pontlliw,Pontardulais.
8059	" Merriman W.J.	Wife	Mrs M.H.Merriman,81 Llangyfelach Rd.S'sea.
7801	" Morgan D.	Father	Mr T.Morgan,28 East Street,Selluloid,Port Talbot.
715	" Murphy A.	Mother	Mrs M.Murphy,55 St.Georges Tce.Swansea.
686	" Nichol W.L.	Mother	Mrs A.W.Nichol,Llwyncelyn,Llandovery,Glam.
757	" Otten W.	Wife	Mrs H.Otten,3 Bridge St,Greenhill,S'sea
741	" Paddison W.E.	Mother	Mrs E.Paddison,32 Little Madoc St,Swansea.
843	" Palmer C.A.L.	Mother	Mrs C.M.Palmer,11 Victoria Place,Highbridge
632	" Parry D.	Wife	Mrs Parry,
786	" Payne R.R.	Mother	Mrs Payne,10 Oakwood St.Port Talbot.
783	" Pearce W.	Wife	Mrs M.Pearce,154 Wellington Rd.Rhyl.
784	" Perry O.G.	Father	Mr J.Perry,5 Hill St,South End,Mumbles,Glam.
262	" Pettican B.T.L.	Wife	Mrs B.Pettican,2 Kynaston Place,Swansea.
716	" Phillips D.	Sister	Mrs L.Evans,24 Middleton St.St.Thomas,Ssea
534	" Phillips M.	Sister	Mrs E.Phillips,40 Vivian Rd.Sketty,S'sea.
533	" Phillips S.G.	Wife	Mrs B.Phillips,22 Ebenezer St.Swansea.
717	" Phillips W.H.	Mother	Mrs E.Phillips,Rhydygwyn,Graigcefnparc, near Clydach,Swansea Valley.
742	" Prescott S.J.	Mother	Mrs A.Prescott,Garnell House,Norfolk St, Swansea
636	" Price D.W.	Mother	Mrs Price,51 Lan St.Morriston,Swansea.
987	" Pritchard D.J.	Wife	Mrs G.I.Pritchard,44 Swyborfach St.Swansea
659	" Pugh H.T.	Father	Mr W.Pugh,Almerly Batch Eardisley. Herefordshire.
056	" D.Reed	Mother	Mrs M.A.Reed,61 Rodney St.Swansea.
765	" Reed J.T.	Wife	Mrs K.Reed,3 White St.Swansea.
314	" Rees A.	Father	Mr G.Rees,43 High St,Clydach-on-Tawe
315	" Rees D.	Mother	Mrs C.Rees,Penrhyden Dairy,Clydach-on-Tawe
316	" Rees N.	Mother	Mrs C.Rees,Penrhyden Dairy,Clydach-on-Tawe.
637	" Rees J.O.	Wife	Mrs Rees,11 Vicarage Ter,St Thomas,Swansea
591	" Rees T.	Wife	Mrs S.Rees,Tai-Ffynone,Trallwyn,Llansamlet
721	" Rees W.	Wife	Mrs F.Rees,13a Chapel St.Swansea.
135	" Rees T.J.	Sister	Mrs Cowell,77 Llangyfelach Rd.Swansea
538	" Rees W.R.	Mother	Mrs L.Rees,Rhydyrafon House,Sketty,Swansea
02	" Regan J.	Mother	Mrs Regan,20 Sandfield Rd.Aberavon,Glam.
539	" Rice A.	Father	Mr Phillip Rice,6 Starron St.Fforestfach, Swansea.
823	" Richards J.	Wife	Mrs E.Richards,43 Bridge St.Chepstow.
722	" Richards S.J.	Mother	Mrs Richards,56 Tymawr St.Port Tennant,Ssea
889	" Richards W.T.	Wife	Mrs L.Richards,74 Oxford St.Swansea.
788	" Roberts F.W.	Aunt	Miss A.Roberts,Llangeorl,Ross,Herefordshire
863	" Roberts H.J.	Wife	Mrs H.Roberts,Penrhyforgan,Manselton,S'sea.

No.	Rank and Name	Relationship	Next of Kin
18030	L/C Romney S.	Mother	Mrs H.L.Romney,13 Manor Rd.Bishopston, Bristol.
17831	" Samuels m.H	Wife	Mrs A.Samuels,76 Byron Crescent,Swansea
17853	" Sandry W.C.	Mother	Mrs C.Sandry,72 Western St.Swansea.
17660	" Shoemake A.E.	Mother	Mrs P.Shoemake,4 Bennett Street,Swansea.
17854	Pte Simons E.	Wife	Mrs E.Simons,17 Maddock St.Swansea.
29296	" Slade N.	Mother	Mrs E.Slade,Pleasant Terr,Walter Road, Llansamlet Swansea.
17789	" Sloper G.W.	Father	Mr G.Sloper,54 Ashley Down Rd,Horfield. Bristol.
17702	" Smith T.C.	Wife	Mrs M.J.Smith,2 Pentwyn Ter,Cwmrhydyceirw. Morriston,Swansea.
17723	" Smith W.T.	Mother	Mrs A.Smith,Sybil St.Clydach,Glam.
17758	" Smitham T.	Wife	Mrs L.M.Smitham,6 Dyfatty St.Swansea.
17760	" Stark A.R.C.	Wife	Mrs A.Stark,3 Weig Terr,Cwmbwrla,Swansea.
18098	" Staton S.	Daughter	Miss Winnie Staton,20 Michna St.Pt.Talbot
17699	" Taylor W.H.	Mother	Mrs A.Taylor,10 Waverlet St.Clydach,Glam
17790	" Thomas A.V.	Aunt	Miss J.Thomas,53 Mysydd Rd.Landore,Swansea.
17791	" Thomas C.C.	Mother	Mrs G.Thomas,36 Station Rd.Llangonwyd,near Bridgend.
17824	" Thomas E.	Sister	Miss S.Thomas,23 Westry St.Morriston,S'sea
29210	" Thomas R.R.	Mother	Mrs Thomas,Cwmphil Ter.Lower Cwmtwrch,Glam.
17687	" Thomas R.	Wife	Mrs E.Thomas,15 Cae Rowlands,Cwmbwrla,S'sea
17821	" Thomas T.R.	Father	Mr Robt.Thomas,148 Wellington Tce.Aberavon.
29052	" Thomas T.	Sister	Mrs C.Hall,30 Osbourne St.Neath,Glam.
17727	" Thomas W.	Mother	Mrs Thomas,Penycion,Little Milt Cottage, Haverfordwest.
17817	" Thomas W.R.	Mother	Mrs R.Thomas,Penrhedyn,Clydach,Glam.
18099	" Thomas W.	Brother	Mr R.Thomas,21 Tydraw Cottages?penycae,Port Talbot.
17728	" Tregaskiss E.J.	Wife	Mrs E.Tregaskiss,5 Heol Draw,Neath Abbey, Glam.
18027	" Truelove W.H.	Wife	Mrs Truelove,North Rd.Loughor,Glam.
17642	" Tucker F.	Wife	Mrs E.Tucker,1 Eversley Rd,Sketty,Swansea
17768	" Tucker W.	Wife	Mrs R.Tucker,174 Rhyddings Tce,Swansea.
17767	" Turner D.J.	Wife	Mrs L.Turner,58 Eaton Rd,Brynhyfryd,S'sea.
17988	" Turner J.T.	Wife	Mrs R.Turner,94 High St.Swansea.
17782	" Vivian F.C.	Mother	Mrs R.Vivian,15 Westbourne Place,Swansea.
29272	" Wadey H.	Wife	Mrs S.Wadey,4 Water Row,Dunvant,Swansea.
29229	" Walters W.H.	Father	Mr Walters,Llandilo Rd.Brynamman,Glam.
17703	" Waters D.G.	Father	Mr S.Waters,1379 Neath Rd.Hafod,Swansea.
17818	" Weston D.C.	Father	Mr A.Weston,Gilwen Row,Lower Cwmtwrch,Glam.
17797	" Wigmore R.	Sister	Miss M.Wigmore,12 Tilchurst Rd.Reading.
17819	" Williams D.J.	Father	Mr J.Williams,Bethal Rd.Lower Cwmtwrch,Glam
17643	" Williams E.	Mother	Mrs Williams,19 Lamberts Cottages,Swansea
17799	" Williams E.	Mother	Mrs A.Williams,13 Vivian Square,Aberavon,
17761	" Williams J.J.	Mother	Mrs N.Williams,4 Margaret St.St Thomas,Ssea
17690	" Williams W.G.	Brother	Mr L.Williams,11 Sea View Terrace,Swansea.
18100	" Williams T.E.	Father	Mr D.Williams,19 Park St.Taibach,Glam.
29275	" Williams T.	Mother	Mrs E.Williams,68 Pentretreharne Rd.S'sea.
17668	" Williams W.	Father	Mr P.Williams,Bryngwyn House,Alltygrug,Rd. Ystalyfera.
17730	" Yendall W.A.	Mother	Mrs B.Collins,4 Rige Ter.Siera.Plymouth.
17650	" Pitman G.W.	Mother	Mrs A.Pitman,52 Fern St.Cwmbwrla,Swansea.
29112	" Pitman W.	Mother	Mrs A.Pitman,52 Fern St.Cwmbwrla,Swansea
17673	L/C Carthew P.G.	Mother	Mrs Carthew,33 Mysydd Rd.Landore,Swansea.
17003	Pte Derricott T.J.	Mother	Mrs Derricott,4 Bargemans Row,Swansea.
29295	" Tanner W.J.	Sister	Mrs L.Hilton,23 Vernon St.Hafod,Swansea
17572	" Collins F.	Mother	Mrs Collins,50 Chili Crescent,Swansea.
17892	" Thomas W.H.	Mother	Mrs Thomas,Lane House,Killay,Swansea.
17949	" Sullivan C.	Wife	Mrs Sullivan,8 Cwm Street,Swansea.
17335	" Kane M.	Father	Mr Wm. Kane,9 Byron Crescent,Swansea.
17157	" Slee R.	Wife	Mrs Slee,1 Duke Street,Swansea.
17258	" Erexson D.	Wife	Mrs M.E.Erexson,19 Greyhound St.Swansea.
17903	" Cottle G.	Father	Mr Cottle,35 Leslie St.Aberavon,Glam.
17685	Sgt Lewis F.	Wife	Mrs Lewis,8 Nelson St.Swansea.
2228.	" Atkinson E.H.	Mother	Mrs E.D.Atkinson,53 Morse St.Swindon.
17806	" Evans R.	Wife	Mrs M.Evans,71 Foxhole Road,Swansea.
17624	" Harris F.D.	Father	Mr Albert Harris,27 New Street,Swansea.
17480	L/Sgt Kennedy A.	Wife	Mrs M.Kennedy,395 Pentregethin Rd.Swansea.
17050	Pte Delanney J.	Wife	Mrs E.Dellanney,1172 Neath Road,Swansea.
17432	" Gilbert G.	Wife	Mrs A.Gilbert,47 Caebricks,Cwmbwrla,Swansea
29168	" Restall W.J.	Wife	Mrs C.Restall,54 Pentregethin Rd.Swansea.
17142	" Lewis T.	Wife	Mrs C.Lewis,20 Grafog St,Danygraig,Swansea
17323	" Tantrun C.	Mother	Mrs E.Tantrun,Jersey Rd.Bonymaen,Nr S'sea
17140	" Jones W.T.	Wife	Mrs C.Jones,29 Llangyfelach Rd.Swansea.
17486	" Rees W.H.	Sister	Mrs M.A.Sheldon,51 John St.Phillipston.Mon.
17082	" Maddocks E.	Wife	Mrs A.Maddocks,1 Pentremawr Rd.Pentre ~~Esty~~ Estyll.
17131	" Harvey F.	Wife	Mrs E.Harvey,56 Llangyfelach St.Swansea.
17024	" Hopkins G.L.	Wife	Mrs A.Hopkins,3 Upper Pentremawr Rd.Nr. Swansea.
17953	" Harris J.	Mother	Mrs E.Harris,Brynau,Blackpill,Nr.Swansea.
29123	" Morgan S.	Wife	Mrs C.Morgan,9 David St.Cwmbwrla,Swansea.
17328	" Cheley W.D.	Wife	Mrs H.Cheley,25 Jersey St.Hafod,Swansea.
17356	" Anderson W.	Wife	Mrs S.Anderson,114 Robert St.Swansea.
17271	" Jones F.	Wife	Mrs M.Jones,1 Peter St.Swansea.
17338	" Pillar J.	Wife	Mrs G.Pillar,49 Argyle St.Swansea.
18021	" Mc Adams G.	Wife	Mrs J.McAdams,1 Wilkinson Place,Swansea.
17350	" Lewis J.	Wife	Mrs M.Lewis,2 Rock Street,Swansea.
17780	" Lewis F.	Mother	Mrs E.Gilbert,71 Courtney Street,Swansea
17662	" Raddenbury D.	Wife	Mrs R.Raddenbury,21 Bull Hill,Bedford (? Bideford)
18091	" Morgan M.	Wife	Mrs E.Morgan,28 Plough Road,Landore,Swansea
17788	" Roberts F.W.	Aunt	Miss A.Roberts,Llangrove,Nr.Ross,Hereford
17825	" Williams R.S.	Sister	Mrs A.Williams,35 Beacon Hill,Denbigh.
29269	" Davies D.W.	Mother	Mrs Ann Davies,High St. St Dogmaels,Pem:

INDEX

Note: ranks are generally given as first encountered in the text. Many changed following later promo